Safety Nets in Africa

Safety Nets in Africa

Effective Mechanisms to Reach the Poor and Most Vulnerable

Carlo del Ninno and Bradford Mills, Editors

A copublication of the Agence Française de Développement and the World Bank

Library of Congress Cataloging-in-Publication Data
  Safety nets in Africa : effective mechanisms to reach the poor and most vulnerable / edited by Carlo del Ninno and Bradford Mills.
    pages cm
  ISBN 978-1-4648-0435-9
  1. Poverty—Government policy—Africa. 2. Poor—Services for—Africa. 3. Poor—Services for—Africa.
I. Del Ninno, Carlo. II. Mills, Bradford F. III. World Bank
  HC800.Z9P62698 2015
  362.5'561096—dc23
                               2014045921

Africa Development Forum Series

The Africa Development Forum Series was created in 2009 to focus on issues of significant relevance to Sub-Saharan Africa's social and economic development. Its aim is both to record the state of the art on a specific topic and to contribute to ongoing local, regional, and global policy debates. It is designed specifically to provide practitioners, scholars, and students with the most up-to-date research results while highlighting the promise, challenges, and opportunities that exist on the continent.

The series is sponsored by the Agence Française de Développement and the World Bank. The manuscripts chosen for publication represent the highest quality in each institution and have been selected for their relevance to the development agenda. Working together with a shared sense of mission and interdisciplinary purpose, the two institutions are committed to a common search for new insights and new ways of analyzing the development realities of the Sub-Saharan Africa region.

Advisory Committee Members

Agence Française de Développement
Jean-Yves Grosclaude, Director of Strategy
Alain Henry, Director of Research
Guillaume de Saint Phalle, Head of Research and Publishing Division
Cyrille Bellier, Head of the Economic and Social Research Unit

World Bank
Francisco H. G. Ferreira, Chief Economist, Africa Region
Richard Damania, Lead Economist, Africa Region
Stephen McGroarty, Executive Editor, Publishing and Knowledge Division
Carlos Rossel, Publisher

Sub-Saharan Africa

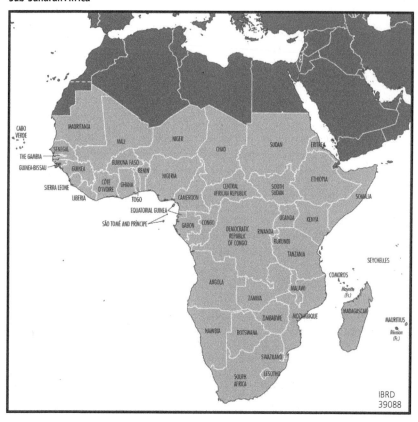

IBRD
39088

Titles in the Africa Development Forum Series

Africa's Infrastructure: A Time for Transformation (2010) edited by Vivien Foster and Cecilia Briceño-Garmendia

Gender Disparities in Africa's Labor Market (2010) edited by Jorge Saba Arbache, Alexandre Kolev, and Ewa Filipiak

Challenges for African Agriculture (2010) edited *by Jean-Claude Deveze*

Contemporary Migration to South Africa: A Regional Development Issue (2011) edited by Aurelia Segatti and Loren Landau

Light Manufacturing in Africa: Targeted Policies to Enhance Private Investment and Create Jobs (2012) by Hinh T. Dinh, Vincent Palmade, Vandana Chandra, and Frances Cossar

Informal Sector in Francophone Africa: Firm Size, Productivity, and Institutions (2012) by Nancy Benjamin and Ahmadou Aly Mbaye

Financing Africa's Cities: The Imperative of Local Investment (2012) by Thierry Paulais

Structural Transformation and Rural Change Revisited: Challenges for Late Developing Countries in a Globalizing World (2012) by Bruno Losch, Sandrine Fréguin-Gresh, and Eric Thomas White

The Political Economy of Decentralization in Sub-Saharan Africa: A New Implementation Model (2013) edited by Bernard Dafflon and Thierry Madiès

Empowering Women: Legal Rights and Economic Opportunities in Africa (2013) by Mary Hallward-Driemeier and Tazeen Hasan

Enterprising Women: Expanding Economic Opportunities in Africa (2013) by Mary Hallward-Driemeier

Urban Labor Markets in Sub-Saharan Africa (2013) edited by Philippe De Vreyer and François Roubaud

Securing Africa's Land for Shared Prosperity: A Program to Scale Up Reforms and Investments (2013) by Frank F. K. Byamugisha

Youth Employment in Sub-Saharan Africa (2014) by Deon Filmer and Louis Fox

Tourism in Africa: Harnessing Tourism for Growth and Improved Livelihoods (2014) by Iain Christie, Eneida Fernandes, Hannah Messerli, and Louise Twining-Ward

All books in the Africa Development Forum series are available for free at
https://openknowledge.worldbank.org/handle/10986/2150

Contents

Tables

Foreword

The need for safety nets in Sub-Saharan Africa is vast. In addition to being the world's poorest region, Sub-Saharan Africa is also one of the most unequal. In this context, redistribution must be seen as a legitimate way to fight poverty and ensure shared prosperity—all the more so in countries where growth is driven by extractive industries that are not labor intensive and often employ very few poor people.

Given that most African countries face difficult decisions about how to allocate limited resources among multiple social programs, evidence is important. Do safety net programs actually benefit the poorest people? This book demonstrates with empirical evidence that it is possible to reach the poorest and most vulnerable people with safety net programs, and it provides lessons for the effective use of targeting methods to achieve this outcome in the region.

The book's introduction presents the rationale for targeting safety net programs to households that are chronically food insecure or vulnerable to food insecurity. A chapter on methods outlines the various ways that targeting can be carried out, along with providing technical details on proxy means test (PMT) and PMTplus methods. Seven case studies are then presented that document a variety of approaches and experiences in country targeting efforts, taking into account country needs and existing programs. Each case study covers the extent of poverty and current safety net coverage, available data, targeting indicators chosen, procedures for long-term (and, in some cases, short-term) targeting, ex ante evaluation of targeting mechanisms, and key lessons learned.

The Mozambique study provides in-depth analysis of the impact of climate-related shocks, while the Kenya, Malawi, and Senegal studies examine how targeting performance varies with exposure to major shocks. Community targeting practices are detailed in the Ghana and Kenya studies. The Cameroon study analyzes the impact of different levels of targeted transfers on the incidence, depth, and severity of poverty; it also highlights the important role that geographic targeting can play in reaching chronically poor people. The Niger study analyzes the strength of the correlation between PMT and alternative targeting indicators and conducts an ex post analysis of the impact of cash transfers implemented under a pilot program. Taken together, these case studies highlight the overwhelming need for safety net programs to assist currently poor households as well as to protect households that may sink into poverty in the future.

In the conclusion, the report discusses future challenges in regarding investments in data, procedures, and methods to improve program targeting. Particular emphasis is placed on the need for countries to invest in targeting methods and procedures to safeguard households against exposure to the negative short-term shocks that are prevalent in African countries.

We hope that this study will prove valuable for governments, policy makers, donors, and the wider development community engaged in the planning, design, and implementation of safety net programs.

Francisco H. G. Ferreira   *Arup Banerji*
Chief Economist   Senior Director and Head of Global Practice
Africa region   Social Protection and Labor

Acknowledgments

This publication has benefited from invaluable contributions from many colleagues and experts within and outside the World Bank. We are especially grateful to participants of the targeting workshop held in Dakar, Senegal, in November 2011, and the Community of Practice face-to-face meeting held in Nairobi, Kenya, in October 2012. The material herein builds on the discussions and feedback received from more than 100 participants and donor partners. We are also grateful to all of the people involved in data collection and the respondents in the data sets that have been used for the country studies.

Overall direction and guidance for this effort were provided by several individuals: the sector managers of the Africa Social Protection Unit, Lynne Sherburne-Benz and Stefano Paternostro; the director of the African Human Development Network, Ritva Reinikka, and Tawhid Nawaz; and staff in the Chief Economist's Office, notably, Shanta Devarajan, Deon Filmer, Punam Chuhan-Pole, and Francisco Ferreira.

In formalizing the publication, we are especially grateful for extensive and thoughtful peer review at the conception stage by Emanuela Galasso, Philip B. O'Keefe, and Hassan Zaman from the World Bank and John Hoddinott from the International Food Policy Research Institute, and by Ambar Narayan and Nithin Umapathi on the final version of the book.

The research and the compilation of this work would not have been possible without the generous financial contribution from the Trust Fund for Environmentally and Socially Sustainable Development, the World Bank's Rapid Social Response Program, which has been generously funded by the Russian Federation, Norway, and the United Kingdom; and the Adaptive Social Protection for the Sahel Multidonor Trust Fund, funded by the United Kingdom.

The work relied heavily on a wealth of expertise and feedback provided willingly across the World Bank. During the entire gestation period, we received excellent contributions, comments, and suggestions from Andrew Dabalen,

Annamaria Milazzo, Anush Bezhanyan, Bassam Ramadan, Celine Julia Felix, Harold Alderman, Louise Fox, Dena Ringold, Ludovic Subran, Margaret Grosh, Ruslan Yemtsov, and Sarah Coll-Black.

Finally, special thanks to Darcy Gallucio and Elizabeth Forsyth for their careful editing of the publication.

About the Editors and Contributors

Editors

Carlo del Ninno is a senior economist in the Africa Unit of the Social Protection and Labor Global Practice at the World Bank, working on safety net policies and programs. He is the manager of the Sahel Adaptive Social Protection Program. Over the past 10 years, he has worked on analytical and operational issues on safety net programs covering several countries in South Asia and Sub-Saharan Africa.

Before joining the World Bank, he worked on food security policy for the International Food Policy Research Institute in Bangladesh, and on poverty analysis in several countries for the Policy Research Division of the World Bank and Cornell University. He received a PhD from the University of Minnesota and has published on safety nets, food policy, and food security.

Bradford Mills is a professor in the Department of Agricultural and Applied Economics at Virginia Tech. He has a PhD in agricultural and resource economics from the University of California at Berkeley. Dr. Mills has extensive international development experience, having worked as a long-term resident technical advisor in government institutes and international research centers in The Gambia, Germany, Guinea, Kenya, and the Netherlands. His research focuses on how social assistance programs, education, and new technologies impact household economic well-being and market outcomes, both in the United States and in low- and middle-income countries. He has published more than 50 journal articles and books.

Contributors

Rodica Cnobloch has been involved directly in both analytical and operational work. She has worked extensively on poverty issues, focusing on linkages with social protection, labor markets and mobility, and health and education in a multi-country context. She has contributed to a number of analytic products assessing the effectiveness of existing programs, as well as studying alternative targeting mechanisms in low- and middle-income countries. She has extensive experience in survey design and implementation, as well as impact evaluation. Operationally, she has designed and led the implementation of the Conditional Cash Transfer pilot in Lesotho.

Kimberly Groover is a PhD student in the Terry College of Business at the University of Georgia. She conducted the research for the Mozambique chapter in this book while she was a graduate student at Virginia Tech in Blacksburg, Virginia. After receiving her Master's degree, Kim worked as a research assistant in the Agricultural and Applied Economics Department at Virginia Tech. Her areas of research include household food security and poverty.

Adea Kryeziu is a consultant at the Social Protection and Labor Global Practice, and the Climate Change VP unit at the World Bank. She has worked on a range of analytical and operational projects related to social safety nets, climate change adaptation, disaster risk management, and political economy of energy subsidies. She has published a dozen background notes, portfolio reviews, briefing notes, and general research on sustainable and human development issues. Prior to the World Bank, she worked at the Global Energy and Environment Initiative (GEEI), Ministry of Economy and Finance in Kosovo, and private sector institutions. She received an MA in international economics and energy policy from the Johns Hopkins University, School of Advanced International Studies, Maryland.

Philippe Leite is a senior social protection economist in the Africa Unit of the Social Protection and Labor Global Practice at the World Bank. Before joining this unit, he worked in the Social Protection and Labor network team, providing technical support on projects in different countries and economies, such as Brazil, Kenya, Mexico, Tanzania, and the West Bank and Gaza, on wide range of topics, including developing social protection systems and designing social safety net programs and impact evaluation. He previously worked for the Development Research Group on determinants of poverty and inequality, poverty maps methodology, and microeconometric simulation models. He holds a BA and MS in statistics from ENCE/Brazil, and an MS and a PhD in economics from the École des Hautes Études en Sciences Sociales (Paris).

Linden McBride is a PhD student at the Dyson School of Applied Economics and Management at Cornell University. She previously worked as a senior research assistant at the International Food Policy Research Institute and as a Peace Corps volunteer in Burkina Faso. Her research focuses on African agricultural development, food price volatility, food security, and social safety net targeting methods.

Pierre Nguetse-Tegoum leads the national development planning process of Cameroon in the Ministry of Economy, Planning, and Regional Development. He is a parttime lecturer at the Central Africa School of Statistics, where he covers impact evaluation techniques, strategic planning, and econometrics. He serves as a consultant on poverty, labor market analysis, and social protection issues. In 2009, he was awarded the prize for the best young statistician of developing countries with his paper estimating the returns to education in the informal sector.

Lucian Bucur Pop is a senior economist in the South Asia Unit of the Social Protection and Labor Global Practice at the World Bank, having served in prior assignments in the global Social Protection Network and in the Eastern Europe and Central Asia Department. He has been involved in investment projects, policy development lending, and analytical work. Prior to joining the World Bank, he was a lecturer at the University of Bucharest. His expertise includes the design and implementation of social assistance programs, poverty analysis, and the evaluation of social programs. He holds a PhD in sociology from the University of Bucharest.

Quentin Stoeffler is a postdoctoral fellow in the Department of Agricultural and Resource Economics at the University of California, Davis, where he works at the Global Action Network on index-based insurance. As a consultant in the Social Protection Unit of the Africa region of the World Bank, he has supported project implementation and conducted impact evaluations of several cash transfers programs. His research focuses on the improvement of household well-being, in particular, through investments in productive activities in rural areas, social safety nets, and index-based insurance products. His research interests include poverty measurement, targeting, and survey implementation in Sub-Saharan Africa. He holds a PhD in agricultural and applied economics from Virginia Tech.

Kalanidhi Subbarao is a senior consultant for the Social Protection and Labor Global Practice at the World Bank. He has been a consultant for the Social Protection and Labor network after being a lead social protection economist in the Africa Region and in the Poverty Reduction Network. Prior to joining the World Bank, he taught and conducted research at the Delhi School of Economics, the Institute of Economic Growth, Delhi, and at the University of California at Berkeley. At the World Bank, he played a major role in the analytical, operational, and policy work in the domain of safety nets and poverty reduction, focusing on equity, efficiency, and fiscal affordability issues. He has published extensively and worked on operational issues on a range of social protection programs in more than 30 countries. He coauthored a report, "Social Protection for Food Security," for the Committee on World Food Security (FAO 2012), and *Public Works as a Safety Net: Design, Evidence, and Implementation* (2012) for the World Bank Directions in Development series. He received his PhD in economics from the Delhi School of Economics, University of Delhi.

Abbreviations

AfDB	African Development Bank
BID	Banque Islamique de Développement or Islamic Development Bank
CARE	Cooperative for Assistance and Relief Everywhere
CBT	community-based targeting
CFAF	African Financial Community franc
CGH	Coady-Grosh-Hoddinott
CLIC	community LEAP implementation committee (Kenya)
CNCAS	Caisse Nationale du Crédit Agricole du Senegal
CRS	Catholic Relief Services
CSA	Commissariat à la Sécurité Alimentaire (Senegal)
CSI	coping strategies index
CT	categorical targeting
CV	cash voucher
DCaS	Programme d'Alimentation Scolaire (Senegal)
DFID	Department for International Development (United Kingdom)
EA	enumeration area
ECAM	Enquête Camerounaise auprès des Ménages (Cameroon)
ENBC	Enquête Nationale sur le Budget et la Consommation des Ménages (Niger)
ESPS	Enquête de Suivi de la Pauvreté au Sénégal
ETE	endogenous treatment effects
FANTA	Food and Nutrition Technical Assistance
FAO	Food and Agriculture Organization (United Nations)

FCDD	food consumption and dietary diversity score
FCS	food consumption score
FCSnt	nontruncated FCS
FEWSNET	Famine Early Warning Systems Network
FGT	Foster-Greer-Thorbecke
FS-CT	Filets Sociaux par le Cash Transfert (Niger)
FSN	Fond de Solidarité Nationale (Senegal)
GDP	gross domestic product
GFD	general food distribution
GLSS	Ghana Living Standards Survey
GPHC	General Population and Housing Census (Cameroon)
GSS	Ghana Statistical Service
HBS	household budget survey
HDDS	household dietary diversity score
HFIAS	household food insecurity access scale
HHS	household hunger scale
HIV/AIDS	human immunodeficiency virus infection/acquired immunodeficiency syndrome
HSNP	Hunger Safety Net Program (Kenya)
IDW	inverse distance-weighted
IOF	Inquérito Sobre Orçamento Familiar (Household Budget Survey, Mozambique)
IPSEV	Initiative de Protection Sociale des Enfants Vulnérables (Senegal)
JHSCCT	conditional cash transfer for junior high school students (Ghana)
KIHBS	Kenya Integrated Household Budget Survey
LEAP	Livelihood Empowerment Against Poverty (Kenya)
MHIS	Malawi Integrated Household Survey
MINADER	Ministère de l'Agriculture et du Développement Rural (Cameroon)
MINAS	Ministère des Affaires Sociales (Cameroon)
MINEDUB	Ministère de l'Education de Base (Cameroon)
MINEPAT	Ministère de l'Economie, de la Planification e de l'Aménagement du Territoire (Cameroon)

MINESUP	Ministry of Higher Education (Cameroon)
MINFI	Ministère des Finances (Cameroon)
MINSANTE	Ministère de la Sante Publique (Cameroon)
MVC	most vulnerable children (Kenya)
NASA	National Aeronautics and Space Administration (United States)
NETS	Nutrition Ciblée sur l'Enfant et Transferts Sociaux (Senegal)
NGO	nongovernmental organization
NIS	National Institute of Statistics
OEV	Bourses d'étude pour les orphelins et autres enfants vulnérables (Senegal)
OLS	ordinary least squares
OVC	orphans and vulnerable children
PAD-Y	Programme d'Assainissement de Yaoundé (Cameroon)
PAPA	Projet d'Appui à la Promotion des Aînés (Senegal)
PMT	proxy means test
PMTplus	proxy means test plus
PNBSF	Programme National de Bourse de Securité Familiale (Senegal)
PPFS-CT	Filets Sociaux par le Cash Transfert (Niger)
PPP	purchasing power parity
PRBC	Programme de Réadaptation à Base Communautaire (Senegal)
PRP	Programme d'Appui à la Mise en Oeuvre de la Stratégie de Réduction de la Pauvreté (Senegal)
PSA	Food Subsidy Program (Malawi)
QR	quantile regression
RGPH3	Recensement Général de la Population et de l'Habitation 3 survey
SFMCH	Supplementary Feeding and Mother and Child Health Program (Kenya)
UCT	unconditional cash transfer
UNICEF	United Nations Children's Fund
WASH	water, sanitation, and hygiene
WFP	World Food Program

Chapter 1

Introduction: Safety Nets in Africa— Effective Mechanisms to Reach the Poor and Most Vulnerable

Carlo del Ninno and Bradford Mills

Life in today's globalized world is fraught with a complex mix of risks and opportunities. As the *World Development Report 2014* highlights, food, fuel, and financial crises generated major disturbances to the world economy in 2008–09 (World Bank 2014). Shocks related to climate change have also affected dozens of countries. In Sub-Saharan Africa, many segments of the population, particularly the poor, remain vulnerable to systemic negative economic shocks, while governments and policy makers struggle to identify population groups most vulnerable to shocks and poverty.

In terms of poverty reduction, Sub-Saharan Africa lags other regions. Europe and Central Asia, Middle East and North Africa, East Asia and the Pacific, and Latin America and the Caribbean have achieved more than 50 percent reductions in poverty since 1990 and already have reached the Millennium Development Goal of halving extreme poverty by 2015. In Sub-Saharan Africa, the poverty rate declined 9 percent (from 56.5 to 48.5 percent) over the last 20 years, before edging upward in response to the world food, fuel, and financial crises (figure 1.1).

Economic growth is needed for countries in Africa to achieve widespread and broad-based reductions in poverty. Fortunately, economic growth has rebounded strongly across the region following the crises in 2008–09 (World Bank 2011). Nevertheless, safety nets can play a role in reducing poverty.[1] Formal safety net programs,[2] particularly cash and in-kind transfers, have been an important mechanism to safeguard minimum levels of consumption during normal times and times of crisis. When effective, such programs protect livelihoods, reduce both the transitory and the chronic poverty and food insecurity of households, and serve as a springboard to more economic opportunities.[3] The Africa Social Protection Strategy 2012–22 highlights

Figure 1.1 Share of Population Living on Less Than US$1.25 a Day, by Region, 1990 and 2010

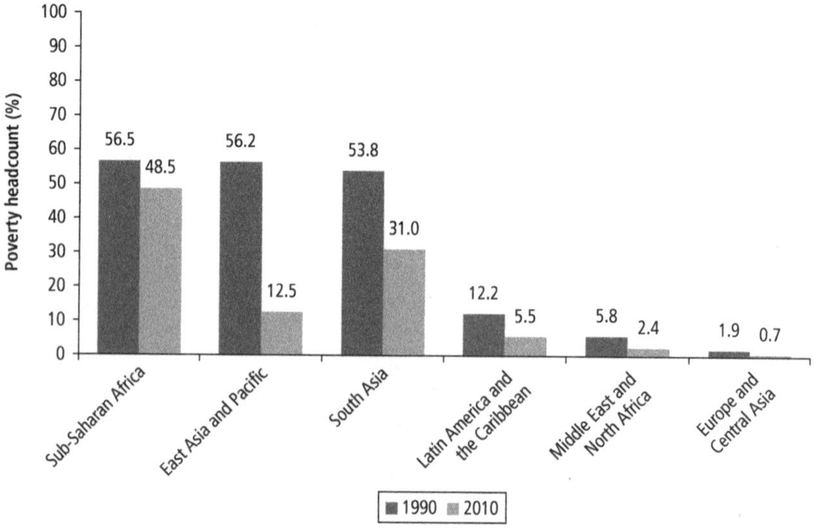

Source: World Bank 2013.

that safety nets are a crucial instrument in reducing chronic poverty and in mitigating the impact of shocks on poor and vulnerable households (World Bank 2012b).

Safety net benefits can be targeted to particular types of households in need or can be universal, in that they are available to all households. Examples of universal benefits include social pensions for the elderly and food subsidies for staple commodities. Universal subsidies that effectively safeguard poor households can be extremely costly, as the benefits are also available to the nonpoor population.[4] Often the fiscal strains associated with universal benefits can substantially erode the level of program benefits as governments attempt to strike a balance between the level of the benefit and fiscal affordability of the social pension.[5] This book focuses on targeted social safety net benefits that are commonly employed in food and cash assistance programs. A broader discussion of the relative benefits of universal programs versus targeted safety net programs is available in the literature. Examples include Acosta, Leite, and Rigolini (2011), Holzmann, Robalino, and Takayama (2009), and Knox-Vydmanov (2013), among others.[6]

Despite the potential, the use of targeted safety nets to combat both transient poverty related to crises and chronic poverty associated with long-term deficiencies in household consumption has been limited and poorly coordinated in Sub-Saharan Africa. As highlighted in a recent review of safety net programs in 22 Sub-Saharan African countries (Monchuk 2013), safety net programs are usually temporary, often created, managed, and financed by donors, and designed primarily to respond to shocks or crises such as natural disasters or conflicts that displace households. As a result, safety nets often do not effectively target the poor. Few safety nets are set up to assist households to manage idiosyncratic shocks—like illness or the death of a household member—that strain the capacity of family or informal community safety nets. Safety net resources are often poorly matched with needs. For example, in Kenya in 2007–08 donors financed more than three-fourths of the total spending on targeted programs, with the majority of funding concentrated in four of eight provinces that did not contain the highest number of poor people (Kenya, Ministry of State for Planning 2012). As a result, safety nets in many Sub-Saharan African countries are an incoherent collection of programs with inconsistent targeting criteria that miss the most disadvantaged households even when donors often spend the equivalent of 2–5 percent of the country's GDP on programs. This was the case in Ethiopia between 1997 and 2002, until the renewed safety net was launched in 2005 (World Bank 2004, 135).

Some countries, encouraged and supported by donors, are seeking to break out of this cycle of "emergency" aid and to develop long-term, sustainable safety nets that are country owned and managed (even if donors still play an important role in financing). For instance, Rwanda, Kenya, and Tanzania have started to reform individual programs and are looking to develop a national social protection system. Ideally, this new generation of safety nets can provide reliable support for the chronic poor and be scaled up in times of crisis. Operationalizing new safety nets has been hampered by many factors, including weak administrative capacity. However, the most important stumbling block has been effective targeting—that is, defining the rules and practice for allocating benefits to the most needy members of society, as identified either by simple indicators of poverty or by other indicators of deprivation such as food insecurity. The extensive experience in middle- and upper-income countries with various types of targeting mechanisms has transferred poorly to the low-income, information-constrained environment of Sub-Saharan Africa, as few programs in Africa have been able to go beyond simple geographic targeting of safety net benefits.[7]

Several key methodological issues constrain the efficient targeting of transitory and chronically poor and food-insecure households in Africa:

- A need for cost-effective and easy-to-implement methods to identify poor and food-insecure households for program participation
- Lack of a clear conceptual distinction between different dimensions of transitory and chronic poverty and food security

- The need to provide objective targeting mechanisms when program participation is often influenced by pressure groups and targeting tends to be based on categorical criteria such as the elderly or orphans
- Difficulty in defining the target population when more than 50 percent of the population are poor and the welfare differences between poor households at any point in time are small (although differences can grow larger when some households are exposed to a negative shock)
- The need for society to accept decisions regarding the allocation of safety net resources.

Government program administrators and organizations such as the World Food Program (WFP), the World Bank, and other donors often face these issues. Difficulties in addressing them limit both the impact of rapid-response safety net programs in emerging crisis situations and the development of acceptable, affordable, and sustainable long-term safety net programs.

The choice of appropriate targeting mechanisms is especially crucial in Sub-Saharan Africa, where the needs are greater relative to funding than in other regions of the world. Therefore, available resources must be concentrated on the population with the greatest need. In practical terms, this often means designing programs that cover only the poorest 10 to 20 percent of the population, even though overall poverty rates are much higher. Methods exist for targeting households that are chronically poor and chronically food insecure; these include geographic targeting (high-poverty areas), categorical targeting (children or orphans), and poverty targeting (low consumption levels). Current best practices usually involve some combination of these methods. Yet implementation of best practices is limited in many countries due to data, knowledge, and capacity constraints.

Knowledge and methods for identifying and reaching households affected by shocks are less developed. For many years the WFP has been providing emergency support, together with recipient governments, and has generated some simple community- and household-based measures of vulnerability to shocks. However, ex post analyses of short-term safety net programs have found relatively high rates of errors of both inclusion and exclusion. The former reflect both information gaps and elite capture, while the latter indicate insufficient budgets to cover an overly broad definition of potential beneficiaries. Common targeting indicators, such as worry about food adequacy, inadequate food quality, and insufficient food quantity, are practical because they can be obtained through limited-scope surveys and in some cases through rapid appraisals, but they are also open to manipulation by potential beneficiaries.

To deal with extreme poverty and vulnerability to poverty, safety net programs need to fit within a broader set of household coping strategies. In Sub-Saharan Africa, most coping mechanisms are of an informal nature and involve family, village, and regional mutual insurance networks. Informal assistance mechanisms often work best for addressing transitory (short-term) and idiosyncratic (household-specific) deficiencies in well-being (Fafchamps 1992). They also have some inherent benefits over formal social protection programs; most important, information for targeting is often more readily available to other network participants than to program administrators. This limits the problems with asymmetric information and moral hazards that are common in formal programs. Yet when compared to formal social assistance programs, informal protection programs also have limitations. In particular, assistance resources are usually rather limited in informal networks where most households are poor or near poor. Furthermore, network members tend to be geographically concentrated, which predisposes the informal support to break down in the face of large covariate shocks such as droughts (Tamiru 2013; World Bank 2012a).[8] When designing formal social assistance programs, it is important to recognize that informal social protection networks play an import role in household coping strategies and to avoid crowding out these mechanisms.

This book explores experiences in Sub-Saharan African with targeting chronically and short-term food-insecure households and tests whether new methods that build on the strengths of existing methods of targeting can improve the identification of potential safety net beneficiaries in times of stability as well as in times of crisis. This introduction provides a general rationale and framework for targeting. However, since targeting is inherently a technical problem, many of the technical "how to" details with respect to implementation are addressed in chapter 2, which describes methods. The most technical sections addressing the use of forefront methods are placed in boxes, and readers not interested in implementation may wish to skim or ignore this material. Case studies focus on the empirical implementation of improved targeting methods using standard household survey data. However, most household surveys currently contain limited information on shocks and the use of safety net programs. Data needs as well as methods to identify and target poor and vulnerable households are, therefore, also addressed in the book.

The book draws several major conclusions. Of particular note, the book demonstrates that it is indeed possible to design and implement viable safety nets in Sub-Saharan Africa. Further, it is possible to target chronically poor households effectively using proxy means tests (PMTs). Nevertheless, further improvements are possible in the design of PMT tools, and the potential exists to improve the performance of targeting substantially by combining PMTs with other targeting methods (geographic targeting and community-based targeting). New methods to identify quickly those affected by a shock and in need of short-term safety nets are promising. But further investments are needed in basic information on shocks, reliable databases on potential beneficiaries' exposure to shocks, and validated methods to measure the impact of exposure to shocks on household consumption.

Concepts: Poverty, Food Insecurity, and Vulnerability

Poverty is a multidimensional phenomenon that combines an economic context focusing on lack of resources to achieve basic needs and a social context that relates poverty to lack of access to basic services and secure social networks. There is an ongoing debate on which dimensions are most important (see Ravallion 2011; Alkire and Foster 2007). But all agree that the multidimensional nature of poverty adds complexity to the identification of beneficiaries of social protection policies. This book acknowledges the debate on the multiple dimensions of poverty and focuses on the simple economic context in which poverty is associated with lack of income or low consumption levels. In this context, poverty is determined relative to a poverty line, which is set as a threshold for the minimum family-adjusted level of expenditures necessary to maintain a defined minimum level of economic well-being.[9]

For food insecurity, the concept and the definition are also complex. The concept of food insecurity, like poverty, has multiple aspects and different associated definitions. The most commonly used, and perhaps broadest, definition of food security was proposed by the World Bank almost three decades ago as "access by all people at all times to sufficient food for an active and healthy life" (World Bank 1986). One decade later, at the World Food Summit in 1996, high-level representatives of the international community agreed with the following statement: "Food security exists when all people, at all times, have physical and economic access to sufficient, safe, and nutritious food to meet their dietary needs and food preferences for an active and healthy life" (FAO 1996).

Workable definitions of food insecurity can be categorized by four key dimensions: (a) food availability, which measures whether a household has sufficient quantities of food of appropriate quality; (b) food access, which measures whether households have adequate resources to acquire appropriate foods for a nutritious diet; (c) food utilization, which measures whether food is accompanied by an adequate diet, clean water, sanitation, and health care and is sufficient to achieve a state of nutritional well-being, highlighting the importance of nonfood inputs in food security; and (d) food stability, which measures whether a household has access to adequate food at all times. This last concept—stability—addresses both the availability and access dimensions of food security (Barrett 2002; del Ninno, Dorosh, and Subbarao 2007).

For the purposes of this book, we focus on the second and fourth dimensions related to food access. Whether a household has adequate resources to acquire appropriate foods for a nutritious diet is akin to definitions commonly used in poverty analysis. A nutritious diet is presented here as the food poverty line derived in most cases from the expenditures needed to satisfy a household's minimum caloric needs.

Food insecurity and poverty are not static. Some households live in a state of constant deprivation, while others are exposed to deprivation only temporarily after experiencing a shock (Hodinott, Rosegrant, and Torero 2012; Tesliuc et al. 2014). Household-specific shocks like illness and job loss are referred to as idiosyncratic shocks, while natural disasters, wars, and economywide crises generate covariate shocks to household economic well-being.

Household vulnerability to shocks can be determined by factors such as household proximity to the (food) poverty line in stable times, the severity and frequency of shocks, and the availability of formal (or informal) coping mechanisms to mitigate the impact of shocks.

In Sub-Saharan Africa, the incidence of poverty is high and inequality is low according to standard measures like the Gini coefficient. Many households reside around the poverty line, and thus a large share of the population is vulnerable to falling into poverty or food insecurity in the face of covariate and idiosyncratic shocks. This is particularly true in the face of natural shocks that recur in the region—droughts, floods, and locust infestations (Mills, del Ninno, and Rajemison 2004).

Further, governments have few resources with which to support affected households. Thus in Sub-Saharan Africa a household's ability to maintain access to sufficient food in the presence of adverse shocks depends almost exclusively on its initial level of assets. Better-endowed households use their assets as buffers against mild shocks (Webb et al. 2006). Low-income households use social networks to buffer against idiosyncratic shocks (Fafchamps 1992). However, these informal social networks often offer limited protection when a community is hit by a strong covariate shock. Thus formal safety net programs are most needed and least likely to crowd out other mechanisms when assistance is required to respond to a strong covariate shock.

Defining Target Groups

The targeting work presented in this book focuses primarily on instruments to identify two population groups:

1. *Chronically food-insecure households,* meaning those whose total expenditure levels consistently fall below the food poverty line. That is, their total expenditure levels are below that needed to secure adequate food, even if all expenditures are devoted to food and the household is not exposed to a significant negative shock. In most cases, the rate of chronic poverty is below the rate of poverty.

2. *Households vulnerable to food insecurity,* meaning those expected to have sufficient expenditures to be above the food poverty line in times of stability

but a high probability of falling below the food poverty line if exposed to a significant negative shock.

A simple change in the cutoff point from the food poverty line to the poverty line allows a similar classification of the population as chronically poor and vulnerable to poverty. Therefore, food insecurity and poverty measures are simple indicators of lack of household resources or ability to meet current household food and basic needs, respectively.

Chronic and vulnerable groups (either poor or food insecure) have different safety net needs. The former require long-term assistance to alleviate hardship and raise their level of assets, while the latter require short-term assistance to ameliorate or protect against the negative impacts of shocks.

As shown in figure 1.2, chronically food-insecure households are a subset of the chronically poor whose expenditures are insufficient to cover basic food needs even without being exposed to shocks. Households that are slightly above the poverty threshold—they can cover food and other basic needs in the absence of a shock—are considered vulnerable to poverty if they face a high probability of being exposed to a negative shock that will move their expenditures below the poverty line. Similarly, households slightly above the food insecurity threshold are vulnerable to food insecurity. Thus households that are chronically poor

Figure 1.2 Relationship between Chronic Poverty and Food Insecurity

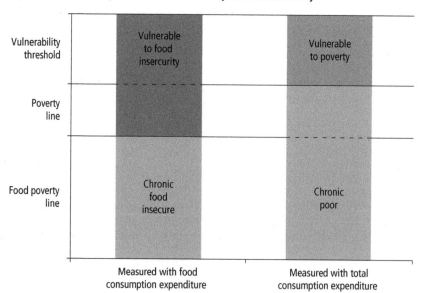

Table 1.1 Simplified Representation of Food Insecurity and Impact of Shocks

| | | Total | After the shock | |
			Not affected	Affected
Before the shock	+			
	Food secure	A	A_1	A_2
Food poverty line				
	Food insecure	B	B_1	B_2
	−			

but not chronically food insecure are likely to be vulnerable to food insecurity. Chronic poverty measures can thus provide sound initial guidance for identifying chronically food-insecure households and households vulnerable to food insecurity.

Table 1.1 presents a simplified representation of figure 1.2 that focuses on the dynamics of food security. In the absence of a shock, households can be classified as either food secure or food insecure according to their relationship to the food poverty line. Those with expenditure levels estimated to be above the food poverty line are classified as food secure and those with expenditure levels below it are classified as food insecure. In table 1.1, groups A and B represent these two populations, respectively. Assuming that shocks are rare events, population B is identified as chronically food-insecure households that require regular social assistance.

When a shock hits, both food-secure and food-insecure populations can be divided into two groups—those affected and those not affected by the shock. Those households that are already chronically food insecure, B_2, will see their situation deteriorate even further. Those households that are not food insecure before the shock, A_2, but that do reside close to the food poverty line are likely to become food insecure after exposure to the shock. Therefore, the challenge is to develop a targeting mechanism that can identify both the population in group B that should receive assistance on a regular basis and the population in A_2 and B_2 that should receive some temporary (additional in the case of B_2) support due to their exposure to the shock.

Basic Concepts of Targeting

Using targeting to narrow the coverage of social programs has three supporting arguments. From an economic point of view, targeting allows policy makers to maximize coverage of the poor for a given budget. From a historical perspective, the poor are often excluded from public spending allocations, and focusing on the poor can reduce this inequality in public spending. From a human capital point of view, the poor have significant human capital deficits. For instance, policies targeted to increase the number of school-age children enrolled in and regularly attending school helps to support long-term reductions in human development inequalities. Overall, targeting reduces waste by concentrating programs on the poorest segment of the population, who traditionally receive a disproportionately small share of government services. Effective targeting can also allow for larger transfers to beneficiaries within a defined group of eligible persons. Trade-offs in target group designation and transfer levels are discussed further in box 1.1.

In theory, the gains from targeting can be large; in practice, difficulties in implementation often lower the gains. Most notably, targeting involves costs, including administrative costs, household costs, and social and political costs.[10] Targeting also can distort recipient and donor incentives and can never be 100 percent accurate—that is, errors may leave some poor households worse off by excluding them from program eligibility.

There are, basically, two types of targeting errors: exclusion errors and inclusion errors.

- *Exclusion errors* occur when eligible populations are not selected by the targeting criteria and are incorrectly excluded from the program.
- *Inclusion errors* occur when ineligible populations are selected by the targeting criteria and are incorrectly included in the program.

Exclusion and inclusion errors result not only from the method used but also from implementation failures. For example, exclusion errors may occur when eligible households do not participate in a program due to lack of information. In contrast, inclusion errors may occur when ineligible households provide incorrect information—for example, if the self-employed claim unemployment benefits or individuals misstate the age of their children or their own age to benefit from family allowances or social pensions.

Exclusion and inclusion errors are key concepts for evaluating the performance of potential targeting schemes.[11] The comparative benchmark for evaluating a proposed targeting scheme is often the status quo—that is, the distribution of safety net resources that occurs without the proposed targeting. Some researchers point to the existence of errors of targeting as the key reason not to employ targeting methods, yet targeting errors occur in all social assistance programs, including universal programs (Barrientos and Hulme 2008; Sluchynsky 2008).[12] Thus the presence of exclusion and inclusion errors in a targeting scheme should not, in itself, be seen as an argument against targeting. Rather, exclusion and inclusion errors should be seen as tools for comparing the status quo with alternative investments that could be made in methods and

BOX 1.1

Targeting: Transfer-Level Trade-offs

Fiscal constraints can have a substantial impact on the level of transfers and the number of beneficiaries in poverty reduction programs. For a fixed program budget, the amount of transfer benefits can be greater if there are fewer beneficiaries—that is, when the program covers only a subgroup of the population. This result holds even in the presence of targeting errors. This book does not explicitly address the optimal level of program benefits, but instead focuses on targeting practices that can lead to lower inclusion errors, allowing higher benefits among program beneficiaries.

The trade-off between number of beneficiaries and level of benefits can be illustrated by comparing the costs of universal and narrowly targeted programs. The book acknowledges that targeting (more specifically poverty targeting) is a controversial topic and that there are trade-offs between universal and targeted programs (for alternative points of view on this topic, see Kidd and Wylde 2011; Coady, Grosh, and Hoddinott 2004; Hanlon, Barrientos, and Hulme 2010; and ECLAC 2000).

Table B1.1.1 shows the level of benefits that can be distributed for a fixed budget that takes into account administrative costs for a universally targeted program and a program targeting the poorest 10 percent of the population. Both targeted and universal programs have significant registration costs, administrative costs, and identification costs. Here we assume a fixed budget of US$500 million and a fixed administrative cost of 15 percent of program costs.

Table B1.1.1 Comparative Costs and Coverage of a Universal and a Targeted Program
US$ unless otherwise noted

Indicator	Uniform benefit	Benefit targeting the poorest 10% of the population
Program budget	500,000,000	500,000,000
Program caseload	20,000,000	2,000,000
Administrative costs	75,000,000	75,000,000
Registration costs	20,000,000	2,000,000
Net budget without costs	405,000,000	423,000,000
Benefit level	20.2	211.5
Annual average poverty gap of the poor	250	250
Estimated size of the transfer relative to the current gap (%)	8	85

A program covering 20 million people would be able to provide benefits of US$20 per person and address 8 percent of the current poverty gap, while a program targeting 10 percent of the population would be able to provide benefits of US$211 per person and address about 85 percent of the poverty gap.

information for targeting. The costs of exclusion and inclusion errors vary across households. For example, incorrectly including a rich household in a program may have greater social costs than incorrectly including a near-poor household. Similarly, incorrectly excluding a household just below the poverty line may have lower social costs than incorrectly excluding an extremely poor household.

Investments in targeting entail costs, particularly administrative costs. These administrative costs can be reduced by using the targeting methods presented in this book—for example, by relying on existing household survey data to generate proxy means tests or community knowledge to infer relative levels of individual household well-being. However, targeting is ultimately meant to be a cost-control exercise. Investments in targeting reduce the program costs associated with inclusion errors as well as the social costs associated with exclusion errors. Trade-offs between the administrative costs of targeting and lower program costs are not well documented; further research is needed in this area. However, available evidence suggests that administrative costs are rather low. For example, targeting a registering beneficiary in Niger using a PMT survey of all households in the villages costs approximately US$25 to US$30 per registered beneficiary, approximately 5 percent of the value of the transfer over a two-year period. Further, investments in data collection for targeting have the added benefits of increasing program transparency and establishing a database[13] that can be used to inform other programs and to enable assistance programs to respond more quickly during a crisis.

Outline of the Book

This chapter has presented the rationale for targeting and the basic concepts associated with safety net targeting. The next chapter explores available methods of targeting and the associated information needs. The strengths and weaknesses of existing targeting methods are explored, with particular emphasis on the current staple method—the proxy means test. The chapter also discusses approaches that combine the standard PMT—a reliable tool for addressing chronic food insecurity—with measures of shocks and other indicators of short-term food insecurity to generate more effective short-term targeting mechanisms. Seven case studies for Cameroon, Ghana, Kenya, Malawi, Mozambique, Niger, and Senegal are then presented in chapters 3–9. The cases studies assess current or proposed targeting mechanisms that can be used to identify chronically poor and vulnerable households. They include country-specific material on the extent of poverty and current safety net coverage, available data, targeting indicators chosen, means of addressing long-term (and in some cases short-term) targeting, ex ante evaluation of targeting mechanisms, and key lessons learned.

The Cameroon case study combines geographic targeting, community-based targeting (CBT), and PMT methods to generate an improved mechanism for targeting assistance to poor and vulnerable households. It also outlines plans to evaluate combinations of CBT and PMT procedures in a designed experiment that should provide further guidance on the efficacy of complementary investments in targeting methods. The Ghana case study evaluates the current targeting mechanism used by its major safety net program (Livelihood Empowerment Against Poverty or LEAP) and discusses potential improvements as the country moves toward a unified procedure for safety net targeting. In doing so it focuses on the role that community participation can play in improving program targeting. The Kenya study explores the possibility of combining different targeting schemes, including food security scores, to identify and distinguish both long-term (chronic) and short-term (vulnerable and transient) food-insecure households. The Malawi case study proposes a PMT model for improving the targeting of poor and vulnerable households. Targeting is conducted conditional on exposure to shocks, and in most cases a PMT is found to improve targeting performance. The Mozambique study combines cross-sectional and climatic data to identify households that are vulnerable to transient poverty induced by climatic shocks and to estimate the impact of potentially endogenous climatic shocks on household expenditures. The results suggest that information on covariate shocks can be valuable in addressing the safety net needs of vulnerable households. The Niger case study explores whether the targeting mechanism employed to identify beneficiaries has successfully identified food-insecure households and whether project assistance has had an impact on the welfare and food security of recipient households. In doing so, it provides a comprehensive analysis of potential measures of household food security. The Senegal case study assesses whether the proposed PMT, which uses short-term indicators of vulnerability in the presence of shocks and quintile regression techniques, is a robust measure for identifying chronically poor households.

The concluding section distills the lessons that arise from the diversity of approaches in the case studies. Particular emphasis is placed on what currently works and what further investments in data, processes, and methods are warranted to improve the targeting effectiveness of social assistance to poor and vulnerable households in Sub-Saharan Africa.

Notes

1. Ravallion, Ferreira, and Leite (2007) show how economic growth and social policies can contribute to poverty reduction in Brazil.
2. Safety nets are often referred to as social assistance. The term "safety nets" is used here for consistency with other World Bank publications.

3. For a definition and a comprehensive treatment of the role of safety nets in social protection programs, see Grosh et al. (2008). For evaluations of effective social protection programs, see de Janvry et al. (2006), Skoufias (2007), and Fiszbein and Schady (2009). For Sub-Saharan Africa, see Woolard and Leibbrandt (2010) and Agüero, Carter, and Woolard (2006).

4. Some universal programs are designed to limit enrollment through self-targeting. See Subbarao et al. (2012) for a review of the role of self-targeted public assistance programs in African social safety nets.

5. For example, a recent report for the Seychelles (Guven 2013) indicates that as the share of elderly in the total population increases over time and benefits are adjusted at 1 percent over the inflation rate to retain their real value, the additional fiscal cost will be on the order of 0.7 percent of gross domestic product (GDP). In Lesotho, social pensions cover all citizens from age 70 on and involve a monthly transfer to about 84,000 people. The transfer accounts for more than 2 percent of GDP and constitutes by far the largest component of social expenditure (even larger than school feeding).

6. The choice of universal or targeted benefits remains an open debate, and more empirical evidence is needed.

7. Smith and Subbarao (2003) argue that information, administrative, and fiscal constraints render the task of identifying and reaching the poorest groups difficult and recommend that programs be self-targeted, with minimal administrative inputs. Nichols and Zeckhauser (1982) show theoretically that ordeal mechanisms, such as time spent applying for programs, or other transaction costs on the use of transfer programs can improve targeting. Alatas et al. (2013) show empirically that, for Indonesia, ordeal mechanisms do improve program targeting among the poor.

8. Tamiru (2013) identifies four groups of informal safety nets: informal mutual insurance arrangements, insurance for major life events, informal savings and credit mechanisms, and traditional social assistance facilities.

9. Well-being is used in this book as a generic term; indicators of well-being focus empirically on household consumption of basic food and housing needs. Moreover, assistance program transfers may have very different impacts among the poor. For example, the very poor may use assistance to meet immediate consumption needs, while slightly better-off poor households may use transfers to invest and increase long-term income flows.

10. Grosh et al. (2008) describe targeting costs as administrative costs to the program of gathering information needed to decide who should be admitted; private costs to the applicant of applying to a program, including the time or cash costs of information gathering, travel, and compliance; incentive (or indirect) costs from eligibility criteria that induce households to change their behavior in an attempt to become beneficiaries; social costs that arise when participation in a program carries some sort of stigma that may affect a household's decision about whether to participate; and political costs that arise if the degree of targeting negatively affects the program's budget.

11. In practice there are several ways to calculate inclusion and exclusion errors. Some authors use the number of observed who are poor and not poor as the base reference, while others use the total population. In addition, some researchers use the concept of leakage as an alternative measure of inclusion errors, referring to the

number of selected beneficiaries who are not poor (Hoddinott 2008). Thus the performance of the targeting will depend on the definition used as well as the number of beneficiaries relative to the poverty rate.

12. Important papers on poverty targeting policies include Coady, Grosh, and Hoddinott (2004); Kidd and Wylde (2011); Ferraz and Finan (2011); and de Janvry, Finan, and Sadoulet (2012), but in Africa few analyses of errors are conducted for universal policies, such as social pensions or family allowances. Guven and Leite (2014) show that universal social pensions are conceptually simple to design but not free of implementation challenges that might result in poor targeting outcomes. For example, in a low-capacity environment in a low- or middle-income country, the elderly might be rejected by a program because they do not have access to an identification card or some other documentation for verifying their age. Moreover, errors and fraud in universal social pension programs are likely to occur in the absence of a strong social registry and a monitoring and evaluation system. Some individuals may collect the benefit before reaching the eligibility age, while others (in most cases surviving relatives) may claim the benefit of a deceased beneficiary. Finally, some beneficiaries might be excluded from the program if payment mechanisms are unable to reach them.

13. Leite, Costella, and Quintana (2012) show the importance of having a database of potential beneficiaries of social safety net programs for the safety net system of a country.

References

Acosta, Pablo, Phillippe Leite, and Jamele Rigolini. 2011. "Should Cash Transfers Be Confined to the Poor? Implications for Poverty and Inequality in Latin America." Policy Research Working Paper 5875, World Bank, Washington, DC.

Agüero, Jorge, Michael Carter, and Ingrid Woolard. 2006. "The Impact of Unconditional Cash Transfers on Nutrition: The South African Child Support Grant." International Poverty Centre Working Paper 39, United Nations Development Programme, Brasilia, September.

Alatas, Vivi, Abhijit Banerjee, Rema Hanna, Benjamin A. Olken, Ririn Purnamasari, and Matthew Wai-Poi. 2013. "Ordeal Mechanisms in Targeting: Theory and Evidence from a Field Experiment in Indonesia." Working Paper 19127, National Bureau of Economic Research, Cambridge, MA, June.

Alatas, Vivi, Abhijit Banerjee, Rema Hanna, Benjamin A. Olken, and Julia Tobias. 2012. "Targeting the Poor: Evidence from a Field Experiment in Indonesia." *American Economic Review* 102 (4): 1206–40.

Alkire, Sabina, and James Foster. 2007. "Counting and Multidimensional Poverty Measurement." OPHI Working Paper 7, University of Oxford, Oxford.

Barrett, Christopher. 2002. "Food Security and Food Assistance Programs." In *Handbook of Agricultural Economics*, vol. 2, edited by Bruce Gardener and Gordon Rausser, 2103–90. Elsevier Science B.V.

Barrientos, Armando, and David Hulme. 2008. *Social Protection for the Poor and Poorest.* Basingstoke and New York: Palgrave.

Coady, David, Margaret Grosh, and John Hoddinott. 2004. *Targeting of Transfers in Developing Countries: Review of Lessons and Experience*. Washington, DC: World Bank.

de Janvry, Alain, Frederico Finan, and Elisabeth Sadoulet. 2012. "Local Electoral Incentives and Decentralized Program Performance." *Review of Economics and Statistics* 94 (3): 672–85.

de Janvry, Alain, Frederico Finan, Elisabeth Sadoulet, and Renos Vakis. 2006. "Can Conditional Cash Transfer Programs Serve as Safety Nets in Keeping Children at School and from Working When Exposed to Shocks?" *Journal of Development Economics* 79 (2): 349–73.

del Ninno, Carlo, Paul Dorosh, and Kalanidhi Subbarao. 2007. "Food Aid, Domestic Policy, and Food Security: Contrasting Experiences from South Asia and Sub-Saharan Africa." *Food Policy* 32 (4): 413–35.

ECLAC (Economic Commission for Latin America and the Caribbean). 2000. "Equity, Development, and Citizenship." United Nations, Santiago, Chile.

Fafchamps, Marcel. 1992. "Solidarity Networks in Preindustrial Societies: Rational Peasants with a Moral Economy." *Economic Development and Cultural Change* 41 (1): 147–74.

FAO (Food and Agriculture Organization). 1996. *Report of the World Food Summit, 13–17 November 1996*. Rome: Food and Agriculture Organization of the United Nations.

Ferraz, Claudio, and Frederico Finan. 2011. "Electoral Accountability and Corruption: Evidence from the Audits of Local Governments." *American Economic Review* 101 (4): 1274–311.

Fiszbein, Ariel, and Norbert Schady. 2009. *Conditional Cash Transfers: Reducing Present and Future Poverty*. Washington, DC: World Bank.

Grosh, Margaret, Carlo del Ninno, Emile Tesliuc, and Azedene Ouerghi. 2008. *For Protection and Promotion: The Design and Implementation of Effective Safety Nets*. Washington, DC: World Bank.

Guven, Melis. 2013. "Long-term Baseline Projections of the Pension System in Seychelles." Mimeo, World Bank, Washington, DC.

Guven, Melis, and Phillippe Leite. 2014. "The Slippery Slope: Explaining the Challenges and Effectiveness of Social Pensions to Fight Poverty in Sub-Saharan Africa." World Bank, Washington, DC.

Hanlon, Joseph, Armando Barrientos, and David Hulme. 2010. *Just Give Money to the Poor: The Development Revolution from the Global South*. Sterling: Kumarian Press.

Hoddinott, John. 2008. "Targeting: Principals and Practice." Technical Guide 9, International Food Policy Research Institute, Washington, DC.

Hoddinott, John, Mark Rosegrant, and Maximo Torero. 2012. *Hunger and Malnutrition*. Copenhagen: Copenhagen Consensus Center.

Holzmann, Robert, David Robalino, and Noriyuki Takayama, eds. 2009. *Closing the Coverage Gap: The Role of Social Pensions*. Washington, DC: World Bank.

Kenya, Ministry of State for Planning, National Development and Vision 2030. 2012. *Kenya Social Protection Sector Review.* Nairobi: Government of Kenya.

Kidd, Stephen, and Emily Wylde. 2011. *Targeting the Poorest: An Assessment of the Proxy Means Test Methodology.* Canberra: AusAID.

Knox-Vydmanov, Charles. 2013. "Should Older People Be Targeted? Social Pensions for the Elderly or Social Assistance for Households." Federal Ministry for Economic Cooperation and Development, Pension Watch. http://www.pension-watch.net/know ledge-centre/?guid=518363d2a5828&order=n.

Leite, Phillippe, Cecilia Costella, and Rodrigo Quintana. 2011. "Developing and Improving Social Safety Net Programs." PowerPoint slides, World Bank, Washington, DC. http:// siteresources.worldbank.org/SAFETYNETSANDTRANSFERS/Resources/281945-1131468287118/1876750-1314735153635/8Leite_SSNSystems.pdf.

Mills, Bradford, Carlo del Ninno, and Harivelo Rajemison. 2004. "Commune Shocks, Household Assets, and Economic Well-Being in Madagascar." Paper selected for the American Agricultural Economics Association meetings, Denver, CO, August 1–4.

Monchuk, Victoria. 2013. *Reducing Poverty and Investing in People: The New Role of Safety Nets in Africa.* Directions in Development. Washington, DC: World Bank.

Nichols, Albert L., and Richard J. Zeckhauser. 1982. "Targeting Transfers through Restrictions on Recipients." *American Economic Review* 72 (2): 372–77.

Ravallion, Martin. 2011. "On Multidimensional Indices of Poverty." Policy Research Working Paper 5580, World Bank, Washington, DC.

Ravallion, Martin, Francisco H. G. Ferreira, and Phillippe Leite. 2007. "Poverty Reduction without Economic Growth? Explaining Brazil's Poverty Dynamics, 1985–2004." Policy Research Working Paper 4431, World Bank, Washington, DC.

Skoufias, Emmanuel. 2007. "Poverty Alleviation and Consumption Insurance: Evidence from PROGRESA in Mexico." *Journal of Socio-Economics* 36 (4): 630–49.

Sluchynsky, Oleksiy. 2008. "Administration of Social Pension Programs." In *Closing the Coverage Gap: The Role of Social Pensions and Other Retirement Income Transfers,* edited by Robert Holzmann, David A. Robalino, and Noriyuki Takayama. Washington, DC: World Bank.

Smith, James, and Kalanidhi Subbarao. 2003. *What Role for Safety Net Transfers in Very Low-Income Countries?* Social Protection Discussion Paper 301. Washington, DC: World Bank.

Subbarao, Kalanidhi, Carlo del Ninno, Colin Andrews, and Claudia Rodriguez-Alas. 2012. *Public Works and a Safety Net: Design, Evidence, and Implementation.* Directions in Development—Human Development. Washington, DC: World Bank.

Tamiru, Kaleb. 2013. "What Is the Role of Informal Safety Nets in Africa for Social Protection Policy?" World Bank, Washington, DC.

Tesliuc, Emil, Lucian Pop, Margaret Grosh, and Ruslan Yemtsov. 2014. *Income Support for the Poorest: A Review of the Experience in Eastern Europe and Central Asia.* Washington, DC: World Bank.

Webb, Patrick, Jennifer Coates, Edward Frongillo, Beatrice Rogers, Anne Swindale, and Paula Bilinsky. 2006. "Measuring Household Food Insecurity: Why It's So Important and Yet So Difficult to Do." *Journal of Nutrition* 136 (5): 1404–08.

Woolard, Ingrid, and Murray Leibbrandt. 2010. "The Evolution and Impact of Unconditional Cash Transfers in South Africa." Working Paper 51, University of Cape Town, Southern Africa Labour and Development Research Unit, Cape Town, South Africa.

World Bank. 1986. *Poverty and Hunger: Issues and Options for Food Security in Developing Countries*. Washington, DC: World Bank.

———. 2004. *Targeting of Transfers in Developing Countries: Review of Lessons and Experience*. Washington, DC: World Bank.

———. 2011. *Africa's Pulse, An Analysis of the Issues Shaping Africa's Economic Future*. Vol. 3. Washington, DC: World Bank.

———. 2012a. "Informal Safety Nets in Eastern and Southern Africa: A Synthesis Summary of Literature Review and Field Studies from Côte d'Ivoire, Rwanda, and Zimbabwe." Africa Region Report 77747-AFR, World Bank, Washington, DC.

———. 2012b. "World Bank's Africa Social Protection Strategy 2012–22." World Bank, Washington, DC.

———. 2013. Povcalnet (database). World Bank, Washington, DC. http://iresearch.worldbank.org/PovcalNet/index.htm.

———. 2014. *World Development Report 2014: Risk and Opportunity; Managing Risk for Development*. New York: Oxford University Press.

Chapter 2

Effective Targeting Mechanisms in Africa: Existing and New Methods

Bradford Mills, Carlo del Ninno, and Phillippe Leite

There are various well-established methods for identifying potential beneficiaries of safety net programs. Grosh et al. (2008) and Coady, Grosh, and Hoddinott (2004) present the pros and cons of targeting methods such as means testing, proxy means testing, community-based targeting, geographic targeting, demographic targeting, and self-selection targeting. After analyzing numerous social protection programs, Coady, Grosh, and Hoddinott (2004) find that interventions using means testing, geographic targeting, and self-selection based on a work requirement are all associated with a larger share of benefits going to the bottom two expenditure quintiles. Further, proxy means community-based selection of individuals and demographic targeting of children show good results on average, but with considerable variation depending on the implementation strategy. Demographic targeting of the elderly and self-selection based on consumption do not appear to be effective in targeting the lowest expenditure quintiles. Handa et al. (2012) provide additional evidence that community-based targeting methods can successfully reach the poor in Sub-Saharan Africa.

Rapid assessment methods have been used to identify vulnerable households affected by shocks. The World Food Program (WFP), for example, has used indicators like food consumption scores (FCSs), dietary diversity indexes, and food frequency indexes to identify food-insecure households. The FCS gives a score for each household that is a linear combination of weights based on the nutrient density of food groups and the level of consumption within groups. The dietary diversity index represents the number of different foods or food groups that households have consumed over a predetermined time period, varying from 1 to 30 days (usually 7 days). The food frequency index considers the frequency of consumption of foods or food groups over a defined period (usually 7 days).

Poverty and food insecurity indicators are intrinsically correlated, but methods for targeting poor and food-insecure households often run independently, with poverty analysis employing household budget surveys (HBSs) and food insecurity work employing rapid assessments. A key challenge for this project has been to find methods that make the best use of data for targeting in specific country contexts. We must design simple but efficient methods that can be used to implement safety net programs targeting both the chronic poor and, possibly using different methods, groups who need short-term emergency assistance to address the adverse impacts of shocks.

The rest of this chapter reviews the commonly used targeting methods and discusses different methods for targeting chronically poor and vulnerable households. Proxy means test (PMT) and PMTplus methods for targeting are then laid out in detail. Many programs combine multiple methods of targeting, and the seven case studies in the next section of the book present lessons that have been gathered from implementing different combinations of the methods discussed in this chapter.

Common Targeting Methods

Five common methods of targeting are reviewed in this section: (1) means testing, (2) proxy means testing, (3) community-based targeting (CBT), (4) geographic targeting, and (5) self-targeting. The combination of targeting methods to support safety net programs is then discussed briefly. Table 2.1 summarizes the five main targeting methods and their associated strengths and weaknesses.

Table 2.1 Summary of Strengths and Weaknesses of Main Targeting Methods

Method	Description	Strength	Weakness
Means tests	Actual consumption or income is compared to eligibility threshold	Very accurate with good income or consumption data	Expensive to collect income or consumption data for all potential beneficiaries
Proxy means test	Consumption is proxied though readily observable and verifiable variables and compared to eligibility threshold	Can accurately and cost-effectively target the chronic poor	Does not address the impact of short-term shocks
Community-based targeting	Groups of community leaders and members determine household eligibility	Incorporates local knowledge and is responsive to short-term shocks; can generate community support	Vulnerable to elite capture, and eligibility decisions can lack transparency
Geographic targeting	Targets are set by location, including all residents within a location	Easy to implement and transparent; can rapidly target in response to natural disasters and other large covariate shocks	Does not account for differences in household well-being in the area
Self-targeting	Benefits and transaction costs are set so that only needy households enroll	Easy to implement and low implementation cost	Stigma and lack of program knowledge may discourage participation

Means Testing

Means testing is the most direct approach for targeting households. In the best of cases it can be extremely accurate if the underlying information on consumption or income is accurate. Under means testing, the actual welfare measure (consumption or income) of each potential beneficiary household is compared to an established threshold for program eligibility. For example, if the assistance program targets food-insecure households, measured household expenditures would be compared to the food-insecurity threshold (the *food share* of the poverty line). This method is administratively demanding. Means testing relies on information provided by the household, and households have a clear incentive to underreport income, assets, and expenditures in order to be eligible for assistance. For this reason, an efficient method of verification must be in place. This is particularly problematic in economies with few formal records of labor market or other economic transactions. Thus in Sub-Saharan Africa, means testing is rarely suitable due to the high costs of collecting verifiable information on household welfare.[1]

Means testing is sometimes used to target particularly vulnerable populations such as malnourished children. In this case, every potentially malnourished child has her or his weight and height measured to identify and target the malnourished population. Means tests are used more frequently to identify food-insecure households, though often not specifically for program targeting. Dietary diversity and food consumption scores can be used to calculate food-security measures rapidly for households with a relatively parsimonious recall of the food items consumed by the household in the last week. These measures are particularly attractive as means tests to identify rapidly those households that have become food insecure due to shocks.

These rapid measures of household food security, nevertheless, are not a panacea for the difficult investments needed to measure household well-being accurately. The issues raised about generating verifiable information when implementing income- and expenditure-based means test measures also apply to using means tests to measure food security and may even be more severe because of the inherent ambiguity associated with measuring food security. Subjective measures of household food security are particularly susceptible to manipulation when used to determine eligibility for assistance. Research also suggests that food diversity scores and food consumption scores often show weak correlation with consumption-based measures of food security.

Proxy Means Testing

Proxy means tests generate a proxy for actual household welfare through fairly easy-to-observe household and individual characteristics. As an alternative to means testing, countries with high levels of poverty and informal information on incomes and expenditures can generate a proxy measure of welfare through statistical models that identify key observable variables (for example, a household's location and quality of dwelling, ownership of durable goods, demographic structure, education, and occupation of adult members, which are highly correlated with household welfare levels). Once this correlation is established, households whose welfare likely falls below poverty and food security thresholds also can be identified.

PMT thus predicts the welfare of an applicant based on a statistical model. PMTs have the same deficiencies as other statistical measures. Notably, statistical measures often generate a great deal of skepticism because they rely on inference rather than direct observation. For example, PMT was developed and performs best for long-term targeting, but critics complain of errors when it is applied to short-term targeting. Many others attribute large errors—both of inclusion and exclusion—to PMT because households can be classified incorrectly. In many instances, poor program implementation (for example, insufficient outreach strategies and failure to enroll the intended population) generates exclusion errors. As a result, instead of proposing new implementation strategies, followed by robust data monitoring, the critics of PMT push for other tools such as categorical targeting. However, dealing with exclusion errors simply by expanding coverage to all members of a certain group can generate large inclusion errors. One of the goals of this book is to help users to understand what PMT measures really mean and when they are the most appropriate targeting tool.

The use of a proxy (that is, PMT) to estimate the welfare or likelihood of a household being poor may be particularly useful when informal economic activities or own-production represent large shares of total household income. Based on statistical models estimated from large and comprehensive household surveys, it is possible to identify the best set of easy-to-verify covariates (variables like age and race) that are correlated with poverty and then to predict relative levels of household expenditures or likelihoods of being poor. The main advantage of the proxy method is that it provides fairly good individual-level targeting results for chronically poor households using a relatively small amount of information. In addition, PMT does not discourage work or distort other incentives for households to increase their level of well-being because applicants do not know which variables, and their respective weights, determine the welfare or poverty level. For these reasons, PMT can be a useful tool for identifying the chronic poor and determing eligibility for programs that provide long-term support.

Community-Based Targeting

Community-based targeting uses a group of community members or leaders, whose principal functions in the community are not related to the social protection program, to determine who in the community is eligible for program assistance. The advantage of CBT is that it relies on local information on individual circumstances, which may be more accurate and less costly to collect than information from other sources. The benefits of enhanced local information have to be weighed against the downside of CBT because the method can politicize eligibility decisions and potentially exacerbate social exclusion.

CBT can be used advantageously for both chronic poverty and short-term interventions. For programs that deal with chronic poverty, CBT requires an effective community structure—clearly defined and cohesive—for targeting. When effectively implemented, CBT can generate widespread program support even if only a portion of the population benefits (FAO 2005). Community-based targeting may also be useful in short-term interventions, as communities (even without a proper structure) can rapidly identify those affected by a covariate, possibly idiosyncratic, shock (World Bank 2013). In all cases, the implementation of CBT must remain vigilant to the tendency of community leaders to disburse benefits in a fashion that supports their own interests.[2]

Geographic Targeting

Geographic targeting uses location to determine eligibility for benefits. That is, people who live in the designated areas (particularly areas with high levels of poverty, food insecurity, malnutrition, or exposure to natural disasters) are identified as eligible and those who live elsewhere are not. Geographic targeting is also frequently used as a social assistance budgetary allocation tool, where areas with high levels of poverty receive larger budgets than other areas.

The key issue for geographic targeting is the geographic resolution used to choose areas. National household budget surveys can be used to identify areas with high incidences of poverty or food insecurity. However, the ability to identify small geographically disaggregated areas with high concentrations of poverty is often limited when using nationally representative surveys. Provinces or districts with high levels of chronic poverty or high levels of food insecurity can be identified, but variations in household circumstances within these broad geo-political designations are likely to be high. Alderman et al. (2003) suggest that lower levels of geographic targeting can be achieved by imputing expenditure levels with census data.

Alternatively, geographic targeting to address short-term needs can be implemented based on indicators of exposure to covariate shocks (for example, flooding or drought). This requires a functional early warning system or community network, but also allows for more geographically refined targeting than is possible using nationally representative survey data. However, not all households within a shock-exposed area will be affected by a shock, and even if exposed to the shock some households will have sufficient resources or access to coping mechanisms to avoid poverty and food insecurity. Thus geographic targeting mechanisms are often combined with other methods that address the circumstances of individual households.

Self-Targeting

Self-targeted programs are technically open to everyone, although they are designed in such a way that only those with a very high level of need will enroll. For example, in public works, wages are set low so that the program is only attractive to those who are willing to work at a low wage. This type of targeting was widely used to alleviate poverty in post-economic crises (as in the Republic of Korea following the 1997 economic crisis and in Argentina following the 1999 economic crisis) and to support reconstruction and employment generation after natural shocks (as in Sri Lanka after the 2005 tsunami). The literature suggests that self-targeting is most appropriate for temporary interventions in response to crisis situations that result in high levels of open and noticeable unemployment or for income support during lean agricultural seasons. However, Alatas et al. (2013) find that self-targeting can improve targeting efficiency in a long-term program in Indonesia when combined with an asset test. The National Rural Employment Guarantee Act in India and Oportunidades in Mexico are also examples of programs that have combined self-targeting with PMT in long-term assistance programs.

Multiple Methods

The literature also suggests that using a combination of targeting methods within a single program can produce better results than relying on a single method (Grosh et al. 2008; Coady, Grosh and Hoddinott 2004; Handa et al. 2012). For example, Mexico's Oportunidades program and Kenya's Orphans and Vulnerable Children (OVC) program combine geographic targeting and PMT; Brazil's Bolsa Familia uses geographic targeting and means testing; and Tanzania uses geographic targeting combined with CBT and PMT. In a well-designed process, multiple methods can bring complementary strengths in order to minimize errors of exclusion and inclusion.

One important element of social assistance targeting that is often overlooked is the development of a centralized database or "registry" of potential social assistance recipients. As Leite, Costella, and Quintana (2011) note, a registry is an accurate and transparent database of potential beneficiaries that can link beneficiaries to multiple safety net programs for which they are potentially eligible. The information investments required for any of the targeting methods discussed here can be reduced significantly over time if systematic, rather than program-by-program, investments are made in information on household conditions as part of a country's investments in safety nets. A well-designed registry can immensely improve coordination across safety net programs. In addition, a registry helps administrators to disseminate information, lowers beneficiary transaction costs, generates savings, and improves efficiency. A functional registry also allows assistance programs to be scaled up and down rapidly in response to shocks. Some costs of data collection in targeting, particularly for means testing and PMTs, are dramatically lowered if the information is contained in the registry. Thus a registry can remove major impediments to the use of these methods and should be considered as an important component in deciding where to invest time and resources in order to improve targeting procedures and performance.

Identifying Chronically Poor and Vulnerable Households

The choice of appropriate targeting methods will depend heavily on who is to be targeted. A key dimension in the choice of who to target is the expected duration of assistance needs. Both the characteristics and needs of chronically poor households are likely to differ from those of households vulnerable to short-term poverty. Table 2.2 highlights different indicators, measures, and data needed to identify and target chronically poor and chronically food-insecure households and to target households vulnerable to short-term poverty and food insecurity.

Chronic Exposure

Detailed measures of chronic poverty and chronic food insecurity are needed to estimate the levels of poverty and food security in Sub-Saharan African

Table 2.2 Indicators and Measures of Chronic and Temporary Poverty and Food Insecurity

Indicators and measures	Chronic poverty (long-term exposure)	Chronic food insecurity (long-term exposure)	Short-term poverty and food insecurity (vulnerability)			
			Short-term exposure	Dynamics of exposure	Household coping mechanism	
					Informal	Formal
Key indicators	Low level of consumption	Chronically weak food access; physical deprivation (stunting or wasting)	Exposure to shocks (covariate or idiosyncratic)	Low asset base; high probability of exposure to food insecurity	Weak access	Weak access
Key measures	Expenditures	Caloric consumption; diet diversity index; anthropometric stunting or wasting	Probability and frequency of covariate and idiosyncratic shocks	Assets and buffers	Household access to informal assistance; adequacy of existing entitlements	Household access to formal assistance
Data	Quantitative[a] household surveys	Quantitative[a] household surveys	Community networks or early warning systems	Survey data; community assessments	Quantitative[a] and qualitative household surveys	Information on program coverage

a. With information on expenditure, quantities consumed, or anthropometric measures.

countries and to inform policy makers and development partners about the needs of populations exposed to long-term deprivation. Chronic poverty and food security statistics are also used to design and implement program interventions to address long-term needs, to monitor the impact of interventions effectively, and to adjust targeting criteria to ensure adequate coverage of chronically poor households.

Households can be classified as chronically poor or chronically food insecure based on different indicators. Most commonly, researchers use low levels of household expenditures as an indicator of chronic poverty. Similarly, indicators of chronic food insecurity often focus on household expenditures that are insufficient to meet food needs. Work by the World Bank in Niger provides an excellent example of the establishment of a minimum expenditure level and the identification of food-insecure households by comparing observed expenditures with that threshold (World Bank 2009). The measurement of these expenditure-based indicators is heavily dependent on the availability of local data and analytical capacity. But household budget surveys and community-level data collected through HBSs provide this type of information in many countries. Detailed survey data of food quantities and anthropometric measurements are sometimes also available and can be used to assess household food security using alternative indicators. Alternatively indicators of chronic food insecurity can be based on subjective measures of quantity and quality of food consumed. Rapid assessment surveys based on self-perceptions of food adequacy and on easy-to-collect questions about the number of days that households consume specific food commodities are used by institutions such as the Food and Agriculture Organization (FAO), WFP, the Food and Nutritional Technical Assistance (FANTA) III Project, and Oxfam to generate such measures.

This book focuses mainly on expenditure-based indicators. Chronic poverty is indicated when expenditures or income are, on average, below the amount needed to purchase a minimum-level consumption bundle that includes food and nonfood commodities. Chronic food insecurity is indicated when expenditures or income are, on average, below the amount needed to obtain adequate food, even when nonfood needs are ignored. The use of alternative indicators of food security is explored in the Kenya and Niger case studies. Box 2.1 provides a brief discussion of several commonly used alternative indicators of chronic poverty and food insecurity.

Vulnerability

Quantitative measures can also be employed to identify those who are likely to be exposed to poverty and food insecurity in response to a negative shock. Often data and resource constraints necessitate a trade-off between developing rigorous measures with information-intensive quantitative methods and

BOX 2.1

Other Indicators of Chronic Exposure

Several alternative indicators of chronic exposure to poverty and food insecurity are commonly employed.

- *Physical signs of poverty and food insecurity: wasting and stunting.* Nutritional indicators such as wasting and stunting can be used to classify households as chronically poor and food insecure. Stunting, as measured by height for age in a standardized way (z-score), indicates long-term malnutrition, while wasting, as measured by weight for height (z-score), indicates severe immediate deprivation.

- *Caloric consumption.* Direct measures of actual household food consumption—most often calories—can be employed to document insufficient food intake and to identify chronically food-insecure households. However, direct measures of household food consumption require accurate and detailed recording of quantities of food consumed. The capacity for such detailed data collection and analysis is unlikely to be available for most safety net programs. Knowledge, attitude, and practice studies, for example, measure what each member of a household eats over six months by weighing intake.

- *Adequacy of caloric availability and food expenditure as a share of the household budget.* Households that do not consume adequate amounts of calories and that allocate a large portion of their budget to food can be defined as food insecure. Households that allocate a high proportion of their budget to food and that consume adequate amounts of calories can be defined as "vulnerable," since they have little scope for increasing the level of food expenditure to meet their caloric requirements if their level of total expenditure is reduced. Finally, households that do not consume adequate amounts of calories but allocate a small portion of their budget to food can be defined as "questionable" with regard to food security status (see del Ninno et al. 2001; Accra Study Team 1998).

employing more qualitatively oriented rapid assessment methods. Speed of implementation is also a primary concern in short-term targeting, as these measures are employed most often in response to emergency needs.

Indicators of short-term exposure to food insecurity are complicated by the dynamic nature of food insecurity. Standard measurements of physical status, household consumption, or household expenditures require in-depth household surveys and substantial analytical capacity to identify households with a high probability of exposure to food insecurity. Most households are not going to be observed to be currently food insecure in standard household surveys. Further, if not chronically food insecure, the household will have asset levels indicating that they can, on average, obtain sufficient food. As such, ex ante indicators of short-term food insecurity focus on measuring two dynamic components of food insecurity: (a) the frequency and severity of adverse shocks to household well-being and (b) the strength of household or community coping mechanisms to mitigate adverse shocks.

As before, standard household surveys such as HBSs, community-level data collected during an HBS or by other agencies, and rapid assessments of food insecurity collected by agencies, such as WFP assessments for vulnerability maps, are the main sources of information for vulnerability indicators. The literature identifies the following main indicators:

- *Exposure to shocks in the past few months.* Information on exposure to shocks can be combined with other household characteristics in order to understand which shocks put households at greatest risk of food insecurity. However, it is difficult to capture the full causal impact of shocks on household well-being using cross-sectional data.

- *Household coping mechanisms.* Accumulated assets, informal assistance networks, and formal assistance networks influence the impacts that shocks have on household food security. However, the complexity of interactions between exposure to shocks and coping mechanisms suggests that cross-sectional data may not capture the causal impact of shocks on household well-being.[3] Variables also should not generate perverse incentives. For example, although having children who are not enrolled in school may be associated with household poverty, including this variable may generate an incentive to remove children from school in order to improve the chances for assistance.

- *Community coping mechanisms.* Community-based informal surveys and community key informants can be used to generate measures of the strength of informal assistance networks and the extent of existing program coverage.

Targeting places an additional constraint on the identification of chronically poor and vulnerable households in that the information used in the analysis must be readily obtainable and easily verifiable. Reducing the set of variables used to identify these distinct chronic and vulnerable groups will lead to an increase in errors of prediction. These increases in prediction errors need to be weighed against the costs of collecting additional information on potential beneficiaries and the errors associated with strategic behavior by program participants when collecting unverifiable information for the purpose of determining program eligibility. The empirical steps involved in generating PMTs and in addressing vulnerable households through PMTplus measures are laid out next.

Using Proxy Means Test for Targeting

Two basic components are involved in generating a proxy means test for targeting. The first component is the establishment of a model for translating readily observable household, community, and regional characteristics into an accurate estimate of household well-being (that is, household expenditures). In other words, weights for selected variables are estimated using a statistical model that regresses an indicator of household welfare on household characteristics using information from a household budget survey. The second component employs the weights obtained from the previous step on the roster of potential program recipients (registry) to estimate expected household well-being and then determine program eligibility. The case studies in this book provide variations on these two steps, but the basic procedures are described here.

The first step is to identify a household budget survey with adequate representation of the country. The measure of household well-being—in most cases person-adjusted household expenditures—is employed as the dependent PMT variable. Covariates are then chosen based on the following factors:

- *Data availability.* Household-level variables come from household budget surveys; however, community or regional information from other sources may be added to the data set.

- *Easily verifiable and readily observable variables.* Households have an incentive to present information strategically to increase their chances of receiving social assistance; therefore, the choice of variables should account for this incentive and be verifiable and readily observable. For example, residential roofing material is easily observed, while the cash savings of a household are not.

- *High correlation with the indicator of household well-being.* The PMT is an exercise not in structural modeling but in accurate prediction. Therefore, the goal is not to generate unbiased structural parameter estimates of the relationships between characteristics and well-being; rather, the goal is to produce the most appropriate model for predicting the welfare of households—in other words, a model with variables that are easy to verify, have a strong correlation with household welfare, and can be easily implemented in the field.

Another major issue in the selection of PMT variables is whether or not to allow for location-specific effects through location indicator variables or the interaction of location indicators with other variables. The advantage of incorporating location-specific indicators is that they can, in many cases, greatly increase the predictive power of the model and lower the number of exclusion and inclusion errors. However, incorporation of location indicators essentially creates separate thresholds and, with location interaction terms, separate PMT weights for each location. The trade-off between capturing location-specific circumstances and maintaining a common threshold for all beneficiaries needs to be addressed explicitly as part of program policy.

Estimation is usually conducted by ordinary least squares (OLS) for the following equation:

$$C_i = X_i \beta + \varepsilon_i, \tag{2.1}$$

where C_i is the expenditure of household i, X_i is a row vector of covariates, β is a vector of parameter estimates, and ε_i is the error term. Measures of household exposure to shocks are usually not included as covariates in standard PMTs and are, thus, part of the error component of the model.

The use of a promising alternative statistical model—quintile regression—that can generate PMT estimates when beneficiary households are likely to be found at the lower tail of the expenditure distribution is discussed in box 2.2, and an application is presented for urban areas in the Cameroon case study.

The second component of the PMT process uses the vector of parameter estimates $\hat{\beta}$ as weights to predict expenditures for households being screened for assistance. This prediction process requires the collection of data for potential applicants through a registry where the same household characteristics used for the model are contained on the registration form. Therefore, a vector Z_j that has

BOX 2.2

Quantile Regression for Estimating PMT Weight

OLS regression generates PMT weights based on the conditional mean of the distribution. In cases where the poverty threshold lies far from the mean, it may be more relevant to estimate PMT weights using quantile regressions that focus on the upper or lower tail of the distribution. For example, the analyst may wish to generate PMT weights based on per capita expenditures, and the poverty threshold may lie at the bottom twentieth percentile of the distribution of per capita expenditures. The rationale for estimating PMT weights around this lower tail of the distribution is that relationships between covariates and the PMT variable may be different (and more relevant) than around the mean.

The basic quantile regression estimator minimizes β_q for the qth population quantile of the distribution:

$$Q_N(\beta_q) = \sum_{i:C_i \geq X_i\beta}^{N} q \, |C_i - X_i\beta_q| + \sum_{i:C_i < X_i\beta}^{N} (1-q) \, |C_i - X_i\beta_q| \tag{B2.2.1}$$

Note that $\hat{\beta}_q$ is now specific to the choice of quantile.

the same variables as in X_i is multiplied by the $\hat{\beta}$ estimate of the parameter vector in equation 2.1 to generate a predicted expenditure for the household. If the predicted expenditure falls below the indicator threshold, the household is determined to be eligible for the program. PMT methods do not explicitly address exposure to shocks. For this reason, they are best used for determining households that are expected to be poor or food insecure on average and are, therefore, most appropriate for targeting chronically poor households.

The PMT score and selection criteria are presented formally as follows:

$$\hat{C}_j = Z_j \hat{\beta}, \tag{2.2}$$

where $\hat{C}_j$ represents the PMT score based on the estimated expenditures of household j, Z_j is a row vector of covariates obtained for applicant households, and $\hat{\beta}$ is a vector of parameter estimates from equation 2.1.

Household j is eligible if $\hat{C}_j \leq cutoff$; it is ineligible if $\hat{C}_j > cutoff$.

Using Proxy Means Testing Plus

The proxy means test plus (PMTplus) is simply a variation of PMT that incorporates the impact that a major shock (a drought, flood, incapacitation, or death of an adult family member) may have on households. Panel data (observations of the same household over multiple time periods) is a first-best option for this type of measurement. However, in line with the data available in Sub-Saharan Africa, the primary focus of this book is on techniques appropriate for cross-sectional (single observation at one point in time) data sets.

With cross-sectional data, household welfare before and after a shock is not observed. Instead, the impact of a shock on changes in consumption is inferred from differences in consumption of otherwise observationally equivalent households.

$$C_i = X_i \beta + S_i \alpha + u_i, \tag{2.3}$$

where S_i is a discrete or continuous measure of exposure to a major type of shock. This specification differs from the standard PMT, where household exposure to shocks is implicitly part of the error component of the model.

The key issue for the PMTplus method is to generate accurate measures of α—the impact of shocks on the PMT score. Several alternative strategies are available. The most straightforward for covariate shocks is to add regional information on shocks directly into the PMT estimator. For instance, the impact of aggregate climatic shocks can be estimated using widely available, continent-wide, and detailed geo-referenced information on historic rainfall from the

National Aeronautical and Space Administration (NASA) Langley Research Center POWER project website.[4] Discrete indicators of drought and flooding events can be generated with the aggregate data and used to estimate impacts on PMT scores (as in the Cameroon case study). Alternatively, variations in rainfall from historic trends can be employed to obtain more nuanced estimates of climatic impacts on PMT scores. The advantages of this approach are that data on aggregate shocks are often readily available and the estimation methods are the same as those used in the PMT. The disadvantages are that the use of aggregate information on covariate shocks is, essentially, a form of geographic targeting. For example, aggregate measures of rainfall are correlated with household exposure to climatic shocks, but they are not direct indicators of household exposure. Micro-climates, geography, soil conditions, as well as farm practices may expose to drought or flooding only a portion of households in the same aggregate climatic conditions.

A second approach is to include discrete indicators of household exposure to shocks directly in the PMT regressions, as is done in the Kenya and Malawi case studies. The advantage of this approach is that estimations of α are based directly on PMT scores from affected households. Disadvantages are twofold. First, household surveys used in PMT estimation often do not have good information on household exposure to shocks. Second, reported household exposure to shocks may be endogenous—for a given shock, poorer households may be more likely to report exposure due to a poorer base of resources or weaker coping mechanisms. This may lead to biased estimates of the impact of shocks on PMT scores.

A third approach builds on the second and uses an endogenous treatment effect model (or other instrumental variable or propensity-matching model) to account for possible endogeneity in the exposure to shocks. The advantages of this approach are that estimates of the impacts of a shock will be unbiased when the model is specified properly. There are two associated disadvantages. First, the estimation method is more technically complex. Second, valid exclusion restriction variables to identify the model (variables that are associated with exposure to shocks, but influence PMT measures only through their impact on exposure to shocks) are often difficult to obtain from survey data.

A more detailed treatment of the endogeneous treatment effect model is provided in box 2.3. Guidance on choosing potential exclusion restrictions is provided in box 2.4.

Once the PMTplus model is estimated, program eligibility of a household after exposure to a shock is easily recovered by incorporating the weight associated with the impact of the shock S_i into the PMT measure. Households whose predicted consumption $\hat{C}_j = Z_j \hat{\beta}$ falls below the cutoff point in the absence of all major shocks are identified as chronically poor. Households that are vulnerable to shocks are then identified by including exposure to shocks in the PMT

BOX 2.3

Implementing an Endogenous Treatment Effect Model

Household shocks may be endogenous and lead to biased estimates of the impacts of a shock on PMT measures for two reasons. First, reverse causality may be present if consumption or wealth levels influence the likelihood of exposure to the shock. For example, richer households are less likely to get sick. Thus in a naive OLS regression, health shocks lead to a poorer PMT score. Reverse causality is more likely to occur with idiosyncratic than with covariate shocks. Second, exposure to a shock may depend on unobserved factors that influence both exposure to a shock and the underlying factors in the PMT score, such as household expenditures or wealth. For example, more affluent households may possess better soils that are less prone to drought. In this case, if soil quality is not accounted for, then estimates of the impact of drought on the PMT measure may be biased.

The most common method of controlling for possible endogeneity in discrete indicators of shocks is the endogenous treatment effects model, with the following PMT equation:

$$C_i = X_i\beta + S_i\alpha + u_i, \tag{B2.3.1}$$

However, household propensity to experience the shock is now jointly estimated. Let S_i^* be the latent propensity to be exposed to a discrete observable shock S_i.

$$S_i = \begin{cases} 0 \text{ if } S_i^* \leq 0 \\ 1 \text{ if } S_i^* > 0 \end{cases}, \tag{B2.3.2}$$

where $S_i^* = \Pi_i\gamma + v_i$.

Two conditions must hold for this approach to yield consistent estimates:

1. A variable appears in row vector Π_i that does not appear in the consumption equation. This is known as the exclusion restriction.
2. The unique variable in Π_i influences consumption only through its impact on household exposure to the shock.

Estimation of the endogenous treatment effects model can be easily performed in STATA using the "treatreg" command.

calculation. This is done by adding $\hat{\alpha}$ to the PMT score. Households that fall below the indicator threshold after exposure to a shock are defined as vulnerable to shocks.

The PMTplus method clearly requires additional information on household exposure to shocks and also often on regional climatic variables. Thus it represents a "higher" level of information investments for short-term targeting.

BOX 2.4

Identification of Plausible Exclusion Restrictions in Treatment Effects Models

Empirical implementation of the endogenous treatment effects model relies on the establishment of plausible exclusion restrictions that are likely to differ based on the type of shock. For large covariate shocks like droughts, floods, and political insecurity, there are limited concerns about true reverse causality, in that the level of household expenditure or wealth is not likely to influence the propensity to be exposed to these types of shocks. However, estimation bias due to unobserved heterogeneity remains a major concern even for covariate shocks.

Several potential instruments exist for measuring covariate shocks. For climatic shocks the best may be local measures of rainfall deviations from long-term averages. These rainfall measures are likely to be strongly associated with household exposure to floods and droughts. At the same time, rainfall deviations from long-term averages are unlikely to influence expenditures or wealth except through the climatic shocks they generate. Local soil characteristics may also be used as instruments, although the concern exists that less well-off households may be more likely to reside on marginal lands. Moreover, significant analytical capacity is required to manipulate geo-referenced climate and soil data into a usable format. Climatic and soil instruments also may not be relevant for some types of covariate shocks, like exposure to political violence.

Another alternative is to use measures of community-level exposure to shocks as instruments (for example, Datt and Hoogeveen 2003). Community-level exposure may be determined through a community questionnaire that is often administered in tandem with the national household-level questionnaire. Community exposure can also be calculated based on the reported exposure of other households in the same survey cluster or geo-political region of the PMT survey. Indicators of community exposure are expected to be strongly correlated with exposure to shocks (by the nature of covariate shocks). Concerns about reverse causation are limited by the fact that community exposure to the shock is not directly associated with the individual household's expenditure or wealth. But concern remains that unobserved heterogeneity may bias estimates of the impacts of a shock, particularly if the source of unobserved heterogeneity is regional.

For example, unhealthy living conditions that are not observed may be correlated with illness and with low household expenditure levels. In this case other community-level conditions can be used as instruments. For example, in the case of household exposure to illness and disease, measures of community health infrastructure may be used as instruments if other measures of community wealth are employed in the expenditure regression to control for the fact that better health infrastructure is often found in more wealthy communities. Active exploration of novel identification strategies is encouraged in future PMTplus applications.

Conclusion

What targeting methods are appropriate will depend on the situation. One method does not fit all needs, and the choice depends on country-specific needs and capacity. If short-term shocks are a dominant driver of safety net needs, then countries may wish to focus investments on methods to enhance the identification of vulnerable households and on the capacity to target short-term needs. Conversely, if chronic poverty generates the greatest need for safety net programs, then methods should focus on identifying and targeting chronically poor households.

In terms of capacity to implement methods, data and human resources are key issues. The choice of methods must be compatible with existing human resources or available resources to invest in training. Identifying and targeting the chronic poor usually require having access to household-level data sets, while targeting households with short-term needs requires additional investments in information on immediate needs or exposure to shocks. Moreover, human resource constraints on the implementation of methods become greater as social safety net systems move toward more structured and quantitative methods. Targeting performance is likely to vary with data availability and human resource capacity. For example, weak administrative capacity may be associated with poor data quality and greater measurement error and, hence, lead to poorer targeting results. The relationship between administrative capacity, data quality, and targeting performance may be particularly strong in the exclusion and inclusion errors of PMTs, given their reliance on household surveys to predict household well-being. Political constraints to improved targeting also need to be recognized and may play a role in the choice of appropriate methods. In this vein, implementation of more quantitative targeting methods may reduce direct elite capture of assistance resources, but lead elites to seek compensation through other leakages.

The next seven chapters of the book provide case studies that demonstrate typical choices made with regard to data and methods for safety net targeting. The concluding chapter provides a synthesis of the case studies, with particular emphasis on where future investments are needed.

Notes

1. The consumption or income data used in means tests are subject to short-term fluctuations. A more consistent long-term measure that smooths these fluctuations may be derived from proxy means tests that infer long-term consumption levels from household assets and human capital characteristics.
2. Alatas et al. (2012) find that CBT performs worse than PMT in Indonesia, particularly near the poverty threshold. However, the relatively poor performance of

CBT does not appear to be due to elite capture. Bardhan and Mookherjee (2006) find that elite capture may play a larger role in across-village than in within-village allocation of benefits in West Bengal. Karlan and Thuysbaert (2013), in contrast, find that a participatory wealth ranking combined with a verficiation household survey performs as well as PMT in targeting the ultrapoor in Honduras and Peru.

3. Generally, more variables will increase the predictive power of the PMT model. However, this may not be true in practice if measurement errors increase with the number of variables collected due to either the difficulty of measuring additional variables or surveyer fatique.

4. See http://power.larc.nasa.gov/.

References

Accra Study Team. 1998. "Promoting Urban Food Nutrition Security for the Vulnerable in the Greater Accra Metropolitan Area." Technical report to the World Health Organization, International Food Policy Research Institute, Washington, DC.

Alatas, Vivi, Abhijit Banerjee, Rema Hanna, Benjamin A. Oklen, and Julia Tobias. 2012. "Targeting the Poor: Evidence from a Field Experiment in Indonesia." *American Economic Review* 102 (4): 1206–40.

Alatas, Vivi, Abhijit Banerjee, Rema Hanna, Benjamin A. Oklen, Ririn Purnamasari, and Matthew Wai-Poi. 2013. "Ordeal Mechanisms in Trageting: Theory and Evidence from a Field Experiment in Indonesia." Working Paper 19127, National Bureau for Economic Research, Cambridge, MA.

Alderman, Harold, Miriam Babita, Gabriel Demonbynes, Nthabiseng Makhatha, and Berk Özler. 2003. "How Low Can You Go? Combining Census and Survey Data for Mapping Poverty in South Africa." *Journal of African Economies* 11 (2): 169–200.

Bardhan, Pranab, and Dilip Mookherjee. 2006. "Pro-Poor Targeting and Accountability on Local Governments in West Bengal." *Journal of Development Economics* 79 (2): 303–27.

Coady, David, Margaret Grosh, and John Hoddinott. 2004. *Targeting of Transfers in Developing Countries: Review of Lessons and Experience*. Washington, DC: World Bank.

Datt, Gaurav, and Hans Hoogeveen. 2003. "El Niño or El Peso? Crisis, Poverty, and Income Distribution in the Philippines." *World Development* 31 (7): 1103–24.

del Ninno, Carlo, Paul A. Dorosh, L. C. Smith, and D. K. Roy. 2001. "The 1998 Floods in Bangladesh: Disaster Impacts, Household Coping Strategies, and Response." Research Report 122, International Food Policy Research Institute, Washington, DC.

FAO (Food and Agriculture Organization). 2005. "Module 8: Targeting." In *Socio-Economic and Gender Analysis for Emergency and Rehabilitation*. Rome: FAO.

Grosh, Margaret, Carlo del Ninno, Emile Tesliuc, and Azedene Ouerghi. 2008. *For Protection and Promotion: The Design and Implementation of Effective Safety Nets*. Washington, DC: World Bank.

Handa, Sudhandshu, Carolyn Huang, Nicola Hypher, Clarissa Teixeira, Fabio V. Soares, and Benjamin Davis. 2012. "Targeting Effectiveness of Social Cash Transfer Programmes in Three African Countries." *Journal of Development Effectiveness* 4 (1): 78–108.

Karlan, Dean, and Bram Thuysbaert. 2013. "Targeting Ultra-Poor Households in Honduras and Peru." Working Paper 19646, National Bureau for Economic Research, Cambridge, MA.

Leite, Phillippe, Cecilia Costella, and Rodrigo Quintana. 2011. "Developing and Improving Social Safety Net Programs." PowerPoint slides, World Bank, Washington, DC. http://siteresources.worldbank.org/SAFETYNETSANDTRANSFERS /Resources/281945-1131468287118/1876750-1314735153635/8Leite_SSNSystems.pdf.

World Bank. 2013. "Building Resilence." Guidance Note 2, World Bank, Washington, DC.

Chapter 3

Generating a System for Targeting Unconditional Cash Transfers in Cameroon

Quentin Stoeffler, Pierre Nguetse-Tegoum, and Bradford Mills

Cameroon has seen robust recent economic growth and is one of the better-off countries in Sub-Saharan Africa. Yet its poverty level has remained persistently high and geographically concentrated in the northern—rural—parts of the country.

Social assistance has been largely reactionary, subsidizing food and fuel prices in response to a crisis, and the results have been regressive (World Bank 2011a). Safety net programs have suffered from limited resources, weak coverage, and poor targeting; excluding subsidies, they account for only 0.23 percent of gross domestic product (GDP), which ranks Cameroon's safety net allocations among the lowest in Sub-Saharan Africa. For these reasons, the government is dedicating a large part of social assistance spending to a unified safety net, moving toward unconditional cash transfers (UCTs) targeted to the poor.

This case study presents an improved mechanism for targeting assistance to poor and vulnerable households in Cameroon. It is based on the work done since 2009 to review the safety net system and draws on documents that describe efforts to identify and target poor and vulnerable households (Nguetse-Tegoum 2011; World Bank 2011a, 2011b; Nguetse-Tegoum and Stoeffler 2012). At present, the outcomes are being piloted in two of the poorest regions, the north and far north.

This case study is organized as follows. First, it presents an overview of poverty and vulnerability in Cameroon as well as current safety net programs. Second, it explains the targeting method employed in Cameroon and the proxy means testing formula generated. Third, it presents ex ante targeting results and details a design for the ex post evaluation of the targeting mechanisms. A final section concludes with lessons learned.

Poverty, Vulnerability, and Social Assistance Response

Cameroon is divided into 10 administrative regions and 58 *départements*, followed by *communes* in rural areas and *arrondissements* in urban areas. Although the country has had strong economic growth in the last decade, the gains have been split largely on a north-south axis, and the incidence of poverty has remained high in the northern half.

Between 2001 and 2007, the poverty rate was virtually constant, at approximately 40 percent of the population. This means that the number of poor increased by 1.1 million as the population grew. In 2007, out of a population of 17.9 million people, 7.1 million were poor.[1] The results are striking when poverty is deconstructed by taking into account the variability in future expected consumption based on the current characteristics of households (Chaudhuri and Datt 2001).

Of the total population, 4.7 million people (26.1 percent) are chronically poor, in that based on their current assets they are expected to be poor in the future (Nguetse-Tegoum 2011). Among the remaining poor, 9.9 percent are transient poor and 4 percent are progressive poor, which means that they are progressing quickly out of poverty.

Chronic poverty is mainly a rural phenomenon: 95.6 percent of the chronic poor live in rural areas, and almost 40 percent of the rural population reside in chronic poverty. In addition, poverty is concentrated in the five northern regions of Cameroon, where 80 percent of the chronic poor are located (and 46.2 percent of the population live). These regions are Adamaoua, the east, northwest, north, and far north. In these last two, the rate of chronic poverty is above 50 percent.

Characteristics of Chronically Poor Households

Table 3.1 shows the characteristics of chronically poor households compared to the entire population for rural areas, urban areas, and five regions selected for a cash transfer project. Poor households tend to have common socioeconomic characteristics with respect to gender of the household head, level of education, labor market attachment, and household size. Chronic poverty increases with the age of the household head and clearly decreases with education level. Since education level and primary activity are related, it is not surprising that being a farmer is strongly correlated with chronic poverty, even in urban areas. Polygamist households have a higher incidence of chronic poverty, and single men and women have a lower incidence of chronic poverty than monogamist married households. Larger household size is also related to a higher rate of chronic poverty.

Chronic poverty also is correlated with lack of access to basic necessities. On the one hand, households with no access to electricity, no toilet in the house,

Table 3.1 Characteristics of Chronically Poor Households in Cameroon
share of the category unless otherwise noted

Characteristic	Rural areas		Urban areas		Five project regions, rural areas	
	All	Chronic poor	All	Chronic poor	All	Chronic poor
Household region						
Adamaoua	0.062	0.061	0.032	0.053	0.10	0.075
Far north	0.24	0.37	0.067	0.14	0.40	0.45
North	0.12	0.18	0.056	0.15	0.20	0.22
Northwest	0.13	0.15	0.054	0.10	0.21	0.18
East	0.061	0.065	0.019	0.021	0.100	0.079
Douala	n.a.	n.a.	0.28	0.088	n.a.	n.a.
Yaoundé	n.a.	n.a.	0.27	0.048	n.a.	n.a.
Center	0.11	0.061	0.020	0.041	n.a.	n.a.
Littoral	0.030	0.011	0.044	0.15	n.a.	n.a.
West	0.11	0.047	0.096	0.19	n.a.	n.a.
South	0.046	0.020	0.0080	0.0061	n.a.	n.a.
Southwest	0.090	0.046	0.050	0.017	n.a.	n.a.
Household head characteristics						
Has no education	0.40	0.55	0.12	0.32	0.57	0.63
Primary school education	0.37	0.34	0.29	0.45	0.31	0.30
Secondary 1 education	0.14	0.083	0.25	0.18	0.079	0.058
Secondary 2 education	0.063	0.021	0.21	0.049	0.031	0.010
Polygamist	0.23	0.29	0.083	0.16	0.29	0.32
Widow	0.11	0.099	0.099	0.16	0.076	0.074
Handicapped	0.064	0.069	0.054	0.061	0.061	0.067
Male household head	0.80	0.84	0.77	0.73	0.85	0.87
Age (years)	45.2	46.9	42.7	48.5	45.0	46.6
Number of household members by age category						
0–4 years old	1.26	1.54	0.93	1.31	1.44	1.61
5–14 years old	2.21	2.96	1.64	2.79	2.49	3.07
15–59 years old	2.95	3.32	3.45	4.11	3.10	3.33
60 years old and older	0.31	0.33	0.18	0.40	0.31	0.33
Household head occupation						
Public sector	0.050	0.018	0.15	0.029	0.036	0.013
Private sector, formal	0.028	0.0076	0.13	0.032	0.013	0.0047
Informal sector	0.15	0.097	0.50	0.49	0.13	0.096

(continued next page)

Table 3.1 (continued)

Characteristic	Rural areas		Urban areas		Five project regions, rural areas	
	All	Chronic poor	All	Chronic poor	All	Chronic poor
Informal, agriculture	0.74	0.85	0.10	0.32	0.79	0.87
No occupation	0.038	0.030	0.12	0.13	0.029	0.020
Housing characteristics						
Owner of the house	0.81	0.91	0.48	0.75	0.90	0.95
Lighting: oil	0.66	0.72	0.094	0.37	0.73	0.73
Lighting: electricity	0.23	0.092	0.90	0.59	0.098	0.039
Cooking fuel: bought wood	0.12	0.063	0.38	0.55	0.14	0.068
Cooking fuel: picked-up wood	0.83	0.93	0.11	0.39	0.84	0.93
Cooking fuel: natural gas	0.028	0.0028	0.39	0.012	0.0063	0.0013
Source of water: forage	0.33	0.32	0.20	0.34	0.32	0.32
Has solid wall	0.12	0.061	0.58	0.28	0.064	0.043
Has solid roof	0.61	0.41	0.99	0.94	0.41	0.30
Has solid floor	0.27	0.13	0.87	0.63	0.17	0.092
Flush toilets	0.0074	0	0.18	0.00062	0.0024	0
Improved latrines	0.12	0.057	0.48	0.29	0.059	0.037
Unimproved latrines	0.71	0.70	0.34	0.69	0.72	0.69
No toilets	0.16	0.24	0.0071	0.029	0.22	0.28
Physical assets						
Phone	0.26	0.11	0.84	0.44	0.16	0.078
Radio	0.48	0.36	0.64	0.50	0.41	0.34
Television	0.13	0.035	0.69	0.29	0.054	0.018
Motorcycle	0.089	0.053	0.087	0.033	0.095	0.051
Bike	0.21	0.27	0.054	0.11	0.30	0.31
Number of observations	5,026	1,240	6,365	345	2,702	951

Source: Calculations based on ECAM3 data.
Note: n.a. = not applicable. Descriptive statistics for households in Cameroon by living areas and poverty status, expressed as a share of the population in the column (unless noted otherwise). Household size and sample weights are used to obtain nationally representative figures in terms of individuals. Chronically poor households are defined as those below 80 percent of the national poverty line.

and less durable housing construction materials are more likely to be chronically poor. On the other hand, households owning a mobile phone are rarely chronically poor.

Table 3.1 also confirms that the chronic poor are concentrated in rural areas, in particular in the five project regions. For instance, in the entire rural population, 12 and 24 percent of households live in the north and far north regions, respectively, but 18 and 37 percent of the rural chronically poor households live in these regions, indicating that the chronic poor are overrepresented in the two northern regions. As expected, the chronic poor possess lower levels of several physical assets: 3.5 percent of them have a television in rural areas (29 percent in urban areas) compared with 13 percent of the whole rural population (69 percent in urban areas). Poor households also have lower levels of human capital: 55 percent of the poor never went to school (no education), but this number rises to 63 percent in the five project regions. Poor households are underrepresented in the public sector (2.9 percent in urban areas) and the formal private sector (3.2 percent in urban areas) compared with the entire population (15 and 13 percent, respectively) and are overrepresented in the agricultural informal sector even in urban areas (32 percent in urban areas compared with 9.8 percent of the entire urban population). They live in larger households on average (more household members in each age category for all areas), and their houses tend to lack equipment and solid material: in urban areas, only 28 percent of the poor have solid walls, compared with 58 percent of the whole urban population.

Differences between rural and urban poverty are also found, with the urban poor having older members and more household heads who are widows, for instance, compared with the rural poor. These differences between poor and nonpoor households, in each living area, can be exploited to design the proxy means testing formula.

Shocks Affecting Households

Cameroonian households are vulnerable to environmental, macroeconomic, and social covariate shocks, in addition to idiosyncratic shocks to employment and health. Climatic risks are the primary source of environmental shocks because they have a direct impact on the livelihoods of the 45 percent of the population engaged in subsistence agriculture. Since climatic events also affect the regional food supply, they affect the food security of the general population. Among these risks, flooding, drought, and desertification are frequent in the poorest provinces (north and far north).

Macroeconomic risks include inflation, exchange rate fluctuations, export price volatility, depressed export demand, and lower remittances and foreign direct investment. All of these have been important shocks in past years. Recently, the fuel and food price crises as well as the financial crisis have been major shocks in Cameroon. Macroeconomic risks are exacerbated by the high reliance of the Cameroonian economy on unprocessed primary goods that are subject to price volatility, by limited diversification of export commodities, and by low agricultural productivity that generates import dependency.

Social covariate risks mainly affect women and children. They include early arranged marriage, human trafficking, and genital mutilation (prevalence rate of 1.4 percent). More broadly, they can include political upheaval and ethnic strife.

Idiosyncratic shocks affect several aspects of household well-being. The largest health shock is death of a household member; disease and disability also influence household well-being. Other idiosyncratic shocks include theft or loss of employment, although the latter probably has a limited impact in rural areas.

Additional information on the frequency of shocks is needed to provide a comprehensive picture of the importance of exposure to shocks for the economic well-being of households. Collection of this information represents an important area for future investment.

Current Social Assistance Programs to Address Short- and Long-Term Needs: Insufficient Scope and Coverage

The number of existing safety net programs is small in Cameroon, and their scope and coverage are limited. The seven safety nets and the principal actors—donors—are presented in table 3.2. Except for price subsidies, the coverage of each program is just above 1 percent of the population and only about two-thirds of the targeted population.

Within the social sector, health and education accounted for 96 percent of total spending or 24 percent of the government budget between 2006 and 2010 (World Bank 2011a). Safety nets accounted for only 0.76 percent of the government budget (0.23 percent of GDP) without including food and fuel subsidies. This compares to an average of 1.9 percent of GDP in developing countries; in Sub-Saharan Africa, Burkina Faso (0.6 percent), Mali (0.5 percent), and Tanzania (0.3 percent) have higher expenditures as a share of GDP than Cameroon. In Ethiopia and Malawi, spending levels are around 4.5 percent of GDP, and Mauritius and South Africa (two countries with higher per capita income than Cameroon) also have higher shares of safety net spending.

Table 3.2 summarizes expenditures of the safety net system in Cameroon by type of program for 2008, 2009, and 2010. As the table shows, when we include universal price subsidies, safety net spending rises to 7.4 percent of the government budget or 1.6 percent of GDP (World Bank 2011a). Indeed, these subsidies are particularly expensive, and costs have risen far above expectations. Further, the subsidies are regressive, because the poor have a lower overall consumption of many of the subsidized products.

Table 3.3 presents details on the targeting criteria (including geographic area), coverage, and costs per beneficiary. In addition to limited scope and coverage, coordination between programs is scant, and response to shocks consists mostly of ad hoc emergency interventions. Targeting is relatively poor overall and is even regressive for universal subsidies, which have represented most of the budget for social protection since 2007.

The proposal to improve the current social protection system by creating an unconditional cash transfer program aims both to expand the coverage and improve the targeting of poor households in a more systematic way.

Table 3.2 Expenditure on Safety Net Programs in Cameroon, 2008–10
CFAF, millions

Program and type of expenditure	Funder	2008	2009	2010
School feeding programs				
School feeding	MINEDUB	50	55	50
School feeding	WFP	1,746	1,746	1,746
Fee waiver programs				
Hospital fees	MINSANTE	4,400	1,600	1,600
School fees	MINEDUB	—	4,800	4,800
Cash transfer programs				
Indigents and street children	MINAS	50	50	50
Price subsidies				
Energy products subsidy	MINFI	136,900	22,500	112,500
Food price subsidies	MINFI	73,000	51,000	51,000
Transport subsidies	MINFI	3,200	3,200	3,200
Public works programs				
Food-for-work	WFP	—	196	196
Yaoundé Sanitation Project (PAD-Y)	MINEPAT	—	600	600
PAD-Y	AfDB	—	2,400	2,400
Emergency				
Cereal stocks	WFP	396	196	196
Emergency, refugees	WFP, UNICEF	25,713	6,354	14,597
Cereal stocks	BID, MINADER	—	215	100
Nutritional support programs				
OVC	UNICEF	47	47	47
OVC	NGOs	100	100	100
Total government of Cameroon		217,600	83,805	173,800
Total government of Cameroon (without subsidies)		1,762	4,500	2,305
Total donors or partners		27,999	11,255	19,383
Total		245,599	95,060	193,183
Total (without subsidies)		32,499	13,560	21,683

Source: World Bank 2011a.
Note: — = not available. MINEDUB = Ministry of Basic Education; WFP = World Food Program;
MINSANTE = Ministry of Public Health; MINAS = Ministry of Social Affairs; MINFI = Ministry of Finance;
MINEPAT = Ministry of Economy, Planning, and Regional Development; AfDB = African Development Bank;
UNICEF = United Nations Children's Fund; BID = Islamic Development Bank; MINADER = Ministry of Agriculture
and Rural Development; OVC = orphans and vulnerable children; NGO = nongovernmental organization.

Table 3.3 Existing Assistance Programs in Cameroon

Type of program	Targeting criteria	Geographic area	Coverage	Cost per beneficiary
School feeding programs				
WFP and MINEDUB	Provinces with low school attainment and high food insecurity	Adamaoua, far north, north	55,366 students (7,180 girls taking home rations) in 367 targeted schools	CFAF 35,000
Nutrition programs				
WFP village granaries		Northern provinces	300,000 people through 410 granaries	
WFP for refugees		North, east, Adamaoua (mostly)	210,000 people with food programs for refugees	
UNICEF Survie (health, nutrition, and WASH)		Far north and north	60,695 people in 60 villages	
UNICEF and NGOs, OVCs	OVCs (micro-credit loans)	All provinces except in the north and far north regions	2,614 children	CFAF 16,190 per child
CARE, assistance to OVCs	Health status of the children and economic status of the family		20,000 people, including 3,000 OVCs	
CRS, assistance program		Mostly northwestern regions	7,500 children countrywide	
Labor-intensive public works programs				
Projet d'Assainissement de Yaoundé	Self-selection (inefficient because of high wage)	Yaoundé	6,000 employees	CFAF 22.3 billion total: daily rate of CFAF 2,400
WFP food-for-work programs	Self-selection	Far north and north regions	16,590 families	Wage equivalent of CFAF 3,147 in cereals monthly
Emergency response initiatives				
WFP and MINADER, village cereal stocks	Area and periods of droughts, food crises, and emergency situations	Northern and western provinces	133 cereal stocks in villages	
WFP assistance to refugees		Eastern borders and Adamaoua	760,940 refugees in 2008 and 227,655 in 2009 in 72 sites	
WFP emergency response to droughts		Far north and north regions	565,400 beneficiaries in 2008 and 94,457 in 2009	

(continued next page)

Table 3.3 (continued)

Type of program	Targeting criteria	Geographic area	Coverage	Cost per beneficiary
Universal price subsidies				
	Universal (proved regressive)	Entire country	Entire population	6.92% of government budget in 2009
Unconditional cash transfers				
MINAS	Specific vulnerable groups (street children, disabled, elderly)			Total estimated around US$10 million
Fee-waiver programs for basic services (by each ministry)				
MINEDUB and MINESUP	Disadvantaged primary school students, disabled university students	Northern and western provinces	69,429 children and 60,000 university students	

Source: World Bank 2011a.
Note: WFP = World Food Program; MINEDUB = Ministry of Basic Education; UNICEF = United Nations Children's Fund; WASH = water, sanitation, and hygiene; NGO = nongovernmental organization; OVC = orphans and vulnerable children; CARE = Cooperative for Assistance and Relief Everywhere; CRS = Catholic Relief Services; MINADER = Ministry of Agriculture and Rural Development; MINAS = Ministry of Social Affairs; and MINESUP = Ministry of Higher Education.

A pilot that employs the targeting method presented here is currently being implemented in the rural *commune* of Soulédé-Roua in far north region and the urban *arrondissement* of Ndop in the northwest region. Different data sets—ECAM3 and General Population and Housing Census (GPHC)—can be used to refine the geographic targeting at the *département* or even *commune* level. For instance, five *départements* (out of 58 in Cameroon) contain about 1.8 million chronic poor, or 49 percent of the total for the country. This pilot will be extended to the five regions where chronic poverty is concentrated—Adamaoua, the east, far north, north, and northwest—and will, given resource constraints and high poverty incidence, target only chronically poor households.

The remainder of the case study provides details on the targeting method generated for this UCT program.

Targeting Methodology Employed in Cameroon

In order to increase both coverage and targeting of the current social protection system, a proxy means test (PMT) formula was developed. In the UCT pilot, the PMT formula is coupled with geographic and community targeting. We first present the PMT formula and then describe how it is combined with two other targeting methods in the pilot.

PMT Formula

In order to implement the program efficiently and with low administrative cost, the number of variables in the PMT formula has to be limited and the accuracy of the responses has to be easy to verify. The variables include sociodemographic characteristics of the household head, demographic composition of the household, housing construction materials, and household equipment and assets. They attempt to cover the maximal dimensions of poverty and correspond to the characteristics of the chronic poor outlined in the previous section. The ECAM3 data were used to select variables associated with chronic poverty and to estimate weights for them. For the PMT formula presented here, chronically poor households are defined as those where adult-equivalent expenditures are below 0.8 of the poverty line, or CFAF 215,554.[2]

We used an ordinary least squares (OLS) regression in order to select the variables and to assign weights, with adult-equivalent expenditures as the dependent variable. In this context, the usual sources of potential parameter bias (omitted variables and endogeneity) are not a concern, since the goal of the PMT is not to determine causality but to establish a correlation between chronic poverty and characteristics of the households. Moreover, we focus on the predictive capacity of the model. Thus the main criteria used to design the formula are the errors of inclusion and exclusion generated by the model. To test the formula in a robust manner, two-thirds of the sample were randomly selected and used for the OLS regression, while the last third was retained to test the formula and compute the errors of inclusion and exclusion.[3] The PMT formula is presented in table 3.4.

When the household's level of well-being increases, the PMT score increases, which means that the household is less likely to be a beneficiary of the program. The demographic composition of the household has a significant effect on its eligibility status, since the weights associated with larger household size are negative. Being a male, uneducated, or an older household head (negative coefficients) also increase(s) the likelihood of eligibility. The PMT score increases—decreasing the likelihood of program eligibility—when a household has access to goods such as electricity or fuel and owns assets like a radio or cart. Some measures of household assets are particularly indicative: refrigerator, motorcycle, and television (positive) or lack of a proper latrine (negative). The R^2 of 0.615 indicates that the model explains 61.5 percent of the variation in the adult-equivalent expenditures.

Table 3.4 PMT Formula for Rural Areas of Cameroon

Variable	Response	Weight
Household head gender	Man	−99
	Woman	0
Household head age	Less than 34 years old	0
	35–49 years old	−100
	50 years old and older	−61
Household head education	No education	−312
	Primary and secondary 1	−291
	Secondary 2 and more	−202
Household head religion	Muslim	144
	Christian	0
	No religion	0
Household head marital status	Monogamist	85
	Polygamist	115
	Other (single)	0
Household head occupational category	Formal sector (public or private)	0
	Nonagricultural informal	0
	Agriculture	−72
	Unemployed	−96
Household size	1 member	0
	2–3 members	−367
	4–5 members	−684
	6–7 members	−794
	8 members and more	−894
Household composition	Members between 0 and 4 years old	23
	Members between 5 and 14 years old	−30
	Members between 15 and 59 years old	−40
	Members 60 years old and older	−43
Size of the house	Small: less than 25 square meters	−90
	Medium: from 25 to 50 square meters	−33
	Large: from 50 to 95 square meters	−22
	Very large: 96 square meters and more	0
Lighting source	AES-SONEL electricity	280
	Oil	185
	Other (natural gas, generator)	0
Main energy source for cooking	Picked-up wood	−150
	Other (bought wood, natural gas, oil, sawdust, coal)	0

(continued next page)

Table 3.4 (continued)

Variable	Response	Weight
Bathroom facility	Equipped latrine	−240
	Unequipped latrine, no latrine	−260
	Flush toilet	0
Main roof material	Cement, sheet metal, tile	51
	Other	0
Main floor material	Soil	−62
	Other	0
Own radio	Yes	67
	No	0
Television or satellite network	Yes	40
	No	0
Own television	Yes	171
	No	0
Own motorcycle	Yes	285
	No	0
Own cart	Yes	117
	No	0
Own refrigerator	Yes	415
	No	0
Own unfarmed land	Yes	46
	No	0
Own house not used by a household member	Yes	105
	No	0
Constant		13,787
Number of observations	1,752	
R^2	0.615	

Source: Nguetse-Tegoum and Stoeffler 2012.

Short-Term Targeting and Data Constraints

The PMT formula presented above does not include a short-term component that would allow programs to address vulnerability by including households affected by temporary adverse shocks. However, adding a short-term component to the PMT targeting is constrained by data limitations. The questionnaires from ECAM3 ask limited questions about shocks faced by the household. Ideally, information would be available on idiosyncratic shocks affecting health (disease and death), loss of employment, and theft, for instance, and on covariate shocks such as agricultural or climatic shocks (pests, floods, storms, and droughts). Further, because of the endogeneity of shocks, data at the individual level and at the community (or regional) level are desirable.

In the absence of such information, we used geo-referenced meteorological data from the National Aeronautics and Space Administration (NASA) on rainfall[4] between 1997 and 2006 to construct long-term rainfall averages and data on the range of rainfall in 2007 to compute the deviation from long-term averages. We also created a dummy variable "drought" for each of our *départements* and included it in our PMT formula estimation to give it a weight. The variable has a coefficient estimate of −0.094 with standard deviations of 0.020; this means that living in an area affected by such a "drought" is associated with 9 percent lower predicted consumption, on average. The weight in the PMT is, for instance, about the same as for being unemployed. The addition of the "drought" variable to the formula does not cause a large change in any of the coefficients presented in table 3.4. Specifically, the weights associated with the variables keep the same magnitude overall, and none of the signs changes.

This "drought" variable, however, has serious limitations. The scale used (*département*) is too large to take into account local variations (real rainfall). Further, 2007, the year of ECAM3, was overall a "good" year with no major drought or flood. Finally, there are no data on household exposure in ECAM3 to combine with this "drought" variable in order to compute an endogenous treatment effect. Thus the impact of "drought" has to be the same for all households in a "drought" area in our model.

Collecting information on covariate and idiosyncratic shocks at the household level is increasingly imperative in order to improve PMT formulas and develop a short-term targeting component. Despite the limitations encountered, our simple "drought" variable provides encouraging results, which are discussed in the next section along with other targeting results.

Urban Formula: Lower Poverty Rates and More Difficult Discrimination

Finding an efficient PMT formula for urban households is a more delicate exercise than working on the rural formula. The urban poverty rate is much lower than the rural rate in Cameroon; the poverty incidence is 55 percent in rural areas and only 12.2 percent in urban areas (Nguetse-Tegoum 2011). In addition, urban poverty might be more diverse in its causes and manifestations than rural poverty. All potential PMT formulas perform poorly in urban areas, particularly in terms of exclusion errors using the ECAM3 data set. Conducting specific research on poor urban households erroneously excluded by the PMT formula would help to identify their attributes.

In light of these difficulties, we adopted a quantile regression (QR) methodology to design the urban PMT formula. Quantile regressions offer three advantages compared to OLS.[5] First, they are less sensitive to outliers, which can be an advantage in urban areas. Second, they allow us to focus on limiting errors at the bottom end of the expenditure distribution; that is, to limit exclusion errors by ensuring that the formula effectively models expenditures of the poorest households—without caring about the imprecision in the formula above the poverty threshold needed for the program. Third, QRs allow us to change easily the threshold used, depending on the needs of the program, such as the number of total beneficiaries or trade-off between inclusion and exclusion errors. For these reasons, the QR model performed much better than the OLS specifications tried for urban areas.

We chose a quantile level of 0.1 for the QR of the urban model (which can be adjusted to reflect the program needs) to reflect the poverty level in urban areas (12.2 percent). The PMT formula for urban areas is presented in table 3.5. This urban formula does not reveal any surprise in terms of signs of the weights associated with each variable. Since the QR minimizes errors at the bottom of the distribution, the PMT weights generated overall are smaller than those of the OLS rural model. Education is not as important in the urban formula, but family composition continues to weigh heavily in the score, with larger households associated with lower expenditures. The urban formula also enables the introduction of new types of assets: cars, compact disk players, and digital video disk players.

Targeting Process: Geography, PMT, and the Community

Proxy means testing is only one component of the information used in the targeting process developed for Cameroon. Here we describe how the geography, the community, and the PMT are combined in the targeting process. The main steps are shown in figure 3.1. After defining the geographic area where the program will be implemented, the community selects potential beneficiaries (that is, those considered as poor by the community). Those households designated by the community then answer a short survey containing all the variables included in the PMT formula (table 3.5). The data set obtained is used to compute the PMT scores. Households with a score below the threshold (12,281 with this formula) are placed on a list for cash transfers. The list is then validated by the community.

For the pilot in Souled é-Roua, in particular, community targeting was an important feature. After Souled é-Roua was geographically targeted, the 15 poorest villages (among the 34 villages of the *commune*) were selected with the community, based on poverty criteria such as poor infrastructure and lack of arable land. In selected villages, the community conducted the first round of a household-level selection, with the aim of keeping around 70 percent of the households as potentially eligible. The selection protocol was established by the pilot project team in collaboration with the community. Selection committees

Table 3.5 PMT Formula for Urban Areas of Cameroon

Variable	Response	Weight
Household head gender	Man	0
	Woman	213
Household head age	Age	11
	Squared age	−0.5
Household head education	No education	−110
	Primary	−136
	Secondary 1	−104
	Secondary 2	−100
	Higher education	0
Household head marital status	Married or union	131
	Single, divorced, or separated	0
Household head occupational category	Public sector	77
	Formal private sector	80
	Nonagricultural informal	15
	Unemployed	24
	Informal agriculture	0
Household size	1 member	0
	2–3 members	−339
	4–5 members	−566
	6–7 members	−634
	8 members and more	−691
Household composition	Members between 0 and 14 years old	−51
	Members between 15 and 59 years old	−49
	Members 60 years old and more	−3
Housing type	Isolated house	0
	House with several housing units	60
	Compound, saré	98
	Modern villa, building with apartments	145
Housing occupation status	Free housing (provided by the employer or by family)	−21
	Tenant	−6
	Owner	0
Size of the house	Small: less than 25 square meters	0
	Medium: from 25 to 50 square meters	12
	Large: from 50 to 99 square meters	42
	Very large: 100 square meters and more	47
Main source of drinking water	Tap or drilling	53
	Other (well, equipped spring, river, rainfall)	0

(continued next page)

Table 3.5 (continued)

Variable	Response	Weight
Lighting source	AES-SONEL electricity	60
	Other (natural gas, generator)	0
Main energy source for cooking	Other (does not cook, sawdust)	0
	Natural gas, electricity	73
	Oil	−16
	Picked-up wood	−133
	Bought wood	−23
Bathroom facility	Flush toilet	280
	Equipped latrine	138
	Unequipped latrine	102
	No bathroom facility	0
Main wall material	Concrete, baked brick, stone	11
	Other (terracotta, simple brick, plank)	0
Main roof material	Cement, sheet metal, tile	137
	Other	0
Main floor material	Cement or tile	45
	Other	0
Own mobile or home phone	Yes	189
	No	0
Own radio	Yes	56
	No	0
Own television	Yes	114
	No	0
Own compact disk or digital video disk player	Yes	46
	No	0
Own refrigerator or freezer	Yes	158
	No	0
Own ventilator or air conditioning	Yes	94
	No	0
Own stove or oil portable stove	Yes	51
	No	0
Own motorcycle or a bicycle	Yes	132
	No	0
Own car	Yes	405
	No	0
Own living room or dining room	Yes	6
	No	0

(continued next page)

Table 3.5 (continued)

Variable	Response	Weight
Own farmed land	Yes	33
	No	0
Own unfarmed land	Yes	53
	No	0
Own house not used by a household member	Yes	1
	No	0
Constant		12,245

Source: Calculations based on ECAM3 data.
Note: Quantile regression (0.1), dependent variable: adult-equivalent household expenditure (in log).

Figure 3.1 Steps Taken in Implementing the Targeting Process

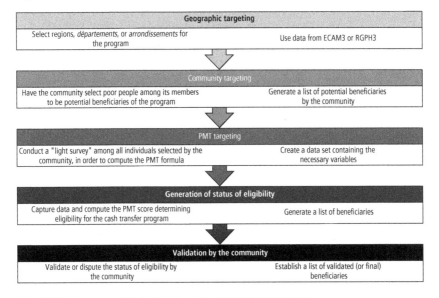

Note: RGPH3 = Recensement Général de la Population et de l'Habitation 3 survey.

were established, with checks and balances, to work with defined poverty criteria: housing conditions, food security, and access to basic health and education services.

By combining community and PMT selection, this pilot allows comparisons to be made. It is especially helpful for measuring errors of inclusion and exclusion for both methods of targeting, as has been done in other countries (for example, Alatas et al. 2010).

Targeting Results

The main indicators used to assess the efficiency of the targeting formula are errors of inclusion and exclusion. The targeting results are relatively sound compared to similar targeting studies or experiences in other countries: inclusion errors are 24.1 percent, and exclusion errors are 24.8 percent. These results are probably due to the variables employed but also to the relative homogeneity of the geographic area where the targeting takes place. Given the high level of poverty in the area, it is important to minimize exclusion errors even further, for instance, with a mechanism allowing people to dispute their eligibility when they are initially registered as nonbeneficiaries. Unfortunately, the available data (ECAM3) preclude identifying specific groups for which exclusion (or inclusion) errors are especially large. However, the ex post evaluation should allow further investigation of what causes some households to have lower consumption than expected in the PMT.

Figure 3.2 shows the proportion of chronically poor households in each decile of the PMT score. The fact that the lower PMT score deciles are associated with a much higher proportion of the chronic poor demonstrates the efficiency of the targeting mechanism.

Adding the "drought" variable slightly reduces the errors, especially exclusion errors, which decrease by about 1 percentage point; errors of inclusion

Figure 3.2 Proportion of Chronically Poor Households in Cameroon Based on PMT Score

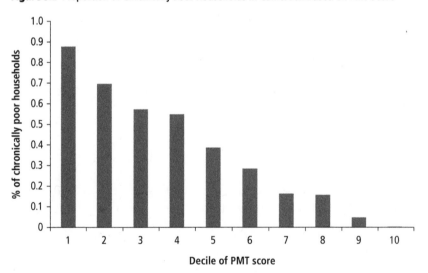

Source: Calculations based on ECAM3 data.

become 23.8 percent and errors of exclusion become 23.9 percent. The results suggest that additional shock variables in general and better meteorological shock variables in particular can improve the efficiency of the targeting. Still, more information is needed on household exposure to shocks.

Errors in the urban formula are also encouraging: 14.5 percent exclusion errors and 35.3 percent inclusion errors. This asymmetry is due to the low quantile level chosen (0.1), which serves to minimize exclusion errors in urban areas.

Ex Ante Performance of the Transfer: A Large Impact on Poverty Indexes

Ex ante simulations were performed, before the start of the pilot, to estimate the potential magnitude of reductions in poverty brought about by unconditional cash transfers in rural areas. The simulations, based on the ECAM3 data, are purely mathematical: the eligibility status of the household is determined using the PMT formula described in the previous section, transfers are added to household consumption, poverty indexes are computed before and after the transfer, and the reduction in poverty is measured. For simplicity, we considered the three Foster-Greer-Thorbecke (FGT) indicators: poverty incidence (headcount ratio), poverty gap, and poverty severity. Since a reduction in poverty incidence only takes into account the number of households crossing a given threshold (the poverty line), it is important to consider the other two indexes (poverty gap and poverty severity) to measure the overall impact on poverty. Here we focus on the impact on chronic poverty—that is, households whose expenditures are below 0.8 of the poverty line.

These simulations also make it possible to compute the Coady-Grosh-Hoddinott (CGH) index, which is an indicator of targeting quality (see Coady, Grosh, and Hoddinott 2004). It measures the part of the transfers actually received by the poorest households, divided by their proportion of the population. Here we consider the part received by the poorest 20 percent of households. Finally, the simulations allow us to estimate the program budget needed when the program is implemented in the entire country.

Different transfer scenarios are considered for the simulations. A usual amount for cash transfer programs (the UCT in Niger) represents 10–20 percent of the beneficiaries' expenditures. According to ECAM3 data, this means monthly transfers per household between CFAF 7,500 and CFAF 15,000. Table 3.6 shows the budget of the transfer depending on the amount per household. For the five targeted regions in Cameroon, this would correspond to a global program budget between CFAF 44.1 billion and CFAF 97.1 billion per year (third column of table 3.6) excluding administrative costs.[6] The last column of table 3.6 shows the reduction in the incidence of chronic poverty (number of households below 0.8 of the poverty line) for each transfer amount, when the PMT presented in table 3.5 is used to target poor households.

Table 3.6 Amount of Transfer per Household and Resulting Global Budget for Cash Transfer Program in Cameroon
CFAF unless otherwise noted

Amount per household per month	Amount per capita per month	Yearly budget of transfer (billions, 2007 data)	Yearly budget of transfer (billions, with projected demographic growth)	Reduction in chronic poverty incidence (%)
7,500	1,000	44.1	49.0	9.15
10,000	1,333	58.8	65.3	13.02
11,250	1,500	66.2	73.4	15.17
12,500	1,667	73.5	81.6	17.64
15,000	2,000	88.2	97.9	21.82
16,500	2,200	97.1	107.7	24.44

Source: Calculations based on ECAM3 data for the 2007 population and RGPH3 data for the projected 2012 population in the target areas.
Note: The budget is based on the number of poor households in Cameroon.

The simulations presented in table 3.6 assume that a fixed amount is transferred to all households below the PMT threshold. However, an alternative is to allocate a different amount to different households. The amount transferred can vary depending on the size of the household, the PMT score, or a combination of these two characteristics.

Varying transfers according to PMT score can lead to greater reductions in poverty indicators, because poorer households receive more resources, which increases the impact of the project on the poverty gap and on poverty severity. Also, if transfers increase with household size, more resources may be transferred to the poor because larger households show a greater depth of poverty. Moreover, if transfers vary by PMT score, having different levels of transfers may increase the perceived fairness of the program by allocating more resources to the poorest households. This also allows the project to phase out participants as they get closer to the PMT threshold, rather than abruptly cutting the transfer as soon as they cross the threshold.

The drawback is increased administrative complexity with regard to computing the list of beneficiaries, registering beneficiaries, and making payments. Also, beneficiaries may not understand why their level of transfers is different from that of other households or may find this difference unfair. Varying the level of payments may generate additional opportunities for corruption. Ultimately, the choice of fixed or varying levels of payments may depend on the country and project administrative capacities as well as on the evaluation of risk (unfairness, corruption) implied by varying levels of payments.

Scenario 1 simulates a transfer of CFAF 12,500 per month per eligible household, which is the upper median amount based on the PMT scale in table 3.6. The associated reductions in the incidence, depth, and severity of poverty are

Table 3.7 Ex Ante Results of Poverty Simulations for Cameroon

Scenario	Amount of transfer per household per month (CFAF)	Reduction of poverty incidence (%)	Reduction of poverty gap (%)	Reduction of poverty severity (%)	Budget (CFAF, billions)
Scenario 1: Fixed amount per household	12,500	17.64	43.35	54.50	72.0
Scenario 2: Different amount per household	5,000–21,000	16.63	45.09	56.96	72.7
Scenario 3: Different amount by household PMT score	7,500–17,500	17.46	45.65	56.82	74.2
Scenario 4: Different amount by household size and PMT score	1,025–2,250[a]	16.09	47.42	59.02	76.2

Source: Calculations with the ECAM3 data.
Note: The budget is based on the number of eligible households in Cameroon.
a. Per member.

presented in table 3.7. The results show a clear reduction in the incidence of chronic poverty and an even stronger impact on both the poverty gap and poverty severity. The CGH index is 2.51, which indicates very efficient targeting. This scenario serves as the benchmark for comparing poverty reduction with variable transfer amounts.

Scenario 2 simulates a transfer similar to the previous one with regard to the average amount received by each household (CFAF 12,500 per month, budget of CFAF 72.7 billion). This time, five household sizes are created, each of which receives a different amount, ranging from CFAF 5,000 per month for a household with 1–3 members up to CFAF 21,000 per month for a household with 10 members or more. This transfer method is fairer in that it gives a similar amount to each person (and not the household).

The result of this simulation is similar to the first, with a slightly lower impact on the reduction of poverty incidence and a higher impact on the reduction of the poverty gap and severity. The shift in impacts toward reductions in the poverty gap and severity measures stems from the fact that poorer households have more family members on average. The CGH index also is higher in this scenario (2.57) than in scenario 1, suggesting better targeting when the transfer amount varies based on household size.

Scenario 3 divides eligible households into three categories depending on their PMT score. The lower category has PMT scores between 11,589 and 12,047.99, the median category has scores between 12,048 and 12,178.39, and the upper category has scores between 12,178.4 and 12,281. The poorer third receives CFAF 17,500 per month, the median third receives CFAF 12,500 per month, and the higher third receives CFAF 7,500 per month. Under this scenario, the incidence measure recovers to the level seen in scenario 1, while the reductions in the depth and severity of poverty seen in scenario 2 are largely maintained. The CGH index is clearly better in scenario 3 than in scenarios 1 and 2, reaching 2.75 in this simulation, suggesting more efficient targeting.

Scenario 4 essentially combines scenarios 2 and 3. The amount received depends on the number of household members and the PMT score of the household. A household in the lower PMT score category receives CFAF 2,250 per household member, the medium category receives CFAF 1,700 per household, and the higher category receives CFAF 1,025 per household. The impact on poverty indexes is mixed, with a slight decrease in the reduction of poverty incidence associated with the transfers and a larger reduction in the poverty gap and poverty severity measures compared to all other scenarios. In addition, the CGH increases to 2.80, suggesting further gains in targeting efficiency.

Overall, these four simulations indicate a high potential reduction of poverty, especially regarding the poverty gap and poverty severity, compared to similar simulations in other contexts (see, for instance, Narayan and Yoshida 2005). The fact that the depth and severity indexes see a larger reduction than the poverty incidence index indicates that the transfers efficiently target the poorer among the poor. The impact also varies by region and is higher in the provinces with the highest chronic poverty rates. A CGH index between 2.5 and 2.8 would rank this transfer program among the most efficient worldwide (see Castañeda et al. 2005). While it is clear that the targeting is more efficient when the transfer amount varies per household, the difference might not justify the increased administrative complexity, as discussed above.

The ex ante simulations suggest the potential for promising gains in terms of poverty reduction. However, the magnitude of the gains can only be captured through an ex post evaluation. The design for such an ex post evaluation is presented in the next subsection.

Design for an Ex Post Evaluation: Further Learning from the Program

A comprehensive evaluation of the unconditional cash transfer program in Cameroon is needed both to generate political support to sustain the program at the national level and to create empirical evidence regarding the economic impact of the transfer. The evaluation would generate knowledge spillovers far beyond the Cameroon project itself, a fact observed in the evaluation literature (Behrman 2007; Rawlings and Rubio 2005). It would also add to the base of knowledge on the design and implementation of safety net programs in Sub-Saharan Africa.[7]

The impact evaluation would focus on the following issues:

- *Is the targeting efficient?* Simple indicators would allow us to answer this question: inclusion and exclusion errors measured after eligibility is determined, but before the first transfer; coverage in terms of the number of beneficiaries and food as a proportion of expenditures of these beneficiaries; and impact on poverty indexes (FGT). These indicators can be compared to the ex ante ones presented above to evaluate the accuracy of ex ante measures as predictors of ex post performance.

- *What is the impact of transfers on short-term consumption and shock-smoothing?* Short-term measurement of expenditures and food consumption would provide a first answer. Variables regarding risk management by the household (ex ante and ex post) would add further insight into the impacts of transfers on household ability to manage shocks.

- *What is the short-term (permanent) impact on asset accumulation and revenue generation?* Data collection on the use of transfers would increase understanding of the impact of transfers on investment and income-generation activities. Variables collected would include changes in assets, changes in agricultural and nonagricultural activity, and changes in marketing behavior, among others.

- *What is the medium- and long-term impact on education, health, and social indicators?* Most of the impact on health and education occurs in the medium or long run. Data would be collected on variables such as diseases, health visits, nutrition, school attendance, and social variables like early marriage of girls or child employment.

A serious evaluation of the UCT pilot and its impact requires a counterfactual using an experimental design with untreated villages (Rawlings and Rubio 2005). Thus it is necessary to collect data in villages where the pilot is being conducted (treatment villages) and in similar villages not included in the pilot cash transfer (control villages) for the evaluation. The literature (Angelucci and de Giorgi 2009; Katayama 2010) recommends using this design rather than using control households in the same community as treatment households because of the indirect effect on ineligible households within a community. The design also would allow us to measure the spillover effect of the transfers. Of course, a qualitative analysis needs to complement this rigorous quantitative evaluation in order to evaluate the full effect of the transfers (Kanbur 2002; Ravallion 2009).

Conclusion: What We Have Learned?

The experience gathered in preparing this unconditional cash transfer suggests that chronic poverty can be effectively targeted for social assistance in Cameroon. Because of the concentration of poverty in the northern provinces and in rural areas, geographic targeting is a crucial component of any targeting mechanism. When geographic targeting is combined with a proxy means testing formula in rural areas, the targeting mechanism generates inclusion and exclusion errors both under 25 percent. Community targeting will be added in the pilot to improve targeting efficiency and community acceptance. An efficient targeting mechanism is harder to find for urban areas, where the incidence of chronic poverty is lower and inclusion errors are considerably higher. However, quantile regression methods have allowed us to overcome some of this difficulty. Current data regarding shocks affecting households are insufficient to assist in program targeting for short-term needs, even in rural areas where covariant shocks have major impacts on household well-being.

The next steps in implementing the targeted UCT in Cameroon are twofold. First, better information regarding risks and shocks has to be collected in order to elaborate a PMTplus targeting approach, which can be employed to scale up assistance programs rapidly in the face of adverse shocks. Second, the UCT pilot has to be evaluated rigorously in order to assess the efficiency of the main (long-term) UCT component.

Annex 3A Detailed Results

Table 3A.1 PMT Formula for in a Pilot Program in Rural Areas of Cameroon

Variable	Response	Weight
Household head gender	Man	1,569
	Woman	0
Household head age	Age	69
	Squared age	−0.5
Household head education	No education	3,647
	Primary	4,103
	Secondary 1	2,826
	Secondary 2 and more	0
Household head religion	Muslim	−423
	Christian and other	0
Household head occupational category	Formal sector (public or private)	0
	Nonagricultural informal	2,408
	Agriculture	4,953
	Unemployed	2,590
Household size	1–3 members	0
	4–5 members	2,646
	6–7 members	4,520
	8 members and more	6,371

(continued next page)

Table 3A.1 (continued)

Variable	Response	Weight
Household composition	Members, 0–4 years old	204
	Members, 5–14 years old	2,084
	Members, 15–59 years old	921
	Members, 60 years old and older	1,000
Housing type	Compound, saré	−679
	Other	0
Housing occupation status	Owner	1,819
	Not owner	0
Main source of drinking water	Tap, drilling	−246
	Other (well, equipped spring, river, rainfall)	0
Main lighting source	AES-SONEL electricity	−3,872
	Other (natural gas, generator)	0
Main energy source for cooking	Bought wood	3,229
	Picked-up wood	6,033
	Other (natural gas, oil, sawdust, coal)	0
Bathroom facility	Equipped latrine, flush toilet	0
	Unequipped latrine	1,851
	No bathroom facility	4,613
Main wall material	Concrete, baked brick, stone	−1,149
	Other (terracotta, simple brick, plank)	0
Main roof material	Cement, sheet metal, tile	−3,210
	Other	0
Main floor material	Cement, tile	−1,377
	Other	0
Own radio	Yes	−844
	No	0
Own television	Yes	−2,686
	No	0
Own car, motorcycle, bicycle	Yes	−506
	No	0
Own farmed land	Yes	−883
	No	0
Own unfarmed land	Yes	−1,595
	No	0
Own house not used by a household member	Yes	−2,522
	No	0
Own a cart or wheelbarrow	Yes	−296
	No	0

(continued next page)

Table 3A.1 (continued)

Variable	Response	Weight
Own cow(s)	Yes	−3,347
	No	0
Own horse(s) or donkey(s)	Yes	−1,656
	No	0
Own sheep(s) or goat(s)	5 and more	−596
	Less than 5	0
Own chicken or poultry	15 and more	−346
	Less than 15	0
Constant		−27,136

Source: Calculations based on ECAM3 data.
Note: Probit regression, dependent variable: "chronic" (status of chronic poverty of the household, as defined in Nguetse-Tegoum 2011).

Notes

1. These rates come from studies using data from the *Enquête Camerounaise auprès des Ménages 2* and *3* (ECAM2 and ECAM3), where the poverty line is established at CFAF 738 (US$1.64) per day (Cameroon's currency is the African Financial Community franc; Nguetse-Tegoum 2011).
2. This threshold is close to the extreme poverty line—US$1.25 per day—and is used in the PMT for econometric reasons. Adult-equivalent consumption levels are defined based on recommended dietary allowances from the National Research Council (1989).
3. A common PMT formula is used in rural areas across the five project regions rather than estimating five different formulas. See table 3A.1 in the annex to this chapter. The reasons include improving project administration by increasing the simplicity and design (and testing) of the formula with a greater number of observations. Including regions (using dummy variables) in the formula does not increase its ex ante targeting efficiency.
4. These data were obtained from the NASA Langley Research Center POWER Project, which is funded through the NASA Earth Science Directorate Applied Science Program.
5. In all our attempts to generate an efficient urban formula, QR produced much lower targeting error rates than OLS, even when OLS was performed on a subsample containing only the poorest households or when PMT variables were regressed on a simple indicator of being above or below the poverty threshold.
6. Taking into account demographic growth, this amount would be between CFAF 49 billion and CFAF 107.7 billion. Administrative costs usually represent 10–20 percent of the budget for this type of program.
7. Several impact evaluations of *conditional* cash transfer programs have been conducted in the last 15 years, regarding indicators of human capital (Behrman and

Hoddinott 2005; Gertler 2004) or production (Gertler, Martinez, and Rubio-Codina 2012). For a comprehensive review of the literature, see Fiszbein and Schady (2009). However, we lack evidence regarding programs in Sub-Saharan Africa, especially unconditional cash transfer programs (Devereux 2006).

References

Alatas, Vivi, Abhijit Banerjee, Rema Hanna, Benjamin Olken, and Julia Tobias. 2010. "Targeting the Poor: Evidence from a Field Experiment in Indonesia." Working Paper 15980, National Bureau of Economic Research, Cambridge, MA, May.

Angelucci, Manuela, and Giacomo de Giorgi. 2009. "Indirect Effects of an Aid Program: How Do Cash Transfers Affect Ineligibles' Consumption?" *American Economic Review* 99 (1): 486–508.

Behrman, Jere. 2007. "Policy-Oriented Research Impact Assessment (PORIA) Case Study on the International Food Policy Research Institute (IFPRI) and the Mexican Progresa Anti-Poverty and Human Resource Investment Conditional Cash Transfer Program." Impact Assessment, International Food Policy Research Institute, Washington, DC.

Behrman, Jere, and John Hoddinott. 2005. "Programme Evaluation with Unobserved Heterogeneity and Selective Implementation: The Mexican Progresa Impact on Child Nutrition." *Oxford Bulletin of Economics and Statistics* 67 (4): 547–69.

Castañeda, Tarsicio, Kathy Lindert, Bénédicte de la Brière, Luisa Fernandez, Celia Hubert, Osvaldo Larrañaga, Mónica Orozco, and Roxana Viquez. 2005. *Designing and Implementing Household Targeting Systems: Lessons from Latin America and the United States*. Social Protection Discussion Paper 0526. Washington, DC: World Bank.

Chaudhuri, Shubham, and Gaurav Datt. 2001. "Assessing Household Vulnerability to Poverty: A Methodology and Estimates for the Philippines." World Bank, Washington, DC.

Coady, David, Margaret Grosh, and John Hoddinott. 2004. "Targeting Outcomes Redux." *World Bank Research Observer* 19 (1): 61–85.

Devereux, Stephen. 2006. "Unconditional Cash Transfers in Africa." IDS In Focus 1, Institute for Development Studies, Brighton.

Fiszbein, Ariel, and Norbert Schady. 2009. *Conditional Cash Transfers: Reducing Present and Future Poverty*. Washington, DC: World Bank.

Gertler, Paul. 2004. "Do Conditional Cash Transfers Improve Child Health? Evidence from Progresa's Control Randomized Experiment." *American Economic Review Papers and Proceedings* 94 (2): 336–41.

Gertler, Paul, Sebastian Martinez, and Marta Rubio-Codina. 2012. "Investing Cash Transfers to Raise Long-Term Living Standards." *American Economic Journal: Applied Economics* 4 (1): 164–92.

Kanbur, Ravi. 2002. "Economics, Social Science, and Development." *World Development* 30 (3): 477–86.

Katayama, Roy. 2010. "Appui à l'equipe de gestion dans le cadre de la mise en œuvre du projet pilote des filets sociaux par le transfert de cash." Rapport de la mission (20 julliet 2010–18 aout 2010), World Bank, Niamey, Niger.

Narayan, Ambar, and Nobuo Yoshida. 2005. "Proxy Means Tests for Targeting Welfare Benefits in Sri Lanka." Report SASPR–7, World Bank, Washington, DC. http://siteresources.worldbank.org/EXTSAREGTOPPOVRED/Resources/493440 -1102216396155/572861-1102221461685/Proxy+Means+Test+for+Targeting+Welfare +Benefits.pdf.

National Research Council. 1989. *Recommended Dietary Allowances,* 10th ed. Washington, DC: National Academy Press.

Nguetse-Tegoum, Pierre. 2011. "Pauvreté et vulnérabilité des ménages au Cameroun." Mimeo, World Bank, Yaoundé, Cameroon.

Nguetse-Tegoum, Pierre, and Quentin Stoeffler. 2012. "Programme de transferts monetaires sociaux: Le ciblage des pauvres chroniques." Unpublished, World Bank, Yaoundé, Cameroon.

Ravallion, Martin. 2009. "Evaluation in the Practice of Development." *World Bank Research Observer* 24 (2): 25.

Rawlings, Laura, and Gloria Rubio. 2005. "Evaluating the Impact of Conditional Cash Transfer Programs." *World Bank Research Observer* 20 (1): 29–55.

World Bank. 2011a. "Cameroon: Social Safety Nets." World Bank, Washington, DC.

———. 2011b. "Social Safety Net Programs in Cameroon: A Feasibility Study." World Bank, Washington, DC.

Chapter **4**

Options for Improving the Targeting of Safety Nets in Ghana

Lucian Bucur Pop

Ghana's safety net system is becoming increasingly complex as new programs are developed and existing ones are scaled up. The system aims to protect the livelihoods of the poor, support their investments in human capital through conditional cash transfers and health insurance fee waivers, and help them to graduate from poverty through productive safety nets such as public works.

Experience in other countries (for example, Armenia, Chile, and Jamaica) shows that, to ensure coherence, effectiveness, and efficiency of safety net programs, having a coherent vision of the right mix of programs may not be enough—programs with common or overlapping target groups need to use a common targeting mechanism and infrastructure rather than develop "proprietary" systems (Grosh et al. 2008). Common approaches give rise to economies of scale, complementarities, and synergies as well as increased coherence and effectiveness of the safety net. Ultimately, the debate around the pros and cons of common versus program-specific targeting mechanisms is an empirical question. Further, the choice of mechanism will depend on the specific country context, including implementation capacity, poverty profile, political economy, and cost-effectiveness.

While it can be argued that one common system might expose multiple programs to the measurement errors of a single targeting mechanism, the advantages of a universal database are likely to offset the risks. Especially in low-capacity contexts, having (at least) a common database can help to reduce the costs and the amount of time needed to identify beneficiaries for multiple programs, avoid duplication, and increase transparency. A common database could allow each specific program the flexibility to reach its intended target

---

This case study is based on a technical assistance note that reviews the options to improve the targeting of safety net programs in Ghana, prepared for the Ministry of Employment and Social Welfare.

group(s) and intended objectives using additional or even alternative targeting criteria[1] and to respond to changes in social policy or socioeconomic conditions.

Ghana has several safety net programs, in different stages of development, that target the poor or specific subgroups of the poor population: (a) the Livelihood Empowerment Against Poverty (LEAP); (b) the health insurance fee waiver for indigents and other vulnerable groups as a component of the National Health Insurance Scheme; (c) the School Uniforms Program; (d) the forthcoming Labor-Intensive Public Works Program; and (e) the forthcoming conditional cash transfer for junior high school students. The various agencies in charge of implementing these programs have expressed strong interest in developing and implementing a common targeting mechanism and a single registry.

Out of these programs, LEAP has the most advanced targeting mechanism and infrastructure and is the best placed on the institutional map to take the lead with respect to a common targeting mechanism (World Bank 2011). LEAP uses a mix of targeting methods—geographic, categorical, community-based, and proxy means test.

- *Geographic targeting.* This type of targeting is not currently used to select districts, but it is used to select communities *within* districts. The selection of "pilot" districts is not necessarily based on poverty criteria, and the number of beneficiaries by district is not correlated with poverty, being the result of a uniform allocation between districts. At the district level, communities are selected by the district LEAP implementation committees using participatory poverty maps (following a methodology elaborated by the German Agency for Technical Cooperation). The distribution of beneficiaries across selected communities is also fairly uniform (that is, quotas are relatively equal across communities).

- *Categorical (demographic) targeting.* LEAP currently targets three types of beneficiaries: the elderly over 64 years of age, the disabled, and orphan and vulnerable children (OVC). However, one-third of beneficiaries are Emergency LEAP[2] beneficiaries, who do not necessarily belong to the three categories targeted by the regular LEAP.

- *Community-based targeting (CBT).* CBT is implemented by the community LEAP implementation committees (CLICs). LEAP (as opposed to the Emergency LEAP) does not allow for open registration; the community identifies the beneficiaries based on the number or quota of questionnaires received. The number (quota) of questionnaires is used as a means to limit demand at each level (that is, the center distributes a limited number of questionnaires to each selected district, and the districts further distribute the questionnaires to each selected community;

the number of questionnaires is typically much lower than the number of potentially eligible people or households). The means of identifying beneficiaries may vary from community to community (through community meetings, consultation, and participation versus preidentification by the CLIC). Because of the very low quotas, it is difficult to assess how the CBT will work once the program's caseload increases, along with the capacity-building needs of the CLICs.

• *Proxy means test (PMT).* The data collected through the questionnaires (providing information about various household characteristics) are entered into a central database. A proxy poverty score (index) is computed for each household by aggregating several indicators from the questionnaire. The score is then compared with a threshold to determine or test eligibility (proxy means test). The current proxy means test is used as ex post selection of the potential eligible beneficiaries submitted by the CLICs. The formula used to compute the score is not available to the public, in an effort to avoid potential fraud such as concealing or falsifying information. The formula uses only some of the indicators collected through the household questionnaires at registration, thus simplifying the existing questionnaire (which is relatively complex and lengthy to administer).

This case study discusses ways to improve the current LEAP proxy means test formula (and implicitly the instrument used to collect information about potential beneficiaries), as the formula is one of the most important building blocks of a common targeting mechanism. The remainder of the chapter is organized as follows. It first reviews the LEAP formula and its targeting performance using data from the latest available round of the Ghana Living Standards Survey (GLSS5).[3] It then presents the methods used to generate a PMT formula using household survey data and assesses the results for Ghana based on the GLSS5; implications are also discussed. This is followed by a presentation of the expected benefit incidence for the current target groups of various programs— poor orphans, the disabled and elderly, school-age children in the case of the School Uniforms Program, and farmers—and a test of the proposed formula in the field and subsequent adjustments. A final section concludes.

Current LEAP Proxy Means Test Formula

In 2010 LEAP covered about 80 of 170 districts and had about 30,000 registered beneficiaries, out of which more than one-third were enrolled in the emergency component of the program (Emergency LEAP).[4] No survey data exist to measure directly the performance of LEAP. Still, according to assessments using imputation techniques (World Bank 2011), the targeting performance of the program is relatively good: 42–48 percent of the beneficiaries belong to the poorest quintile of the population. This case study does not attempt to assess the program's outcomes, which are the result of the multiple targeting mechanisms used and their implementation in practice. Instead it simulates the performance of the current PMT formula under the assumption of "perfect implementation."

The current LEAP formula includes about 36 indicators related to agricultural assets (livestock) and equipment, ownership of durable goods (household appliances), dwelling conditions, and income from remittances (external support). The characteristics of household members are used as additional criteria for demographic or categorical targeting. With few exceptions (income from remittances), the indicators are easy to verify, although some (radio, mobile phone, and cassette player) could easily be concealed by potential beneficiaries. The LEAP score is computed as a weighted sum of the indicators:

$$s = \Sigma w_i x_i, \tag{4.1}$$

where s is the score, x_i is the indicator i, and w_i is the weight of the indicator i. The indicators were selected and their weights were established based on expert opinion and thus contain a certain degree of subjectivity.

The LEAP formula can be simulated with relatively high accuracy using the GLSS5. However, the simulation cannot capture two indicators: the condition of the dwelling's roof and walls; these indicators are assessed during the household visit to potential LEAP beneficiaries and are not captured in the GLSS5. Their exclusion from the simulation is likely to lead to an overestimation of LEAP exclusion and inclusion errors (that is, the simulated score is likely to misclassify some of the cases that are correctly classified by the full formula). However, these two indicators have a low weight in the total score, and thus the overestimation of the errors is likely to be small.

If the current PMT formula and categorical targeting (that is, the elderly, the disabled, and OVC) were the only targeting mechanisms used by LEAP, about 11 percent of households in Ghana would be eligible to benefit from the program, comprising about 9 percent of the population. The program would cover about 12 percent of extremely poor households and 16 percent of households below the poverty line but above the extreme poverty line. The current selection algorithm is thus expected to exclude more than 80 percent of poor households (exclusion error). At the same time, only 24 percent of households participating in the program would be extremely poor or poor, while the remaining 76 percent would be nonpoor (inclusion error). If the demographic filters or selection criteria (that is, the elderly, the disabled, and OVC) are not used, the targeting performance would not change significantly, but the coverage of poor households would increase to 20 percent of extremely poor households and 24 percent of households below the poverty line but above the extreme poverty line. Without demographic targeting, about

19 percent of households would be eligible for LEAP (see table 4A.1 in the annex to this chapter).

Because of the low correlation of the current PMT score with welfare, the combined selection mechanism—PMT and categorical targeting (CT)—has high inclusion errors in the regions where the poverty rate is lower and better targeting performance in the regions where the poverty rate is very high. At the same time, the current formula seems to have a pro-urban bias, probably due to the higher weights attributed to the ownership of agricultural assets, which "inflate" the score in rural areas. As a result of this bias, program coverage is expected to be higher in urban than in rural areas (figure 4.1).

Under the assumptions of "perfect implementation" of the PMT and demographic targeting, full program rollout, and no other selection mechanisms, LEAP is expected to cover about 25 percent of extremely poor households with an orphan, 19 percent of extremely poor households with a disabled member, and 20 percent of households with an elderly member.

This section summarizes the expected performance of the LEAP PMT formula from a poverty reduction perspective, not taking into account the categorical (demographic) targeting (that is, the elderly, the disabled, and OVC). For this purpose, table 4.1 presents percentages of the population, not households, and reports the following performance indicators: *coverage of the poor* (percentage of the poor covered by the program), *targeting* (percentage of program beneficiaries who are poor), *exclusion error* (percentage of the poor

Figure 4.1 Expected Coverage and Targeting Performance of LEAP PMT and CT in Ghana, by Area of Residence and Region

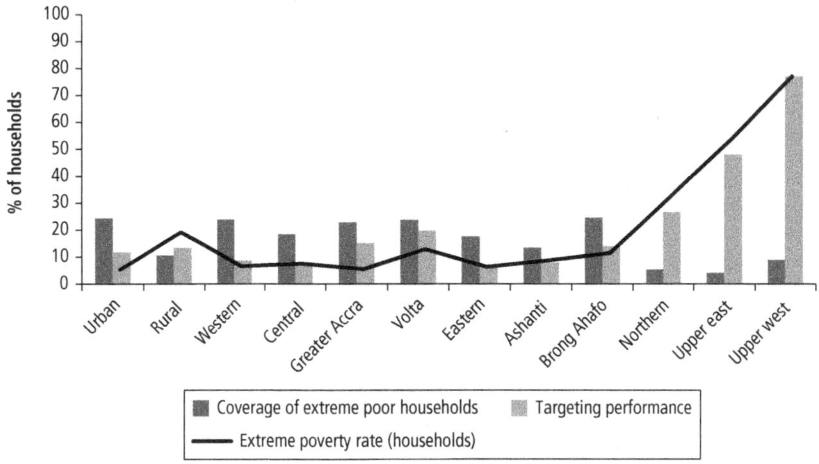

Source: Calculations based on GLSS5.

Table 4.1 Expected Performance of LEAP Formula in Ghana
% of population

Area of performance	National			Rural			Urban		
	Extreme poor	All poor	Total population	Extreme poor	All poor	Total population	Extreme poor	All poor	Total population
Targeting performance	19	33		20	35		16	27	
Coverage	15	16	14	13	15	17	30	26	11
Inclusion errors	81	67		80	65		84	73	
Exclusion errors	85	84		87	85		70	74	

Source: Calculations based on GLSS5.
Note: Blank cells are not applicable.

who are missed by the program, referred to as *undercoverage*), and *inclusion error* (percentage of beneficiaries who are nonpoor, referred to as *leakage*, especially when looking at the distribution of funds and benefits).

Since the last two indicators can be derived from the first two and provide basically the same information, for the remainder of this chapter we use the first ones: coverage (of the poor) and targeting performance.

Improving the LEAP PMT Formula

This section lays out the methodological approach, the selection of indicators, and the options for determining eligibility.

Methodological Approach

The main difference between the design of the current LEAP PMT and the standard approach used in most countries stems from the selection of indicators included in the formula and their corresponding weights (or coefficients). In general, when programs target the poor, the indicators are selected based on their observed correlation with a welfare indicator that is estimated using survey data. In brief, it is an *empirical formula*, derived from a regression model of the *observed relationship between observable household characteristics and household welfare*—as opposed to the expert opinion approach (which is not to be dismissed or disregarded, as it can bring significant value added in guiding the process).[5]

In this case, the ordinary least squares regression model is employed using the latest round of the Ghana Living Standards Survey, which is a nationally representative sample of 8,687 households conducted by the Ghana Statistical Service (GSS) from September 2005 to September 2006.[6] The dependent variable (Y) is the (natural log of) household consumption per equivalent adult.

The PMT approach is consistent with the generic objective of the programs mentioned in the introduction, which is to provide cash or in-kind (uniforms) *income support* to the *poor* (or specific categories of the poor). The methodology provides an "operational instrument" for identifying persons who lack the necessary resources to meet basic needs (an adequate level of consumption) and is less appropriate for identifying persons who are the transient poor as a result of their exposure to other types of risks and vulnerabilities (except if these risks are strongly correlated with poverty). Since the method is based on selecting a limited number of easy-to-verify and easy-to-measure indicators, and most of these indicators are usually time-insensitive (housing or dwelling characteristics, including access to utilities and ownership of durable goods), the derived formula is usually "biased" toward the chronic poor and is less effective in identifying the "transient" poor or the vulnerable.[7]

Selection of Indicators

The proxy indicators (set of variables X) were chosen based on the ultimate objective of this exercise, which is to identify a set of targeting indicators that are (a) easy to verify (easy to observe and measure), (b) difficult for households to manipulate, (c) significant correlates with welfare, and (d) not numerous (to allow for cost-effective data collection). To build the model, we started with the same categories of indicators that are currently included in the LEAP formula: household composition or demographics, housing or dwelling characteristics, agricultural assets, and durables ownership. Given the significant geographic dimension of poverty in Ghana, we added one more indicator—location—using two alternative sets of indicators. The first set of indicators includes area of residence (rural or urban) and administrative region (10 regions). The second set includes seven ecological zones: six zones defined by the combination of area of residence (rural or urban) and three broad ecological zones (forest, coastal, and savannah) plus the metropolitan area of Greater Accra. The inclusion of location variables in the model is expected to increase its "predictive" performance. The PMT model was also run with and without location variables. The indicators selected after running the models (and testing for the statistical significance of the coefficients[8]) are shown in table 4.2, while the detailed results are reported in tables 4A.2 and 4A.3.

The selection of variables implies a trade-off between maximizing the model "performance" and including only those indicators that are easy to verify (in view of designing a simple and easy-to-implement PMT instrument). Thus, although being self-employed outside of agriculture and receiving remittances (external support) are good predictors of welfare, they were dropped because they are difficult to verify. The same applies to ownership of a mobile phone, radio, and cassette player. Not only are they problematic to verify, but the values of their coefficients in 2010 were likely to be lower than in 2006 (that is, we do

Table 4.2 Indicators Used to Calculate the PMT Formula for Ghana

Element	Indicator
Household composition	Household size (number of members)
	Presence of elderly members (over 64 years old)
	Share of adult household members (over 18 years old)
	Occupational status of the household head
Housing	Number of persons per room
	Presence of electricity
	Source of drinking water
	Toilet facility
	Construction material of the walls
	Construction material of the roof
	Construction material of the floor
Agricultural assets	Landownership
	Livestock ownership
Durables ownership	Stove
	Refrigerator or freezer
	Television
	Motorcycle
	Car
Location	Area of residence (rural or urban) *and* administrative regions
	or
	Seven ecological zones: rural or urban areas of coastal, forest, and savannah zones plus the metropolitan area of Greater Accra

not expect their coefficients to be stable over time). Other variables that might seem of interest were excluded simply because the number of observations is low (less than 1 percent of households have a disabled member in the survey) or because their coefficients are not "statistically significant" (for example, having orphan children in the household).

Who is most likely to be eligible according to our model(s), presented in tables 4A.2 and 4A.3? First are persons living in large households, in crowded dwellings, and in households with a high dependency ratio. Having elderly members also increases the probability of being eligible. However, because the model "favors" rather large households, multigenerational households are more likely to be eligible than a single elderly person or an elderly family. Households headed by the self-employed in agriculture are poorer, while those headed by an employee in the formal sector are better off. Lack of access to basic housing utilities such as a toilet and electricity, are important selection criteria, together with the source of drinking water. Out of the more than 10 possible sources of drinking water, only three are strong correlates of poverty in the GLSS5: bore-holes and protected and unprotected wells. Mud, earth, asbestos, or slate construction materials for the roof and walls also indicate a lower level of welfare. Owning more than 4 acres of land or more than two head of livestock (cattle, sheep, and goats) decreases the likelihood of being eligible, but not as much as the ownership of durables. Owning a car almost always excludes a household from the program, while owning a stove, television, refrigerator, freezer, or motorcycle decreases considerably (although to different degrees) the chances of being enrolled. Finally, location is an important factor, as being located in the upper regions of the country is a significant indicator of lower levels of welfare.

Assessing the Options and Setting the Eligibility Threshold

The proposed models were assessed against two types of criteria: (1) model fit or "explanatory power" and (2) accuracy in identifying the poor (expected coverage of the poor and targeting performance). As in any regression model performed using cross-section survey data, and given the constraints in selecting the independent variables (proxy indicators), our model does not fully "explain" the variance of the welfare indicator (the dependent variable). The R^2 statistic is 0.54 for the national model with ecological zones and 0.55 for the model with administrative regions (tables 4A.2 and 4A.3).[9] These values compare well with models developed elsewhere, which range from 0.20 (Armenia) to 0.57 (Bangladesh).[10] The models containing regional location variables also perform better.

Since none of the models perfectly predicts the welfare indicator, it is normal to expect inaccuracies in identifying the poor. Moreover, the "accuracy" also depends on the cutoff point (or threshold) chosen. LEAP and the other programs are geared toward extreme poverty, so we chose a threshold at the twentieth percentile of the predicted welfare indicator (the PMT index), which is consistent with the extreme poverty rate estimated in the GLSS5 (18 percent in 2006).[11] Figure 4.2 illustrates the trade-offs associated with the choice of cutoff point. As the threshold becomes more generous, the coverage of the extreme poor increases, but the targeting performance of the formula decreases.

The accuracy of the three national models in identifying the poor using a cutoff point at the twentieth percentile is presented in table 4.3.

So far we do not have strong evidence to prefer one model over another. Model A has the highest statistical fit and performance, but the difference is small. To make a decision we looked at a second criterion, the accuracy of the model for lower cutoff points. This is an important element if, for example, the program needs to be limited to the first 10 percent of the population and not the first 20 percent (that is, with a cutoff point at the tenth percentile, not the twentieth). This analysis shows that model A (including the administrative

Figure 4.2 Trade-offs between Coverage and Targeting Performance on the Basis of Alternative Choice of Cutoff Point in Ghana

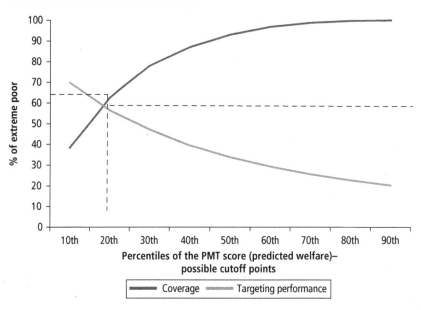

Source: Calculations based on GLSS5.

regions as location variables) also has the best accuracy for a lower cutoff point. We therefore decided to drop model B (with the ecological zone location indicators) from further analysis.

Finally, we carried out a test to assess how well our models perform by area of residence and region. Table 4.3 also shows that the models, including the "preferred" one (model A), have low coverage of the urban poor (that is a rural bias). The analysis of the regional distribution of the eligible population indicates that our preferred model has good targeting performance overall in all regions (around 60 percent of those eligible according to the PMT are poor), but the coverage of the poor is lower in the southern, better-off regions of Ghana than in the northern, poorer regions (table 4A.4). This is largely a result of the very low consumption levels in the northern regions (over 60 percent extreme poverty rate in the upper east and upper west), which have a strong influence on the predicted levels of well-being.[12]

The uneven coverage of the poor across area of residence and regions[13] can be addressed in two ways. One option is to work with PMT formulas derived from separate models; the regional samples, however, are relatively small for this purpose. A second option is to use different cutoffs (thresholds) that reproduce

Table 4.3 Accuracy of the Models in Identifying the Poor in Ghana
% of population

Model and indicator of performance	National			Rural			Urban		
	Extreme poor	All poor	Total population	Extreme poor	All poor	Total population	Extreme poor	All poor	Total population
Model A									
Targeting performance	57	72		57	72		50	69	
Coverage	62	50	20	67	55	30	29	21	3
Model B									
Targeting performance	55	72		55	72		54	64	
Coverage	61	50	20	66	56	30	25	16	3
Model C									
Targeting performance	53	70		53	71		53	65	
Coverage	59	49	20	62	54	30	30	19	3

Source: Calculations based on GLSS5.
Note: Blank cells are not applicable. All three are national models. Model A includes indicators for regional location, model B includes indicators for ecological zone location, and model C does not include any location indicators.

the distribution of poverty by regions and urban or rural location.[14] An additional advantage of this latter approach is its simplicity—one model, one formula.

Using different regional thresholds slightly worsens the overall coverage and targeting outcomes at the national level, but this is an acceptable trade-off to achieve horizontal equity, which may be an important policy consideration. In our case, using regional and rural or urban thresholds is similar to adjusting the regional coefficients estimated by the regression model. In practice, this adjustment translates into a decrease in the absolute value of the initial weights of the regions. Table 4.4 and table 4A.4 present the outcomes of applying the adjusted regional and rural or urban weights when using the same national cutoff point at the twentieth percentile.

After introducing regional and rural or urban thresholds (that is, adjusting the regional weights), we obtained higher coverage of the extreme poor in urban areas and in the southern regions (table 4A.4), but lower overall performance with respect to both targeting and coverage of the extreme poor. The distribution of potential beneficiaries by welfare deciles shows that only about 11 percent belong to the richest five deciles, while 70 percent belong to the poorest three deciles (figure 4.3). Coverage of the first decile (the poorest) is also relatively good (about 70 percent), while exclusion is higher in the second decile (about 58 percent).

Table 4.4 Accuracy of Model D in Identifying the Poor in Ghana
% of regional thresholds

	National			Rural			Urban		
Indicator of performance	Extreme poor	All poor	Total population	Extreme poor	All poor	Total population	Extreme poor	All poor	Total population
Targeting performance	53	70		56	73		35	53	
Coverage	57	48	19	59	50	27	45	36	7

Source: Calculations based on GLSS5.
Note: Blank cells are not applicable. Model D is a national model with adjusted regional weights.

Figure 4.3 Distribution of Beneficiaries in Ghana, by Welfare Deciles

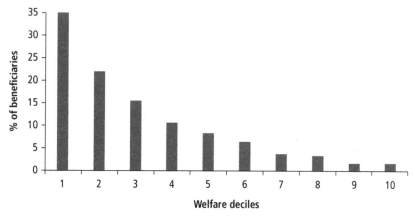

Source: Calculations based on GLSS5.

Expected Coverage of the Target Groups of Various Programs

The proposed PMT formula is expected to improve the ability of LEAP to target specific groups and help the other safety net programs to reach their own target groups more accurately. According to simulations, the proposed PMT (and corresponding cutoff point) may be able to cover 50–60 percent of the extreme poor orphans, the elderly, the disabled, and school-age children (table 4.5). The targeting performance by group is comparable with performance overall, being around 50 percent for the extreme poor and about 65 percent for the poor in each category or target group. Under "perfect implementation," the proposed PMT is expected to cover about half of extremely poor adults of working age and half of extremely poor farming households.

Table 4.5 Simulated Coverage of Target Groups in Ghana

Target group	Expected coverage	
	Number of persons	% of target group
Extreme poor		
Orphans	250,283	50.7
Children, 7–14 years old	488,321	62.3
Elderly, over 64 years old	63,031	48.5
Disabled	23,054	62.5
Work age, 19–64 years old	641,464	52.3
All poor coverage		
Orphans	333,413	39.8
Children, 7–14 years old	644,900	52.7
Elderly, over 64 years old	81,977	41.6
Disabled	45,700	65.2
Work age, 19–64 years old	828,538	42.5
Total coverage		
Orphans	531,949	15.9
Children, 7–14 years old	947,338	25.7
Elderly, over 64 years old	122,553	15.0
Disabled	70,596	44.3
Work age, 19–64 years old	1,156,625	14.5

Source: Calculations based on GLSS5.

Testing the PMT Formula

Since the regression coefficients are not straightforward for implementation purposes, we built the indicators' weights by transforming and rescaling the coefficients to obtain a PMT score that increases with the degree of poverty (that is, the higher the score, the poorer the household) and a cutoff point corresponding to a score of 1,000. This means that *a household has to have a total score of at least 1,000 to be considered eligible for the program.*[15] The resulting PMT formula is referred to as the "*initial* PMT" or "*initial* formula" throughout the remainder of the chapter.

To test the initial formula, we designed a PMT form (or poverty scorecard) to do the following:

- Use the same GLSS questions for the proxy indicators
- Coordinate with the GSS on the questionnaire design and accompanying guidelines

- Avoid complex, specialized modules (for example, on health or disability) that may complicate data collection and not be useful for the purposes of a common targeting mechanism
- Establish with the GSS clear guidelines for enumerators.

The initial PMT formula was pilot tested in the field in the spring-summer of 2011. The pilot had several objectives:

- Test the PMT questionnaire in the field and assess the targeting performance of the new PMT formula (against a poverty measure based on consumption expenditures)
- Assess the outcomes of the community-based targeting
- Assess the outcomes of the CBT-PMT combination
- Test the feasibility or cost-effectiveness of implementing a combination of census sweep (door-to-door survey), PMT, and community validation as an alternative to the CBT-PMT approach
- Elaborate clear and detailed guidelines for the household targeting mechanism
- Evaluate the possibility of using a food consumption score built using the World Food Program methodology to target the poor.

Methods

To assess the performance of the PMT formula, a small random survey (sample size 487) was carried out in March 2011 in 12 enumeration areas (EAs) of the 2010 census in the three ecological zones in Ghana (forest, coastal, and savannah). The number of EAs and the total sample size were dictated by budget constraints. The Ghana Statistical Service selected the EAs based on the follow-ing criteria: (1) no more than two EAs could be selected per administrative region (Ghana has 10 regions) and (2) the EAs selected had to be among the poorer hamlets or communities in a given region or area. As a result, the survey was implemented in six districts in six regions. Three EAs out of the 12 were selected from urban areas—2 in the savannah and 1 in the coastal zone. About 40 households were selected in each enumeration area. The resulting sample is not representative at the national level or for the poor communities in Ghana; however, it is considered satisfactory for testing PMT performance in poor communities across the three ecological zones.

To address the next four objectives, 6 out of the 12 enumeration areas were fully surveyed (census sweep or door-to-door survey). According to the GSS, the boundaries of the EAs overlap to a large extent with the boundaries of villages, hamlets, and compact rural settlements and with the boundaries of neighborhoods in urban areas. For the purposes of the pilot, the six EAs were considered to represent communities. The average size of an EA is around 150 households. The six communities were selected based on a single criterion: to achieve maximum heterogeneity or regional dispersion (table 4.6).

The pilot included three components, implemented in sequential stages: (a) a survey or census of households, (b) community-based targeting, and (c) community validation. In the first stage, the survey was implemented in all EAs. Community-based targeting was carried out in the second stage in three of the six communities subject to the census—one from each ecological zone. Finally, the community validation was carried out in all six communities where the census was implemented.

During the survey, three types of questionnaires were applied in each community: PMT questionnaire, validation questionnaire, and community questionnaire. The PMT questionnaire included only the indicators used by the PMT formula. The validation questionnaire measured mainly consumption expenditures (1-month recall period), consumption of food from own production, food security (1-week recall period), and shocks (12-month recall period). The community questionnaire collected information about food prices, covariate shocks in the last 12 months, and sources of livelihood in the community. The fieldwork was carried out by the Ghana Statistical Service in March 2011.

The community-based targeting was carried out by community committees formed and trained for this purpose, similar to the LEAP model.[16] Each committee implementing the CBT was instructed to select the poorest 40 households in the community. The committees were not provided with guidance regarding selection criteria (household characteristics or indicators of poverty) but were simply instructed to divide the community into four

Table 4.6 Geographic Distribution and Number of Households Surveyed in the EAs Census Sweep in Ghana

Community	Ecological zone	Region	Area (urban or rural)	Number of households surveyed
New Town (hamlet)	Coastal	Western	Rural	166
Anyamam (village)	Coastal	Greater Accra	Rural	133
Ehiamakyene (village)	Forest	Eastern	Rural	102
Samproso (village)	Forest	Ashanti	Rural	152
Nakpanduri (neighborhood)	Savannah	Northern	Urban	173
Chiana (neighborhood)[a]	Savannah	Upper east	Urban	170

Source: Calculations based on the Pilot Targeting Survey, 2011.
a. Classified as rural in the sample design stage.

areas and make sure they identified the poorest households ("the worst off and struggling, compared to everyone else in your community") in each of these four areas.

Finally, during the validation process the communities were asked to validate only the households that were selected either by the PMT or by the CBT, but not by both. In other words, the households for which the CBT and PMT converged were not subject to the validation process. In the census communities where the CBT was not implemented, all households selected by the PMT were subject to validation. In the CBT communities, the validation was carried out only for those households for which the CBT and the PMT selections were not consistent. The validation process consisted everywhere of community meetings in which 25–30 community members participated, including 2–5 CLIC members. Women represented about half (in some cases more than half) of participants, and according to the field reports, in some cases they were more active than men. The district social welfare officer for the area and the village chiefs also attended the meetings.[17] The households subject to validation were discussed in all cases one by one, but the validation rules (consensus or majority) as well as the role of the CLIC members in the process (active participation or vote versus facilitation) varied from community to community.

None of the pilot components was free of errors:

- The quality of the household survey was seriously affected by data collection errors (missing data) on a few important indicators (the number of rooms in the dwelling and the units of measurement for some items that were part of the consumption indicator). To not lose observations, the errors were fixed by univariate or multivariate imputation methods.
- The names or identification of households also caused problems. In some communities, the census lists and the CBT or validations lists did not match completely because different names were used or because the community committees went beyond the EA boundaries (in one case).
- The guidelines for the community-based targeting were not always followed, and the implementation team was obliged to revise the guidelines slightly and repeat the process.
- Finally, the community validation process was carried out differently across communities.

Results

The PMT performance was tested using two criteria: (1) comparison against poverty measures based on the consumption aggregate, using both the random sample in 12 EAs (N = 487 households) and the census in 6 communities (N = 896 households) and (2) consistency with community preferences (through community validation) in the six census communities.

The consumption aggregate includes expenditures on food, nonfood, and services, as well as the value of food consumed from own-production. Consumption and expenditures were collected for a reference period of one month—February 2011—just before the start of the lean season (usually March–April).[18] Poverty was estimated using the same national thresholds used in the analysis of GLSS5, adjusted for a change in prices: a high poverty line of ¢59 per adult equivalent per month (¢1.9 per adult equivalent per day) and a lower one of ¢46 per adult equivalent per month (¢1.5 per adult equivalent per day) based on January 2011 prices in Accra.[19] Most analyses in this chapter use only the low poverty line.

The pilot used two thresholds for the PMT: a conservative one, which according to simulations would select about 19 percent of the Ghanaian population, and a more generous threshold that is 10 percent higher than the conservative one. Table 4.7 presents the outcomes of the PMT in the sample of 12 EAs.

As expected, the estimated poverty levels in the sample are high—about 60 percent of the individuals are estimated to be extremely poor.[20] Overall, the PMT has low inclusion errors (good targeting performance), but high exclusion errors: 88 percent of those selected by the PMT using the conservative threshold are extremely poor, but only about one-third of the extreme poor in the sample are captured using this cutoff. When the more generous PMT threshold is used, the exclusion errors decrease (coverage, 42 percent), but at the expense of slightly higher inclusion errors (targeting, 82 percent). Even

Table 4.7 PMT Performance and Consumption Expenditures Poverty in a Sample of 12 Enumeration Areas in Ghana
% of population

PMT threshold	Extreme poverty	Poverty	Total sample of PMT selected households
Conservative			
Targeting performance	88	97	
Coverage	29	26	20
Generous			
Targeting performance	82	92	
Coverage	42	38	30
Total sample (2,068 persons)	60	74	

Source: Calculations based on the Pilot Targeting Survey, 2011.
Note: Blank cells are not applicable.

when using the more generous PMT threshold, poverty is underestimated. The generous PMT threshold estimates a 30 percent poverty rate against the 60 percent estimated by the consumption aggregate.

The PMT does not perform the same in all ecological zones (table 4.8). Both inclusion and exclusion errors are higher in the coastal zone, where poverty rates are lower. This result is consistent with the simulations done on GLSS5, but the observed errors are higher than the simulated ones.[21] When using the more generous PMT threshold, both errors decrease. These results are consistent with the ones estimated for the six census communities (table 4.9).

However, the six communities vary greatly with regard to poverty and inequality (table 4.10). The two urban communities in the savannah zone are poorer and more unequal than the others (except New Town in the coastal zone, which has the highest inequality). At the same time, one of the two communities in the coastal zone, Anyamam, is less poor and less unequal than all other communities.

Table 4.8 PMT Performance in a Sample of 12 EAs in Ghana, by Ecological Zone
% of individuals who are extremely poor

PMT threshold	Coastal	Forest	Savannah
Conservative			
Targeting performance	58	83	94
Coverage	9	22	41
Generous			
Targeting performance	65	71	92
Coverage	23	33	53

Source: Calculations based on the Pilot Targeting Survey, 2011.

Table 4.9 PMT Performance in Six Census Communities in Ghana, by Ecological Zone
% of individuals who are extreme poor

PMT threshold	Coastal	Forest	Savannah
Conservative			
Targeting performance	43.1	70.9	94.2
Coverage	23.8	18.7	41.1
Generous			
Targeting performance	50.0	70.1	92.1
Coverage	39.1	32.0	52.3

Source: Calculations based on the Pilot Targeting Survey, 2011.

Table 4.10 Poverty and Inequality in Six Census Communities of Ghana

Community	Extreme poverty (%)		Inequality: Gini	
	Individuals	Households	Individuals	Households
New Town (western, rural)	51	43	.46	.48
Anyamam (Greater Accra, rural)	24	20	.32	.36
Ehiamakyene (eastern, rural)	43	33	.37	.41
Samproso (Ashanti, rural)	62	43	.32	.36
Nakpanduri (northern, urban)	79	70	.41	.46
Chiana (upper east, urban)	76	59	.42	.47

Source: Calculations based on the Pilot Targeting Survey, 2011.

Table 4.11 PMT Performance in Six Census Communities in Ghana
% of population

	Coastal		Forest		Savannah	
PMT threshold	New Town, western, rural	Anyamam, Greater Accra, rural	Ehiamakyene, eastern, rural	Samproso Ashanti, rural	Nakpanduri, northern, urban	Chiana, upper east, urban
Conservative						
Targeting performance	64	32	49	83	93	95
Coverage	19	36	15	20	32	55
Generous						
Targeting performance	79	28	52	86	91	94
Coverage	39	43	27	34	41	70
Extreme poverty rate (individuals)	51	24	43	61	79	76

Source: Calculations based on the Pilot Targeting Survey, 2011.

The PMT seems to perform better in the communities with higher poverty (and inequality) and worse in the communities with lower poverty (and inequality) (table 4.11).

CBT Performance

Community-based targeting was carried out in three communities: New Town in the Jomoro District of the western region, Ehiamankyene in the Fanteakwa District of the eastern region, and Chiana in the Kassena-Nankana West District of the upper east region. The district social welfare officers were given instructions on training the CLICs to carry out the exercise over a two-day period.

The initial guidelines required the CLICs to pick the poorest households in the community, based on their own criteria of poverty and without an upper limit for the number of households to be selected. Forms were distributed asking information on a wide range of household characteristics as a means of identifying the kinds of characteristics that communities used as indicators of poverty. These included information on the number of nonworking adults, children, elderly, orphans and vulnerable children, household members with severe disabilities, household source of income, assets, other benefits that the household was currently receiving, and brief reasons why the household was considered poor or vulnerable.

In all three communities the results of this first round of CBT yielded long lists of names (over 100) indicating, in most cases, household members rather than household heads. This made it difficult to match the results to the census survey data (which identified households by the name of the household head). In addition, the area covered by the CBT in Chiana did not match the area covered by the census. Therefore, poor households could not be compared using the two targeting processes, and the process had to be repeated in that community; still, the list of names provided by the CLIC was again a long one.

Consequently, a new round of the CBT was carried out. This time, a population-based ceiling was placed on the number of households that could be chosen—40 households each from New Town and Chiana and 30 households from Ehiamankyene. In addition, district social welfare officers for these communities were brought to the headquarters of the Department of Social Welfare for more thorough training. They were also given the census lists to ensure that the CBT names matched those in the census. The guidelines were further strengthened to explain more clearly the objectives of the program. However, despite these instructions only 20 households in Ehiamankyene could be matched with the census lists.[22]

The CBT performs well in two communities (New Town and Chiana) and less well in the third one (Ehiamankyene). In the first two communities, the inclusion errors are not extremely high (34 and 17 percent, respectively), while in Ehiamankyene they are about 60 percent (table 4.12).[23] The coverage of the poor in the case of CBT was determined by two factors: (a) the imposed quotas (40 households in New Town and Chiana and 20 in Ehiamankyene, respectively) and (b) the targeting performance. The resulting coverage of the poor varies between 24 and 35 percent (again, coverage is lower in Ehiamankyene, where the quota was also low).

Table 4.12 CBT Performance against Consumption Expenditure Poverty in Ghana
% of population

Coverage of extreme poor	New Town (western, rural)	Ehiamakyene (eastern, rural)	Chiana (upper east, urban)
Targeting performance	66	40	83
Coverage	35	24	33

Source: Calculations based on the Pilot Targeting Survey, 2011.

When comparing the two targeting methods (CBT and PMT) against extreme poverty, we find that the performance of the CBT has a pattern similar to that of the PMT (using the conservative threshold). However, the targeting performance of the CBT is (slightly) lower in all cases, while the coverage is higher (except in Chiana, where the PMT performs better on both dimensions). The differences in coverage are partially explained by the different "thresholds" used by the two methods: in the case of CBT, we used quotas (uncorrelated with the poverty level in the community), while in the case of PMT, we used the same (restrictive) threshold for all communities. Since the PMT is correlated with consumption, the number of selected households varies by region proportionally with poverty—which means that the PMT is more "generous" in poorer regions (Chiana) and less generous in better-off regions (New Town, Ehiamankyene).[24] Indeed, in Chiana, the PMT selected 37 percent of the total number of households (compared with 24 percent in the case of CBT), while in the other two communities it selected only around 11–13 percent (half of the CBT figure; figure 4.4).

These results (which are limited by the number of cases and other methodological caveats) seem to imply that one targeting method is not necessarily better than the other. However, the objective of the pilot was not to compare the two methods but, rather, to look at their combination. Before doing that, we briefly compare the results of the community validation for the two methods and find rather mixed results. In four communities, more than

Figure 4.4 Comparison of Targeting Performance and Coverage in Ghana

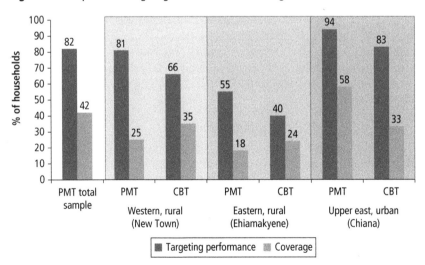

Source: Calculations based on the Pilot Targeting Survey, 2011.
Note: The figures are not fully comparable; however, the pattern is the same when imposing an equal number of selected households by both methods (per community).

Figure 4.5 Validation of PMT and CBT in Community Meetings in Ghana

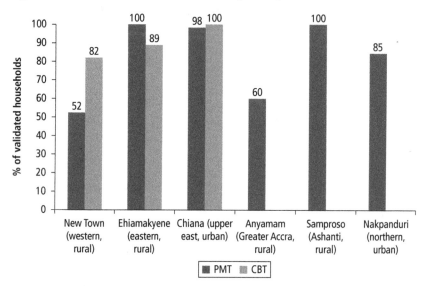

Source: Calculations based on the Pilot Targeting Survey, 2011.
Note: In the case of CBT communities, only lists that did not overlap were submitted for validation.

80 percent of the PMT-selected households were validated, while in two communities the corresponding figures ranged between 50 and 60 percent. In the case of CBT, the percentage of validated households was higher than 80 percent everywhere. The communities gave the following main reasons for not validating households: (a) the existence of "external support" (relatives), (b) ownership of agricultural or fishing equipment, (c) existence of incomes from small trade or employment, and (d) the ability of household members to work (figure 4.5).

Community Preferences and PMT
The underlying principle of combining the two methods (CBT and PMT) is that the PMT would reduce the inclusion errors of the CBT. It is generally assumed that the CBT is more exposed to inclusion errors, since the process is not always transparent, at least for program administrators and, in some cases, even for community members. Using the community (committees) as a first layer in household targeting implies a principal-agent dilemma—the program administrators (the principal) delegate the targeting to the communities (committees) who act as agents. This is usually exacerbated by the low capacity of the program to monitor and control implementation at the local level and, in many cases, also by the lack of functional grievance mechanisms.

Figure 4.6 Outcomes of PMT When Applied to CBT-Selected Households in Ghana

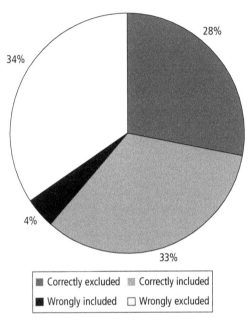

Source: Calculations based on the Pilot Targeting Survey, 2011.

In other words, the PMT, if used in combination with the CBT, is a "control and feedback tool" expected to correct the inclusion errors of the CBT. However, used in this combination, the PMT cannot be expected to correct the CBT exclusion errors.

Is the PMT effective in reducing the CBT inclusion errors? The survey found that the PMT does a good job of reducing the number of inclusion errors, although it also leads to high exclusion errors (that is, it excludes the poor who were correctly selected by the CBT). After applying the PMT to the households preselected by the community committees, the inclusion errors of the CBT are reduced to 4 percent, yet at the same time about half of the correctly identified poor are excluded. Figure 4.6 presents the final outcomes of applying the PMT to the households preselected through the CBT.[25]

The main reason for this outcome is that the two methods target different profiles of the poor. The CBT favors small households, usually composed of the elderly without support (and, in particular, elderly widows) and the disabled (see also the segmentation analysis in figure 4A.1), while the PMT better captures large, poor families and, in particular, those with more than two working-age adults.

Final PMT Formula

The analysis suggests that all previous PMT simulations or models[26] are biased toward excluding small households such as elderly widows and are "favoring" large households with working-age adults. A closer review of the construction of the welfare indicator[27] suggests that the equivalence scale, which is a caloric scale, does indeed "disadvantage" the elderly (in particular, women). In addition, since the equivalence scale does not factor in the household economies of scale, smaller-size elderly households are, in particular, excluded, while the large households with no elderly adults are more likely to be included (table 4.13).

While the use of a calorie-based equivalence scale is legitimate for measuring poverty (in particular, when food is the largest share of consumption and is very high), in order to estimate a PMT that is more "inclusive" and closer to community preferences, the most efficient approach is to replace the current

Table 4.13 Equivalence Scale Used in GLSS5 in Ghana

Category and age (years)	Average energy allowance per day (Kcal)	Equivalence scale
Infants		
0–0.5	650	0.22
0.5–1	850	0.29
Children		
1–3	1,300	0.45
4–6	1,800	0.62
7–10	2,000	0.69
Males		
11–14	2,500	0.86
15–18	3,000	1.03
19–25	2,900	1.00
25–50	2,900	1.00
51+	2,300	0.79
Females		
11–14	2,200	0.76
15–18	2,200	0.76
19–25	2,200	0.76
25–50	2,200	0.76
51+	1,900	0.66

Source: National Research Council 1989.

equivalence scale with one that increases the "weights" of the elderly and decreases the "weights" of large, working-age adult families. After reviewing the literature and performing a few sensitivity tests, we decided to use the following scale:

$$AE = (A + 0.5{*}C)^{0.8}, \tag{4.2}$$

where AE is the number of equivalent adults, A is the number of working-age adults, C is the number of children 0–14 years of age, and 0.8 is the economies of scale factor.

The regression coefficients for the revised model are presented in table 4A.5. The overall performance of the revised PMT is similar to that of the initial PMT, while the coverage of poor elderly households and female widows is higher, being closer to the GLSS5 poverty estimates for these groups (figure 4.7).

Conclusions

Community-based targeting is a prominent feature of the design of safety net programs in low-income countries. In Africa alone, at least 71 percent of conditional cash transfer and 49 percent of unconditional cash transfer programs,

Figure 4.7 Overall Performance of Initial and Revised PMT in Ghana

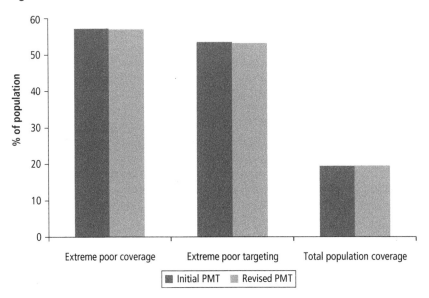

Source: Calculations based on GLSS5.

including those that are now being piloted, employ some sort of CBT combined with geographic, categorical, or proxy means test targeting (Garcia and Moore 2012). The evidence so far seems to indicate that in low-capacity settings with significant barriers related to geography and administrative capacity in reaching the poor, the governments and donors turn first to some form of CBT in implementing safety nets. Community-based targeting has several advantages over other approaches to identifying the poor (poverty census surveys) when implementation capacity is low, including the use of local knowledge, faster implementation, and, not least, lower administrative cost. There is evidence that CBT can be effective (for example, in Ethiopia), is better accepted by communities than other targeting methods (Alatas et al. 2010), and can contribute to strengthening local capacity (for example, in Uzbekistan's Mahallas). Conversely, CBT may come with limitations or risks, including lack of transparency, discriminatory practices, exclusion of the poor who are considered as "undeserving," elite capture, or horizontal inequity. To avoid these risks, the approach promoted in some cases is to combine community-based targeting with geographic targeting, proxy means test methods, or both. This case study has aimed to discuss the steps undertaken to improve LEAP's targeting mechanism and to present the findings from testing the revised mechanism in the field. In particular, the second part of the chapter has focused on the outcomes of combining community-based targeting with proxy means tests in the Ghanaian context. Although this approach is not necessarily new, most countries are now piloting the approach in an effort to "correct" the potential limits of CBT by adopting a more "objective" approach, while containing the administrative costs.

The evidence presented in this study, though limited in scope, provides some indication with respect to the potential outcomes of combining the two targeting methods. First, we find that in Ghana CBT seems to be working relatively well. While its targeting performance appears to be lower than that of PMT, the inclusion errors are not significantly higher or worrying when compared with PMT. Nevertheless, the "community" preferences are directed mostly toward traditionally vulnerable groups such as the elderly and tend to exclude the households with adults who are able to work. Second, we find that the combination CBT-PMT seems to work better when communities are not restricted to preselecting a small number of households. Still, limits need to be provided for CBT to act as a primary "filter" and thus reduce the administrative cost of conducting the PMT survey. Third, the study finds that, when applied over CBT, PMT is very effective in reducing the inclusion errors but also excludes some of the poor who were correctly preselected by the CBT, particularly those living in small households (usually the elderly and widows). This is influenced to some extent by the choices made when constructing the welfare (consumption) aggregate used to estimate the PMT weights, including the choice of an equivalence scale. Finally, the study confirms that the CBT requires thorough training of and guidance for community committees and that adequate grievance and appeal mechanisms should be in place to compensate for the inherent errors and limitations occurring in implementation.

Annex 4A Detailed Results

Table 4A.1 Simulation of LEAP PMT Performance in Ghana

	Poverty status: households (GLSS5)			
Indicator	Extreme poor	Poor	Nonpoor	Total
LEAP PMT score and categorical targeting				
Not eligible				
Number	430,064	277,732	3,169,615	3,877,411
% of row	11	7	82	100
% of column	88	84	90	89
% of table	10	6	73	89
Eligible				
Number	60,363	53,045	352,734	466,142
% of row	13	11	76	100
% of column	12	16	10	11
% of table	1	1	8	11
LEAP PMT score and no categorical targeting				
Not eligible				
Number	390,999	249,758	2,896,865	3,537,622
% of row	11	7	82	100
% of column	80	76	82	81
% of table	9	6	67	81
Eligible				
Number	99,429	81,018	625,484	805,931
% of row	12	10	78	100
% of column	20	24	18	19
% of table	2	2	14	19
Total				
Number	490,427	330,777	3,522,349	4,343,553
% of row	11	8	81	100
% of column	100	100	100	100
% of table	11	8	81	100

Source: Calculations based on GLSS5.
Note: Gray indicates coverage of poor, dark gray indicates exclusion errors, light gray indicates targeting performance, and mid gray indicates inclusion errors.

Table 4A.2 PMT Regression Models for Ghana, with Consumption per Equivalent Adult (ln) as Dependent Variable—(Models with Administrative Regions)

	Models with administrative regions		
Variable	National (preferred)	Rural (dropped)	Urban (dropped)
Household composition			
Household size (number of household members)	−0.0792***	−0.0658***	−0.105***
	(0.0045)	(0.0054)	(0.0066)
At least one household member is elderly (65 years old or more)	−0.0821***	−0.0980***	−0.0688**
	(0.0190)	(0.0248)	(0.0291)
Share of adult members (more than 18 years old)	0.136***	0.271***	—
	(0.0350)	(0.0472)	—
Household head is employee in the formal sector	0.0379*	—	0.0495**
	(0.0202)	—	(0.0241)
Household head is self-employed in agriculture	−0.114***	−0.128***	−0.126***
	(0.0215)	(0.0279)	(0.0382)
Housing			
Two persons per room (1.5–2.49)	−0.204***	−0.208***	−0.172***
	(0.0217)	(0.0304)	(0.0306)
Three persons per room (2.5–3.49)	−0.247***	−0.224***	−0.242***
	(0.0229)	(0.0330)	(0.0297)
Four persons per room (3.5+)	−0.324***	−0.312***	−0.296***
	(0.0286)	(0.0460)	(0.0358)
No electricity	−0.105***	−0.0688**	−0.153***
	(0.0225)	(0.0329)	(0.0268)
Source of drinking water is borehole	−0.0638*		—
	(0.0352)		—
Source of drinking water is well	−0.110**		−0.103**
	(0.0429)		(0.0489)
Source of drinking water is borehole, well, river, stream, dugout, pond, lake, dam, rainwater		−0.0950*	
		(0.0503)	
Toilet facility: pit latrine	−0.104***	—	−0.111***
	(0.0358)	—	(0.0411)
Toilet facility: Kumasi ventilated improved pit	−0.0796**	—	−0.0849**
	(0.0344)	—	(0.0397)
Toilet facility: public toilet	−0.126***	—	−0.118***
	(0.0350)	—	(0.0392)
No toilet facility	−0.168***	—	−0.197***
	(0.0408)	—	(0.0590)

(continued next page)

Table 4A.2 (continued)

Variable	Models with administrative regions		
	National (preferred)	Rural (dropped)	Urban (dropped)
Walls of mud, mud bricks, sheet metal, slate, asbestos, thatch	−0.0678***	−0.0528**	—
	(0.0262)	(0.0262)	—
Roof of asbestos, slate, mud bricks, earth	−0.109***	−0.262***	—
	(0.0416)	(0.0658)	—
Floor of earth, mud, mud bricks	—	—	−0.277***
	—	—	(0.0889)
Agricultural assets			
Owns more than 4 acres of land	0.0518**	0.0562*	
	(0.0252)	(0.0295)	
Owns more than two head of livestock (cattle, sheep, goats)	0.0514**		
	(0.0217)		
Owns more than five head of livestock (cattle, sheep, goats)		0.0551*	
		(0.0288)	
Owns land or livestock			0.0716**
			(0.0279)
Durables ownership			
Stove	0.237***	0.255***	0.228***
	(0.0213)	(0.0398)	(0.0230)
Refrigerator or freezer	0.164***	0.151***	0.174***
	(0.0189)	(0.0284)	(0.0238)
Television	0.119***	0.162***	0.108***
	(0.0176)	(0.0249)	(0.0253)
Motorcycle	0.337***	0.380***	0.248***
	(0.0471)	(0.0710)	(0.0460)
Car	0.580***	0.572***	0.598***
	(0.0491)	(0.0727)	(0.0633)
Location			
Western	0.269***	—	0.192**
	(0.0574)	—	(0.0757)
Central	0.263***	—	0.433***
	(0.0556)	—	(0.0725)
Volta	0.159**	—	0.251***
	(0)	—	(0.0779)

(continued next page)

Table 4A.2 (continued)

Variable	Models with administrative regions		
	National (preferred)	Rural (dropped)	Urban (dropped)
Eastern	0.227***	—	0.270***
	(0.0512)	—	(0.0646)
Ashanti	0.204***	—	0.281***
	(0.0477)	—	(0.0492)
Brong Ahafo	0.137**	−0.0968*	0.214***
	(0.0554)	(0.0513)	(0.0729)
Northern	—	−0.310***	—
	—	(0.10)	—
Upper east	−0.350***	−0.653***	—
	(0.0954)	(0.0946)	—
Upper west	−0.632***	−0.941***	—
	(0.1000)	(0.0920)	—
Rural	−0.127***		
	(0.04)		
Constant	14.86***	14.71***	14.95***
	−0.0535	−0.0698	−0.0476
Number of observations	8,686	5,069	3,617
R^2	0.552	0.474	0.495

Source: Calculations based on GLSS5.
Note: — = not statistically significant. Standard errors in parentheses.
*** $p < .01$, ** $p < .05$, * $p < .1$

Table 4A.3 PMT Regression Models for Ghana, with Consumption per Equivalent Adult (ln) as Dependent Variable—(Models with Ecological Zones, and without Location)

	Models with ecological zones			Models without location		
Variable	National (dropped)	Rural (dropped)	Urban (dropped)	National (dropped)	Rural (dropped)	Urban (dropped)
Household composition						
Household size (number of household members)	−0.0862***	−0.0747***	−0.108***	−0.0917***	−0.0796***	−0.110***
	(0.0047)	(0.0054)	(0.0066)	(0.0045)	(0.0053)	(0.0069)
At least one household member is elderly (65 years old or more)	−0.0989***	−0.114***	−0.0668**	−0.0875***	−0.106***	−0.0646**
	(0.0195)	(0.0253)	(0.0283)	(0.0201)	(0.0256)	(0.0304)
Share of adult members (more than 18 years old)	0.114***	0.223***	—	0.0928**	0.222***	—
	(0.0371)	(0.0501)	—	(0.0369)	(0.0491)	—
Household head is a paid employee in the formal sector	0.0353*	—	0.0494**	—	—	0.0501*
	(0.0201)	—	(0.0242)	—	—	(0.0274)
Household head is self-employed in agriculture	−0.128***	−0.139***	−0.120***	−0.149***	−0.166***	−0.122***
	(0.0221)	(0.0254)	(0.0410)	(0.0231)	(0.0271)	(0.0429)
Housing						
Two persons per room (1.5–2.49)	−0.206***	−0.220***	−0.168***	−0.219***	−0.223***	−0.188***
	(0.0227)	(0.0324)	(0.0308)	(0.0229)	(0.0327)	(0.0310)
Three persons per room (2.5–3.49)	−0.245***	−0.231***	−0.239***	−0.246***	−0.225***	−0.238***
	(0.0235)	(0.0335)	(0.0300)	(0.0238)	(0.0343)	(0.0312)
Four persons per room (3.5+)	−0.303***	−0.299***	−0.280***	−0.282***	−0.265***	−0.272***
	(0.0282)	(0.0415)	(0.0348)	(0.0296)	(0.0446)	(0.0366)
No electricity	−0.117***	−0.111***	−0.141***	−0.126***	−0.111***	−0.165***
	(0.0232)	(0.0329)	(0.0267)	(0.0228)	(0.0321)	(0.0277)

(continued next page)

Table 4A.3 (continued)

Variable	Models with ecological zones			Models without location		
	National (dropped)	Rural (dropped)	Urban (dropped)	National (dropped)	Rural (dropped)	Urban (dropped)
Source of drinking water: borehole	-0.114***	-0.135***	—	-0.108***	-0.137***	—
	(0.0356)	(0.0416)		(0.0361)	(0.0411)	
Source of drinking water: well	-0.131***	-0.140**	-0.0986**	-0.0918**	-0.126**	—
	(0.0418)	(0.0611)	(0.0493)	(0.0424)	(0.0625)	
Toilet facility: pit latrine	-0.0822**	—	-0.0984**	—	—	—
	(0.0364)		(0.0429)			
Toilet facility: Kumasi ventilated improved pit	-0.0616*	—	-0.0748*	—	—	-0.0668*
	(0.0341)		(0.0392)			(0.0386)
Toilet facility: public toilet	-0.122***	—	-0.107***	-0.0785***	—	-0.101***
	(0.0354)		(0.0399)	(0.0267)		(0.0376)
No toilet facility	-0.249***	-0.163***	-0.232***	-0.255***	-0.261***	-0.176***
	(0.0405)	(0.0377)	(0.0568)	(0.0358)	(0.0415)	(0.0653)
Walls of mud, mud bricks, sheet metal, slate, asbestos, or thatch	-0.0613**	-0.0664***	-0.0886*	-0.0823***	-0.0963***	—
	(0.0245)	(0.0254)	(0.0520)	(0.0261)	(0.0257)	
Roof of asbestos, slate, mud bricks, or earth	-0.121***	-0.261***	—	-0.155***	-0.239***	-0.113**
	(0.0413)	(0.0656)		(0.0393)	(0.0690)	(0.0459)
Floor of earth, mud, or mud bricks	—	—	-0.232***	—	—	-0.275***
			(0.0812)			(0.0780)
Agricultural assets						
Owns more than 4 acres of land	0.0871***	0.0906***		0.0787***	0.0838**	
	(0.0291)	(0.0344)		(0.0285)	(0.0339)	

(continued next page)

Table 4A.3 (continued)

Variable	Models with ecological zones			Models without location		
	National (dropped)	Rural (dropped)	Urban (dropped)	National (dropped)	Rural (dropped)	Urban (dropped)
Owns more than five head of livestock (cattle, sheep, goats)	0.0697*** (0.0251)					
Owns more than 10 head of livestock (cattle, sheep, goats)		0.0653* (0.0332)		0.0744** (0.0311)		
Owns land or livestock			0.0733*** (0.0277)			0.101*** (0.0300)
Durables ownership						
Stove	0.242*** (0.0207)	0.240*** (0.0402)	0.234*** (0.0232)	0.247*** (0.0217)	0.236*** (0.0403)	0.241*** (0.0243)
Refrigerator or freezer	0.167*** (0.0182)	0.144*** (0.0286)	0.180*** (0.0241)	0.176*** (0.0192)	0.142*** (0.0286)	0.200*** (0.0246)
Television	0.121*** (0.0172)	0.157*** (0.0247)	0.108*** (0.0241)	0.113*** (0.0185)	0.169*** (0.0249)	0.0791*** (0.0258)
Motorcycle	0.290*** (0.0491)	0.358*** (0.0774)	0.214*** (0.0475)	0.271*** (0.0490)	0.309*** (0.0778)	0.209*** (0.0482)
Car	0.588*** (0.0490)	0.577*** (0.0723)	0.599*** (0.0633)	0.579*** (0.0498)	0.591*** (0.0770)	0.574*** (0.0614)
Location						
Greater Accra metropolitan area	−0.150*** (0.0538)	— —				

(continued next page)

Table 4A.3 (continued)

Variable	Models with ecological zones			Models without location		
	National (dropped)	Rural (dropped)	Urban (dropped)	National (dropped)	Rural (dropped)	Urban (dropped)
Urban coastal	0.240***		0.399***			
	(0.0540)		(0.0573)			
Urban forest	0.0822**		0.273***			
	(0.0377)		(0.0472)			
Urban savannah	—	—	0.177**			
			(0.0779)			
Rural savannah	−0.232***	−0.242***				
	(0.0542)	(0.0543)				
Rural				−0.0700*		
				(0.0363)		
Constant	15.00***	14.84***	14.93***	15.04***	14.85***	15.11***
	(0.0554)	(0.0701)	(0.0490)	(0.0461)	(0.0690)	(0.0373)
Number of observations	8,686	5,069	3,617	8,686	5,069	3,617
R^2	0.54	0.44	0.50	0.52	0.42	0.46

Source: Calculations based on GLSS5.
Note: — = not statistically significant. Standard errors in parentheses.
*** $p < .01$, ** $p < .05$, * $p < .1$

Table 4A.4 Performance of Models A and B in Ghana, by Region
% of population

Region and model	Extreme poor		All poor		Total coverage
	Targeting	Coverage	Targeting	Coverage	
Western					
Model A	50	36	73	22	6
Model D	41	52	68	38	10
Central					
Model A	45	31	70	23	7
Model D	33	40	68	39	12
Greater Accra					
Model A	29	25	54	24	5
Model D	26	27	50	28	7
Volta					
Model A	33	24	71	25	11
Model D	31	32	65	33	16
Eastern					
Model A	35	32	46	18	6
Model D	34	43	46	25	8
Ashanti					
Model A	45	36	58	25	9
Model D	40	48	55	36	13
Brong Ahafo					
Model A	38	45	63	38	18
Model D	38	42	65	36	16
Northern					
Model A	54	68	69	64	49
Model D	56	58	68	52	40
Upper east					
Model A	68	95	77	92	84
Model D	76	65	84	61	51
Upper west					
Model A	82	100	91	99	96
Model D	83	93	92	93	88
Total					
Model A	57	62	72	50	20
Model D	53	57	70	48	19

Source: Calculations based on GLSS5.
Note: Model A is a national model with location indicators. Model D is a national model with adjusted regional weights.

Table 4A.5 Comparison of the Initial and Revised PMT Models for Ghana

Variable	Initial lnwelfare	Revised (new equivalence) scale lnwelfare
Household size: number of household members	−0.0792***	−0.0443***
At least one household member is elderly (65 years old or more)	−0.0821***	—
Share of elderly (65 years old or more) in the total number of household members	—	−0.306***
Share of children younger than 5 years old in the total number of household members	—	−0.139***
At least one household member is disabled		−0.126
Hosusehold head is female widow over 65 years old		−0.105***
Share of adult household members (more than 18 years old)	0.136***	—
Household head is employee in the formal sector	0.0379*	0.0591***
Household head is self-employed in agriculture	−0.114***	−0.106***
Number of persons (household members) per room	—	−0.0420***
Two persons per room (1.5–2.49)	−0.204***	—
Three persons per room (2.5–3.49)	−0.247***	—
Four persons per room (3.5+)	−0.324***	—
No electricity	−0.105***	−0.114***
Source of drinking water is borehole	−0.0638*	−0.0562
Source of drinking water is well	−0.110**	−0.113**
Toilet facility: pit latrine	−0.104***	−0.101***
Toilet facility: Kumasi ventilated improved pit	−0.0796**	−0.0804**
Toilet facility: public toilet	−0.126***	−0.128***
No toilet facility	−0.168***	−0.168***
Walls of mud, mud bricks, sheet metal, slate, asbestos, thatch	−0.0678***	−0.0697***
Roof of asbestos, slate, mud bricks, earth	−0.109***	−0.115***
Owns more than 4 (5+) acres of land	0.0518**	0.0494*
Owns more than 2 (3+) head of livestock (cattle, sheep, goats)	0.0514**	0.0402*
Owns agricultural or fishing equipment (including canoe)		0.140**
Stove	0.237***	0.226***
Refrigerator or freezer	0.164***	0.166***
Television	0.119***	0.140***
Motorcycle	0.337***	0.326***
Car	0.580***	0.591***
Region1	0.269***	0.274***

(continued next page)

Table 4A.5 (continued)

Variable	Initial Inwelfare	Revised (new equivalence) scale Inwelfare
Region2	0.263***	0.267***
Region4	0.159**	0.159**
Region5	0.227***	0.221***
Region6	0.204***	0.204***
Region7	0.137**	0.134**
Region9	−0.350***	−0.373***
Region10	−0.632***	−0.663***
Rural	−0.127***	−0.131***

Note: — = not statistically significant. Standard errors in parentheses.
*** $p < .01$, ** $p < .05$, * $p < .1$

Figure 4A.1 CBT Selection for Ghana: Classification Tree (Segmentation Analysis)

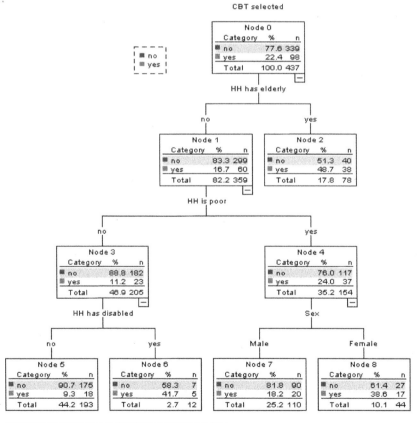

Source: Calculations based on the Pilot Targeting Survey, 2011.

Notes

1. The data collected through a single instrument and stored in a common database can be used for proxy means test targeting, simple categorical targeting, or a combination of both. For example, one program can select households based on categorical criteria such as families with children under the age of two, and another can use the data to calculate a poverty score based on proxy means testing.
2. In 2009 an emergency response package was introduced in response to floods and rising food prices. This component targeted households in 20 of the most food-insecure districts and offered a flat grant of ¢15 (Ghanaian cedi) per household. It was financed by the World Bank and implemented for seven months (Ayala 2009).
3. Since the reference period of the GLSS5 is September 2005–September 2006, the data are probably not fully consistent with the current demographic or poverty profile (the poverty rate is likely to be lower and the population larger than in 2006). However, the basic poverty correlates are not expected to be different.
4. The Emergency LEAP uses a different selection mechanism and does not use PMT.
5. When the survey data do not contain the necessary information to allow the construction of an income or consumption aggregate or when the program intends to target beneficiaries based on more "complex" definitions of "deprivation," other techniques may be used, such as principal component analysis or similar approaches. We used the regression model approach because LEAP, as well as the other programs, targets mainly the (extreme) poor and the GLSS5 includes information on household consumption.
6. For a detailed description of the survey, see GSS (2008).
7. The PMT proposed here could be complemented with a smaller set of indicators for targeting groups vulnerable to shocks using data from the 2008 World Food Program Vulnerability Survey.
8. Standards errors were computed by taking into account the sampling design (two-stage stratified random sampling) and sample weights. Cross-validation was used to test for over-fitting.
9. As expected, the model with no regions has a lower fit. The rural-urban models have a lower fit as well.
10. For a brief review and references, see Sharif (2009).
11. A cutoff at the twentieth percentile means that the program will cover 20 percent of population, the poorest population as identified by the PMT index.
12. We also ran the national models with regional interaction terms to test (and allow) for different effects in the north, but the targeting or coverage outcomes were not significantly different.
13. This issue translates into a regional or horizontal equity issue: a higher undercoverage rate in some regions means that the poor do not have the same probability (opportunity) to be selected in the program across regions—that is, a poor person in the southern regions does not have the same probability of being included as a poor person in the northern regions.
14. Another option, similar to building separate models for each region or residence area, is to build one model including geographic or location interactions. This option was tested, but the results (not shown here) are the same.

15. This approach was chosen in order to be consistent with the original scoring algorithm and threshold used by LEAP. The LEAP's original poverty score formula, based on expert opinion, was designed to increase with poverty and had a threshold of 1,000.
16. The targeting in LEAP is implemented by the CLICs.
17. In one community the field team decided to add three random names to the original validation list, one of which happened to be the Zongo chief present at the meeting. The community members agreed straightaway that, given his assets, he had to be excluded from the list of poor.
18. Measuring consumption or expenditures for a reference period of just one month provides a weak or imperfect estimate of welfare, since such a measurement is affected by seasonality. However, using February as the reference month reduces the risk of significant over- or underestimation of poverty.
19. The two thresholds correspond to approximately ¢53 and ¢41, respectively, per adult equivalent per month at national prices. The high poverty threshold corresponds roughly to a threshold of US$2 purchasing power parity per day per adult equivalent.
20. The sample was not weighted.
21. The confidence intervals for the pilot survey estimates are relatively large due to the small sample size.
22. The names that households provided to the interviewers were different from the names used in the community.
23. Both the PMT and CBT have high inclusion errors in Ehiamankyene, which may imply that something is wrong with our measure of welfare in that community, with the survey data collection, or with both.
24. The PMT also has built-in regional "weights" (by region and by urban or rural area), which were adjusted for the conservative PMT threshold to reproduce the regional poverty distribution in 2006.
25. Cost is another aspect of combining various methods that deserves attention. Based on this small pilot, it was estimated that the cost of applying a combined CBT and PMT approach is about 60 percent lower than the cost of conducting a door-to-door PMT census. Adding community validation to the PMT was estimated to increase the cost by about 20 percent.
26. Including those using alternative modeling approaches such as quantile regression, among others.
27. Another option would be to set more generous thresholds for specific groups, but this approach did not prove robust either and did not solve the inclusion errors for large households with working-age adults.

References

Alatas, Vivi, Abhijit Banerjee, Rema Hanna, Benjamin Olken, and Julia Tobias. 2010. "Targeting the Poor: Evidence from a Field Experiment in Indonesia." Working Paper 15980, National Bureau of Economic Research, Cambridge, MA.

Ayala, Francisco. 2009. "LEAP Operational Assessment Report." Unpublished, yala Consulting.

Garcia, Marito, and Charity Moore. 2012. *The Cash Dividend: The Rise of Cash Transfer Programs in Sub-Saharan Africa*. Washington, DC: World Bank.

Grosh, Margaret, Carlo del Ninno, Emile Tesliuc, and Azedene Ouerghi. 2008. *For Protection and Promotion: The Design and Implementation of Effective Safety Nets*. Washington, DC: World Bank.

GSS (Ghana Statistical Service). 2008. *Ghana Living Standards Survey, Report of the Fifth Round*. Accra: Government of Ghana.

National Research Council. 1989. *Recommended Dietary Allowances*, 10th ed. Washington, DC: National Academies Press.

Sharif, Iffath. 2009. *Building a Targeting System for Bangladesh Based on Proxy Means Testing*. Social Protection Discussion Paper 0914. Washington, DC: World Bank. http://go.worldbank.org/AC1Z563GK0.

World Bank. 2011. "Republic of Ghana: Improving the Targeting of Social Programs." Report 55578-GH, World Bank, Washington, DC.

Chapter 5

Short- and Long-Term Targeting in Kenya

Phillippe Leite

Kenya's economy is smoothly transitioning toward stability after several years of turbulence. Severe price increases, climaxing with inflation peaking at 19.7 percent in November 2011 and with depreciation of the Kenya shilling, dampened economic growth at the outset of 2012. By the end of the year, however, the economy had made solid gains supported by declining inflation and interest rates that enabled the central bank to loosen monetary policy in an effort to stimulate growth. The projected growth rate of gross domestic product (GDP), at 4.3 percent, came in slightly lower than the 2011 rate of 4.4 percent (World Bank 2011), but compared relatively well to the 2012 macroeconomic growth rates of 5.3 and 6 percent in Sub-Saharan Africa and the East African Community, respectively (IMF 2011). This period of economic instability and declining infrastructure produced persistently high poverty, which hampered Kenya's ability to address increased hardship, discrimination, and inequality of opportunity in accessing good-quality jobs in urban areas and deterred the benefits of economic growth from reaching the rural population.

Poverty and vulnerability to climate change remain the most critical development challenge facing Kenya. At the height of the Horn of Africa drought emergency in 2011, more than 3.7 million Kenyans were affected; this year the number declined to 2.2 million. Even so, the number of people in need of food, medicine, and other aid is significant, at about 5.5 percent of the population. This is especially the case in the northern and eastern parts of the country, some of the poorest regions in Kenya.

Poverty, Vulnerability, and Social Assistance Response

Despite diverse government initiatives over the last four decades, poverty in Kenya remains high (World Bank 2012). Although poverty declined between 2000 and 2005/06, the incidence of poverty at the end of that period was

47 percent, and the actual number of poor people increased slightly from 15.1 million to 16.5 million due to population growth. Further, 6.9 million Kenyans were food poor in 2005/06, in that their expenditures were insufficient to meet their nutritional needs even when nonfood essentials were excluded.[1] An individual or household is described as being food poor when they cannot meet all of their nutritional needs because of their expenditure on other basic nonfood essentials.

However, poverty is not evenly or randomly distributed in the country. For example, as shown in table 5.1, poverty rates were markedly higher in rural areas (49.7 percent) than in urban areas (34.4 percent). This unevenness is due to and reinforced by various factors, including regional disparities in access to services and income-generating opportunities. The distribution of poverty depends on the viability of the livelihoods that households depend on and on the susceptibility of these livelihoods to economic, environmental, and security shocks.

National poverty figures camouflage significant regional differences. For instance, the most recent poverty maps for Kenya show that poverty incidence on the coast and in the northeastern provinces is 70 and 74 percent, respectively, compared with 22 percent in Nairobi and 31 percent in the central province. Rural and urban areas offer different income-generating opportunities, with poverty rates being higher in rural areas because livelihoods in rural Kenya tend to be heavily reliant on agriculture.

Although poverty incidence tends to be higher in rural areas than in urban areas, residents of informal settlements within cities experience high levels of deprivation, sometimes far greater than in rural areas. The Kenya Poverty and Inequality Assessment (World Bank 2009) shows that the poverty incidence in informal settlements in Nairobi was about 63 percent in 2006, which was above the national average of 46.7 percent for the same period.

Vulnerability

The current macroeconomic environment contributes to poverty and vulnerability in different ways. An often-cited definition of household vulnerability is "exposure to contingencies and stress and the difficulty of coping with them."

Table 5.1 Changes in Poverty Levels in Kenya, 1997–2005/06
% of population

Location	Headcount (P0)			Poverty gap (P1)			Poverty severity (P2)		
	1997	2005	Change	1997	2005	Change	1997	2005	Change
Rural	52.7	49.7	−3.0	19.0	17.8	−1.2	8.9	8.9	0.0
Urban	49.9	34.4	−15.4	15.8	11.7	−4.2	6.9	5.6	−1.3
Total	52.2	46.6	−5.6	18.5	16.6	−1.9	8.6	8.2	−0.3

Source: Ndirangu 2010.

This draws attention to how the future well-being of households or individuals is shaped by their capacity to cope, the presence of risks, and the overall political, social, and economic context that conditions risks and coping capacity.

Households in Kenya have reported experiencing a range of shocks with different effects on their well-being. For instance, data from the Kenya Integrated Household Budget Survey (KIHBS) 2005/06 show that increases in food prices were the most common shock experienced by households during the study period (2000–05). Of all severe shocks, the most frequently reported shock was a rise in food prices, but, while common, this was considered to be less destructive than the death of a family member or drought (15 percent of households). The study also reveals that extremely poor households are 78 percent more likely to report experiencing a negative effect of a shock than their wealthier counterparts. Among adults facing unemployment, a slightly higher proportion of unemployed men are in chronic poverty than unemployed females. Households reported having used various coping mechanisms to respond to shocks, including, most frequently, drawing on household savings or selling assets or produce. However, better-off households were more likely to draw on savings, while poor households were more likely to sell off their assets. Transfers from family and friends were an important way of coping with death and illness-related shocks. Borrowing from informal or formal sources in response to shocks was limited, and few households reported receiving public support.

Kenyan households in rural areas are more likely to be exposed to agro-climatic shocks, while those in urban areas are more likely to be exposed to insufficient entrepreneurial activity and job creation. Different income-generating opportunities exist in rural and urban areas. Previous studies have shown a concentration of more remunerative activities in urban areas than in rural areas. As shown in table 5.2, rural households in Kenya, especially in arid areas, appear to be much more vulnerable (Christiansen and Subbarao 2005; Suri et al. 2009). Although poverty incidence is higher on average in rural than in urban areas, residing in an urban slum predisposes people to particularly high poverty levels. World Bank (2009) finds that poverty incidence in informal settlements in Nairobi was about 63 percent in 2006. As the World Bank has pointed out in the *World Development Report 2013*, a job creation strategy is needed to move more Kenyans into better wage jobs; policy makers, especially at the local level, should accept informal household enterprises as a legitimate part of the Kenyan economy that contribute to increasing productivity in urban areas (World Bank 2013).

Household composition also affects vulnerability to poverty and food insecurity. World Bank (2009) finds that poverty in Kenya has a predominantly young face—half of the population in 2005/06 was under 20 years old, and young people accounted for two-thirds of the poor. Suri et al. (2009) find that every additional young member of a household decreases the probably of the

Table 5.2 Spatial Distribution of Households Falling into and Rising out of Poverty in Kenya, 2000–07

% of households

Location	Non-poor	Chronic poor	Rose out of poverty	Fell into poverty	Moved in or out of poverty
Coastal lowlands	13	28	12	5	41
Eastern lowlands	34	12	14	3	37
Western lowlands	7	39	16	8	30
Western transitional	25	16	7	7	45
High-potential maize area	41	17	12	5	24
Western highlands	17	32	12	8	32
Central highlands	70	6	8	1	15
Marginal rain shadow area	41	8	19	3	30
Overall	36	19	12	5	29

Source: Suri et al. 2009.

household rising out of poverty. Households with high dependency ratios may have fewer opportunities to diversify their income because they have fewer employable members.

Female-headed households are more likely to be vulnerable and poor. World Bank (2009) reports that female-headed households tend to run bigger households and to experience higher poverty levels. Female-headed households may be more vulnerable because they have fewer income-generating opportunities (Hall 2005). However, other studies have found that there is no difference between female-headed households and male-headed households in terms of their vulnerability to aggregate sources of risk (Glewwe and Hall 1998).

Households with older heads are very vulnerable to poverty. Suri et al. (2009) show that a household headed by a 60-year-old is nearly 20 percent less likely to rise out of poverty than one headed by a 30-year-old. Figure 5.1 shows poverty rates (absolute, food, and extreme poverty) by household type, and it is evident that households composed of elderly people and children have the highest poverty rates.

A lack of education may also increase vulnerability, as it may hinder an individual's ability to adapt quickly and adequately to economic or natural shocks (Schultz 1975). Similarly, households headed by a well-educated person may be less vulnerable, because better-educated individuals have more labor market flexibility and economic mobility, and they tend to have higher-paying jobs. World Bank (2009) shows that households with more education and vocational skills are less likely to be poor.

In examining factors associated with movements in and out of poverty in rural Kenya, Burke et al. (2007) show that selling livestock products

Figure 5.1 Poverty Headcount in Kenya, by Type of Household

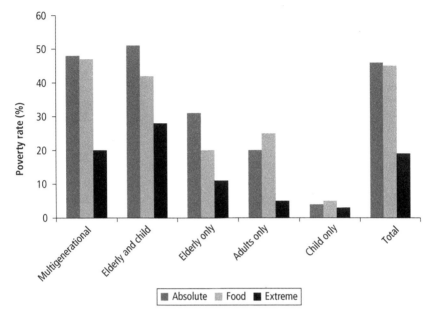

Source: Ndirangu 2010.

(especially milk) and cattle is key to keeping households out of poverty.[2] They estimated that, with all else being equal, a household that is initially land poor and has no cattle or milk to sell has a 62 percent probability of remaining consistently poor and only a 1 percent probability of being nonpoor. By contrast, a household with more than 3.25 acres of land that is producing milk and selling cattle has a 51 percent chance of being consistently nonpoor and almost no chance of being consistently poor.

Households that depend largely on rain-fed agriculture are highly vulnerable to rainfall shocks (Dercon 2002). The Tegemeo panel analysis shows that the level of rainfall during the main growing season increases the probability of exiting from poverty, indicating that rural Kenyan households remain dependent on stable agricultural outcomes to maintain their standard of living. As noted in Suri et al. (2009), exiting from poverty is dependent on stable livelihood sources, such as salaried work and business activities, and is negatively related to unstable income sources, such as casual farm labor. Christiansen and Subbarao (2005) observe that households with access to nonfarm employment consume more on average and tend to face less fluctuation in their income, especially in the arid and semiarid areas. Vulnerability among households headed by a member employed in the informal sector is accentuated by a lack of formal and reliable safety nets for workers in that sector. Moreover, risk-averse households in agriculture and the informal sector may be victims of risk-induced poverty traps, as they may adopt low-return activities in order to mitigate risks (Chaudhuri 2003).

Increased Vulnerability to Shocks among the Poor

Agriculture-related shocks like droughts and loss of crops and livestock are mainly rural problems, while shocks such as the loss of salaried employment, business failures, inflation, carjacking, and burglary, are largely urban problems (figure 5.2, panel a).

Poverty incidence is closely associated with a higher relative incidence of agriculture-related shocks (figure 5.2, panel b). About 13.3 percent of Kenyan households reported drought as the most severe shock they had experienced. In relative terms, the incidence of the shock is 78 percent higher for the extremely poor and 37 percent higher for all of the poor than the nationwide average. Droughts and livestock shocks also were reported more frequently by poor households (figure 5.2, panel b). The incidence of other shocks, despite being less severe, is also higher for extremely poor households. Inflation, illness, and death of a family member seem to be problems for the better-off, as the reported incidence of large rises in food and agricultural input prices is higher among the nonpoor.

Coping Mechanisms

Households use a range of coping mechanisms to react to shocks (figure 5.3). Resorting to the household's own savings seems to be a major coping mechanism, followed by self-insurance. These two mechanisms are a form of dis-savings, as is the sale of household assets and produce. Very few households reported having borrowed either from informal or formal sources in response to a shock. Public support is also limited and most likely to be available after the occurrence of a covariant shock such as a drought or flood. A large proportion of households (about 40 percent) respond to high food prices by reducing their consumption. Transfers from family and friends are an important mechanism for coping with the death or illness of a household member.

Coping mechanisms vary between the rich and the poor. The use of savings as a coping mechanism increases with household wealth because richer households have higher disposable income. A larger proportion of poorer households dispose of their assets and work more in response to a shock.

Social Assistance Response

Kenya has passed various sector-specific laws aimed at improving the welfare of poor and vulnerable members of society but lacks a coherent national strategy

Figure 5.2 Incidence of Shocks in Kenya, by Area of Residence and Poverty Status of the Household

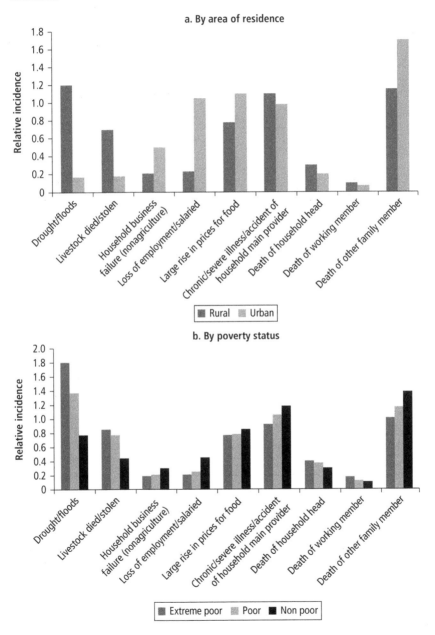

Source: Ndirangu 2010.

Figure 5.3 Household Coping Strategy in Kenya, by Consumption Quintile

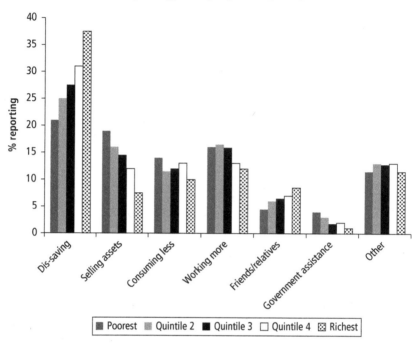

Source: Ndirangu 2010.

to meet the needs of the poor. An analysis of safety nets in the country was recently carried out to document the scope of current programs. The range of safety net interventions in Kenya is wide, but, in the absence of a coherent national strategy, these interventions lack the capacity to offer an integrated or systematic response to the needs of the poor. An uncoordinated range of interventions has been created in response to both domestic and donor pressures and external shocks (for example, droughts). The main aim of these programs has been to protect "vulnerable groups," a vague aim that has not led to a comprehensive, equitable, or efficient use of funds. While the country has responded to *acute* vulnerability with repeated emergency efforts, the responses to *chronic* vulnerability have been piecemeal and geographically limited. While the ongoing and repeated distribution of food to poor families in arid and semiarid lands has been keeping people alive, it has not contributed to a sustained reduction in poverty. Thus interventions are characterized as "a series of disparate and fragmented responses, with ongoing support to some vulnerable groups, while others remain outside the safety net" (World Bank 2012).

We examined 20 safety net programs that operate in four sectors and cover a range of objectives. These safety net programs were categorized by sector, covering agriculture, education, social cash transfers, and relief and recovery programs. Even within the sectors, programs have a range of objectives. These include (a) increasing the access to inputs, skills, and other resources to increase agricultural productivity; (b) providing school meals to improve educational outcomes and increase food consumption among children generally or marginalized children specifically; (c) preventing malnutrition among women; (d) improving health and nutritional outcomes among women, children, and vulnerable groups; (e) increasing adherence to HIV/AIDS (human immumodeficiency virus/acquired immune deficiency syndrome) treatment and reducing infant and maternal mortality; (f) promoting the foster care and human capital development of orphans; (g) improving the livelihoods of older people and people in informal settlements; (h) supporting people with severe disabilities; (i) reducing poverty and high rates of malnutrition among pastoralists in northern Kenya; and (j) helping households to recover from drought. These programs are implemented through the ministries of agriculture, education, and health as well as the World Food Program (WFP) and nongovernmental organizations (NGOs). Some of these programs were designed as pilots to learn lessons, for example, about the provision of cash transfers as a response to chronic food insecurity, extreme poverty, and vulnerability or about how best to enable households to find sustainable livelihoods and thus graduate from assistance. In summary, Kenya has numerous programs designed to protect the poor population. Some programs are cash transfer programs, some are in-kind transfer programs, some are targeted to households or individuals, and others are targeted to geographic areas. Despite the large number of poor and vulnerable individuals in Kenya, the current safety net system is limited, funded largely by donors, and, consequently, fragmented.

Twelve ongoing targeted programs cover more than 1 million people.[3] As shown in table 5.3, the most important cash transfer program targeted to poor households is the Orphans and Vulnerable Children (OVC) Program, which reached 27,000 households in its first phase. It has now been expanded and is expected to cover 47 districts and more than 400,000 individuals in 2011. The OVC is a conditional cash transfer program designed to encourage the fostering and retention of OVC within their families and communities, increase their access to health care and education, and increase their birth registration. The program is financed by the government of Kenya, the U.K. Department for International Development (DFID), the United Nations Children's Fund (UNICEF), and the World Bank. Another important cash transfer program is the Hunger Safety Net Program (HSNP), an unconditional cash transfer program financed by DFID in the arid and semiarid lands of northern Kenya; it aims to protect chronically food-insecure households. The HNSP covered

Table 5.3 Number of Households and Individuals Covered by Targeted Programs in Kenya, 2008/09 and 2011

| | 2008/09 | | 2011 |
Program	Households	Individuals	Individuals
OVC	44,668	134,000	412,000
Hunger Safety Net	12,000	60,000	346,000
Food Distribution: Emergency Operations		2,581,000	21,801,000
Regular and Expanded School Feeding		1,076,000	1,900,000
Home Grown School Feeding		743,000	538,000
Most Vulnerable Children		200,000	1,778,000
Supplementary Feeding and Mother and Child Health		340,000	455,000
HIV/Aids Nutrition Feeding		77,000	72,000
Health Voucher Schemes			60,000
Njaa marufuku Kenya		31,000	37,000
National Accelerated Agricultural Inputs Access			121,000
Older Persons Cash Transfer			33,000

Source: Ndirangu 2010.

12,000 households in four districts during its pilot phase and is gradually being expanded by DFID, in partnership with the government, with the goal of covering 346,000 individuals. These two programs plus support for older persons are the only cash transfer programs in the country targeted to households.

Other important programs include the Most Vulnerable Children (MVC) Program, the School Feeding Program, the General Food Distribution (GFD) Program, and the Supplementary Feeding and Mother and Child Health (SFMCH) Program. The MVC is financed by DFID, UNICEF, and the World Bank, while the School Feeding Program is financed by the government, DFID, the WFP, and the World Bank. Both the GFD and SFMCH programs are financed by the WFP. All of these programs have one feature in common: they are basically geographically targeted. The exception is the OVC Program, which has three levels of targeting, including a proxy means test (PMT) for identifying poor households. Furthermore, both the GFD and the SFMCH are emergency relief operations undertaken as a humanitarian response during food shortages and cover the chronically food-insecure population in the arid and semiarid lands. Together with the School Feeding Program and the Home Grown School Feeding Program, which started in May 2009, these programs jointly cover about 4.4 million people. These safety net programs are concentrated mainly in rural areas, particularly the arid and semiarid lands, while only a few interventions target the vulnerable in urban areas.

Overall spending on social protection in Kenya is low, although this masks variations in levels and patterns of spending within different subsectors. A range of stakeholders, including the government, multilateral and bilateral donor agencies, private firms, and workers (as members of contributory schemes) finance the various programs in the country. Total spending for fiscal 2008/09 on the 12 targeted programs reviewed was about K Sh 20 billion (Kenyan shillings), including both government and donor contributions (table 5.4).

As presented in table 5.5, external donors largely fund Kenya's safety nets. Most of the programs are implemented by development partners on behalf of the government. However, a few, such as *Kazi kwa Vijana* or Older Persons Cash Transfer, are fully financed by the government. This is not a sustainable long-term arrangement. Policy makers recognize these challenges and have introduced or are planning to introduce several reforms to extend the coverage and increase the sustainability of safety nets. The intention is to free up resources that could be reallocated to other poverty and vulnerability reduction programs.

Even though there have been many safety net initiatives to protect the poor and vulnerable, their scale, coverage, targeting mechanisms, target population, and delivery methods have differed substantially. The geographic, household, and individual targeting methods used by the OVC cash transfer, the HSNP, emergency relief operations, and school feeding programs have all been shown not to capture many of the poor and vulnerable. They are biased

Table 5.4 Fiscal Cost of Targeted Programs in Kenya, 2008/09

Indicator	Cost
GDP (K Sh, billions)	2,299
Total revenue (K Sh, billions)	513
Total expenditure (K Sh, billions)	673
Expenditure for targeted programs (K Sh, billions)	21
Government of Kenya	5
Donor	16
Targeted programs	
% of GDP (total)	0.9
Government of Kenya contribution	
% of GDP	0.2
% of total expenditure	0.7
% of revenue	0.9

Source: Government of Kenya 2009.
Note: Shares decline in the medium term because the growth rates of GDP and total expenditure are higher than the growth rate of spending on targeted programs.

Table 5.5 Expenditure Levels of Targeted Programs in Kenya, 2008/09
K Sh, millions

Program	Government of Kenya	Donor	Total
OVC	95	803	898
Hunger Safety Net	—	155	155
Food Distribution: Emergency Operations	258	10,025	10,283
Regular and Expanded School Feeding	206	2,387	2,593
Home Grown School Feeding (estimates)	400	180	580
Most Vulnerable Children	—	1	1
Supplementary Feeding and Mother and Child Health	—	1,833	1,833
HIV/AIDS Nutrition Feeding	—	640	640
Health Voucher Schemes	—	—	—
Njaa marufuku Kenya	128	30	158
National Accelerated Agricultural Inputs Access	300	400	700
Kazi kwa Vijana	3,400	—	3,400
Older Persons Cash Transfer	4	—	4

Source: Ndirangu 2010.

toward certain districts to the detriment of poor provinces (western and Nyanza). Rural areas also account for the dominant share of total safety net spending. There are plans to scale up the cash transfer programs (OVC and HSNP) and, budget permitting, other programs as well. Given the diversity of the food-insecure population (which includes both the chronic poor and the transient poor who are vulnerable to shocks), much more must be done to identify the specific population that suffers from short-term poverty associated with covariate shocks.

Why Targeting?

Poverty imposes costs on communities in several ways. The chronic poor are usually asset constrained, have low productivity, and therefore draw on community resources to meet basic needs. Vulnerability[4] to shocks forces families with limited resources to use coping strategies, many of which may involve inefficient use of resources just to reduce the uncertainty of future incomes. Spells of sudden impoverishment can have long-term consequences. To maintain minimum consumption, the poor are forced to sell their assets and forgo investment in the human capital of their children by cutting spending on care, nutrition, or education. Losses to children's development during a crisis tend to be irreversible and can undermine their future prospects in life, locking families in poverty.[5] Therefore, in a volatile world prone to natural and economic shocks, policy makers may choose to target their actions to protecting the poor and the vulnerable.

Targeting Methods

Various targeting methods are discussed in this case study: food security assessment, PMT, and PMTplus.

Food Security Assessment

Chapter 2 of this book provides valuable guidance on how to identify food-insecure households in safety net programs by combining different targeting schemes in order to identify and distinguish both long-term (chronic) and short-term (vulnerable and transient) food-insecure households. Quantitative and qualitative data and human resources are the key requirements for identifying food-insecure households. However, there is a trade-off between rigor and speed in designing emergency response programs in the aftermath of a covariate shock. It is important to identify the neediest households quickly to ensure that they receive immediate assistance, and this necessitates using qualitative rapid assessment methods rather than quantitative methods based on household survey data (which would take much more time to develop and employ). Also, the dynamic dimensions of exposure to food insecurity are particularly difficult to capture in surveys and often depend on respondents' subjective responses to questions about household exposure to shocks and food insecurity. However, if qualitative measures are used to save time, they should be validated to ensure that they are strong indicators of actual exposure to food insecurity.

Indicators of food insecurity are easy to collect but often involve measurement errors. Despite the usefulness of such indicators in times of crisis or shocks, the collection of field data can be subject to bias. For example, just one adult per household provides the information; whether this is the adult male or female household member can affect responses, particularly when subjective assessments are involved. Second, the context can affect the indicator. For example, answers about the frequency with which the household consumes certain items can be influenced not only by the shock itself but also by a lack of money with which to buy the commodities, which is a situation that is related to poverty rather than directly to the shock. Therefore, even quick surveys aiming to identify short-term changes due to shocks have measurement errors that might lead to excluding extremely poor households.

According to the results of the KIHBS 2005/06, despite the improvement in the country's economy in the five years prior to the household survey, food insecurity measured by caloric intake and food dietary diversity remains high. In rural areas, food dietary energy consumption was 1,690 Kcal per person per day, while in urban areas it was 2,060 Kcal per person per day. The proportion of the population without enough income to acquire a balanced food basket was estimated to be 22 percent in rural areas and 15 percent in urban areas. Breaking down this critical food poverty indicator by province, the highest level of food poverty (35 percent) was in the western province, followed by the northeastern, Nyanza, and Rift Valley provinces.

Proxy Means Test

The OVC Program originally used a two-step approach consisting of a mix of community-based targeting (CBT) and a poverty scorecard. However, this resulted in inclusion errors where recipients were being chosen who were not poor (13 percent even came from the top quintile) and performed only marginally better than random selection. An impact evaluation also suggested that about 43 percent of the poorest households had not been reached (exclusion errors). As a result, policy makers decided to modify the program's targeting process, most notably by replacing the poverty scorecard with a more conventional proxy means test applied to data from the KHIBS 2005/06 (Hurrell, Ward, and Merttens 2008). In a PMT, beneficiaries are chosen based on a weighted combination of characteristics that are believed to be highly correlated with either well-being or deprivation.

The KHIBS 2005/06 household survey provides a wide range of indicators that help to explain poverty status in Kenya. Certain determinants of poverty, however, can be manipulated if households know that their answer might render them eligible for social assistance, for instance, and others are difficult to observe or verify in the field. After a careful analysis of the correlation of household characteristics (demographic and infrastructure) and poverty in Kenya, six main PMT variables were selected for the OVC Program: (a) size of household measured by the adult-equivalence scale used by the National Statistical Office, (b) number of children under five years old per household, (c) main source of drinking water of the household, (d) main source of cooking fuel used by the household, (e) type of household toilet, and (f) type of roofing material.

The PMT is expected to have an acceptable level of targeting errors. Simulations using the KIHBS 2005/06 data show that, if the proxy means test were applied to the whole Kenyan population, 1.6 million households would be classified as chronically food insecure—that is, living under the food poverty line. This proxy would have both exclusion and inclusion errors estimated at 30 percent when compared to household per capita expenditure (and when applied nationwide with no additional geographic targeting or community validation). A targeting assessment of the OVC Program is currently being conducted, but the government is generally satisfied with the level of targeting errors found by the program's monitoring activities.

Proxy Means Test Plus

Given Kenya's vulnerability to climate change and international price fluctuations, it is not surprising that the levels of poverty and vulnerability vary across the country. Further, the current PMT used for the OVC Program is not a good instrument for identifying households suffering temporarily from idiosyncratic shocks.

While droughts and price increases are the two main shocks in the country, a significant share of the affected households are also chronically food insecure. According to the KIHBS 2005/06, droughts affected 16 percent (1.3 million) of 6.7 million Kenyan households. Among these 1.3 million households, 388,000 (30 percent) were indeed chronically food insecure because their household per capita expenditure was below the food poverty line. Droughts and food crises affect Kenyans' welfare in two main ways: first, through the increased mortality of livestock in the drought-affected areas and, second, through the high price of food, especially maize, as a result of the drought (but also worsened by the recent rise in global prices).

PMTplus is a method that allows small shock-related adjustments to the PMT to reduce inclusion errors in times of shocks. Simply applying the value of $\hat{\alpha}$ (the estimated impact of the shock on welfare) to correct the cutoff point for the PMT and using an indicator of food insecurity, such as the WFP food consumption score, makes it possible to identify households that are vulnerable to poverty. For this reason, the best way to increase the precision of the targeting would be to examine the most up-to-date geographic data to identify the shock-affected areas (geographic targeting) and then carry out a quick data collection exercise to gather food-insecurity indicators to improve the precision of the model.

For emergency support linked to large covariate shocks, it would be more efficient and possibly more politically acceptable to provide universal aid than to target the poor specifically. We agree on this point of view in certain cases. However, PMTplus is not developed as a tool for emergency interventions. In regular times poor households are already being supported by social programs according to the PMT selection. The goal of PMTplus is to allow the existing program to expand rapidly in response to a shock to cover other households and, thereby, mitigate the impact of the shock. Given that household information and characteristics are already known, the PMTplus identifies households that may need additional assistance during a crisis. The proposed shock adjustment for the PMTplus would only be implemented in areas identified as having been affected by the shock. By geographically targeting areas affected by the shock, program administrators can increase the number of beneficiaries by simply shifting up the PMT cutoff point and classifying those new households as eligible for support. Then a means test would be applied to measure food insecurity in the areas affected by the shock using the data obtained from a quick survey (using the household's food consumption score and dietary diversity, among other indicators), the results of the PMT and the means test would then be cross-tabulated to identify those households in need of temporary assistance. In this case, the graphic representation of the targeted population is given in table 5.6.

Combining the original PMT with new geographic targeting and a means test based on food-insecurity indicators would increase the coverage of current programs in the short term without adding any inclusion errors. This strategy makes it possible to identify those families in need of temporary support to mitigate the impact of a covariate shock. The Republic of Yemen used this strategy in the aftermath of last year's political turmoil, where the Social Fund for Development (a) redefined its priorities by emphasizing cash-for-work programs; (b) selected areas of intervention based on current maps of malnutrition and vulnerability; (c) enlisted the help of communities to identify food-insecure households; and (d) added a means test to the then current targeting strategy that combined community-based targeting, self-selection, and a proxy. As a result, the Social Fund for Development was able to increase the number of people benefiting from cash-for-work programs in a short period.

Performance of Targeting Mechanism

Simulations of the PMTplus method have had encouraging results for Kenya. Simulations using KIHBS 2005/06 data show that, if the proxy means test alone were applied to the whole Kenyan population, approximately 1.6 million

Table 5.6 Targeting Post-Shock Food-Insecure Populations through PMTplus

| | | | After the shock | | |
| | | | Areas not affected by the shock | Areas affected by the shock | |
		Total		Food secure	Food insecure
Before the shock					
	Food secure	A	A20	A21	A22
			A10	A11	A12
Food poverty line					
	Food insecure	B	B10	B11	B12

Note: B represents chronically food-insecure households and regular beneficiaries of safety nets. A_{12} represents households vulnerable to food insecurity due to the shock—that is, those who need immediate assistance because of the shock. A_{22} represents households that are not chronically poor but are food insecure as a result of the shock, so they may be in need of a shorter-term intervention. A_{10} and A_{20} represent households living in areas that are not affected by the shock and so are not eligible for the shock-related intervention.

households would be identified as chronically food insecure—that is, living under the food poverty line. This proxy would have both exclusion and inclusion errors estimated at 40 percent when compared to household per capita expenditure and when applied nationwide with no additional geographic targeting or community validation (table 5.7).

To measure the role of PMTplus for targeting the chronically poor and vulnerable among households affected by a drought, we performed the following simulation exercise.

1. We assumed that all of the 1.6 million households identified by the PMT were included in the single registry approach—that is, information was collected when individuals applied for a given program (where 972,000 were correctly classified as poor and 639,500 were wrongly classified).

2. We identified areas that had suffered from droughts in the previous six months (1.3 million households out of the total 6.7 million nationwide), in which 388,000 were actually poor. The PMT identified 371,000 households, but only 227,000 correctly. This translates to 38 percent inclusion errors and 41 percent exclusion errors.

3. We estimated the shocks modeled on the KIBHS 2005/06 data and found that household expenditures would decline by a factor of −0.216 due to a drought, meaning that on average this shock reduces expenditures 19.4 percent: $1 - \exp(-0.216)$.

4. We adjusted the PMT targeting using the shocks model, setting the cutoff point 19.4 percent higher in areas affected by droughts than elsewhere.

5. We used KIBHS 2005/06 nutritional indicators to calculate the means test as a proxy for food consumption scores that cannot be estimated with the KIBHS 2005/06 data. In other words, since food consumption scores cannot be estimated with the KIBHS data and because nutritional indicators are

Table 5.7 Results of PMT Estimation in Kenya with No Other Targeting Method
number of persons, unless otherwise noted

Indicator	PMT		Total
	Nonpoor	Poor	
Actual nonpoor	4,553,751	639,508	5,193,259
Poor	739,961	972,695	1,712,656
Total	5,293,712	1,612,203	6,905,915
Errors (%)			
Inclusion		40	
Exclusion		43	

correlated with food insecurity, we considered that any household with at least one malnourished child in the particular drought area was deeply affected by the drought and, as a consequence, was food insecure.[6] As a result, we estimated that 324,000 households would be classified as food insecure due to the shock.

6. We estimated the coverage of the new temporary program using the PMTplus method by cross-tabulating the results of the adjusted PMT and the means test (table 5.8) and found that (a) group B, which represents chronically food-insecure households and regular beneficiaries of safety nets, continued to consist of the 1.6 million households identified by the PMT, (b) group A_{12}, which represents households that are vulnerable to food insecurity due to the shock and food insecurity—that is, those who need immediate assistance because of the shocks—consisted of 66,000 households, and (c) group A_{22}, which represents households that are not chronically poor but are food insecure as a result of the shock, so that they may be in need of a shorter-term intervention, consisted of 98,000 households.

7. We estimated the new caseload of potential beneficiaries of safety nets using two approaches: (a) adding group A_{12} (66,000) to the original 371,000 households identified by the original PMT, resulting in 437,000 beneficiaries, and (b) adding group A_{12} and group A_{22} to the original 371,000 households identified by the original PMT, resulting in 536,000 beneficiaries.

8. We estimated the targeting errors for both approaches using household consumption as a benchmark. In the first approach (8a), there were 28 percent inclusion errors and 42 percent exclusion errors, while in the second (8b), there were 35 percent inclusion errors and 35 percent exclusion errors.

9. An alternative approach that avoids adding short-term data collection to the means would be simply to adjust the PMT score by $\hat{\alpha}$—that is, increase

Table 5.8 Ex Ante Simulation of PMTplus for Kenya

| | | | After the shock | | |
| | | | | Areas affected by the shock | |
		Total	Areas not affected by the shock	Food secure	Food insecure
Before the shock					
	Food secure	5,062,557	4,352,707	611,479	98,371
Food poverty line			—	164,791	66,364
	Food insecure	1,612,203	1,241,028	211,499	159,676
	Total	6,674,760	5,593,735	987,769	324,411

Table 5.9 Number of Food-Insecure Households Identified in Areas of Kenya Affected by Drought

Areas affected by drought	Number of beneficiaries	Inclusion errors (%)	Exclusion errors (%)	Food-insecure households %	Food-insecure households Number
Original PMT	371,175	39	41	43	159,605
(1) Adjusted PMT only	602,330	35	28	38	226,054
(2) PMTplus = (1) + group A_{22}	437,539	28	42	52	226,033
(3) PMTplus = (2) + group A_{21}	535,910	35	36	61	324,386

the PMT cutoff point by the size of the shock. In this case, we would have 600,000 households in the program. The estimated inclusion errors would be 35 percent, and exclusion errors would be 28 percent.

However, despite the similar inclusion errors in the alternative approach (9) and the second approach (8a) and the much lower exclusion errors in the alternative approach (9), the share of households that are food insecure because of the shock (identified by child malnutrition) differs markedly (table 5.9). The PMTplus approach would be preferable to a single PMT adjustment because the standard PMT does not properly identify the food-insecure households.

We carried out a similar exercise for areas affected by price increases and crop or livestock losses. In both cases, the PMTplus findings were similar.

Conclusion

In this case study, we have explored a robust measure to identify chronically poor households with short-term vulnerability indicators to deal with identification errors in times of shock in Kenya. The main findings of an ex ante simulation show that, in the presence of shocks, the combination of geographic targeting to identify areas affected by the shock, a proxy means test for targeting the chronic poor, and a means test to identify those vulnerable to shocks would help to expand a program in the short term and, at same time, reduce overall inclusion and exclusion errors.

As a result, better targeting outcomes in Kenya would be achieved by combining these two measurements. In times of crisis, the government of Kenya could better address the short-term needs of the population affected by the shock (transient poor) by using its current well-developed PMT and its national registry of potential beneficiaries, combined with short-term food insecurity (means test) measures.

Notes

1. Most statistics on poverty come from the Kenya Integrated Household Budget Survey (KIHBS) of 2005/06. The KIHBS was designed to provide data that could be used to update poverty, welfare, and employment statistics, derive the consumer price index, and revise the national accounts information. The survey also gathered socioeconomic data on the Kenyan population, including education, health, energy, housing, and water and sanitation indicators. These data provide the government and the private sector with crucial information to guide their investment and national development policy decisions. The data for the KIHBS 2005/06 were collected during a 12-month period starting on May 16, 2005. The survey was fielded in 1,343 randomly selected clusters across all districts in Kenya: 861 rural and 482 urban clusters. In addition to the basic questionnaire, the KIHBS 2005/06 contained a market price questionnaire and a community questionnaire that make it possible to identify areas affected by shocks. See Kenya National Bureau of Statistics (2007).

2. Substantial evidence shows that households subject to income shocks and facing imperfect insurance markets use their assets to smooth their consumption (Deaton 1992). In addition to land, another important asset for rural livelihoods is livestock. Several studies show that livestock is commonly used to smooth consumption in developing countries (Fafchamps, Udry, and Czukas 1998; Kinsey, Burger, and Gunning 1998; and Ndirangu 2007). The findings of Kinsey et al. (1998) suggest that livestock is held by the rural population as a buffer stock, especially for drought, and that the households most exposed to the adverse effects of drought are those without livestock. In Kenya, Christiansen and Subbarao (2005) note that the possession of goats or sheep helps households to smooth their consumption in the face of idiosyncratic shocks.

3. This is a rough estimate assuming an average household size of seven. Further, some households may be covered by more than one program, which would imply double counting.

4. The elderly, disabled, widows, and children and orphans are especially vulnerable and need special treatment and attention. For example, (a) children have needs that are markedly different from those of adults and require age-appropriate care; (b) the elderly have unique needs due not only to the increased incidence of illness and disability, but also to the multiple and complex interactions of other types of physical and social consequences of aging; and (c) orphans can be too young to manage an inheritance or do not even know they have access to an inheritance.

5. The need to help the poor and destitute imposes costs on communities and strains neighborhood and family support networks, often at the times when everyone is struggling. Poverty may also result in socially harmful behavior (crime, begging) that imposes costs on all members of the society.

6. This step does not suggest that "having malnourished children" is included in the model for many reasons, mainly to avoid any bad incentives it may provide. We are simply using "having malnourished children" as a proxy for food insecurity to illustrate the case of PMTplus. In reality, in the areas affected by the drought, we would

need to visit all households registered for the current program to collect food insecurity indicators so that we could identify the ones that are indeed food insecure for applying PMTplus in full.

References

Burke, William, T. Jayne, H. Ade Freeman, and P. Kristjanson. 2007. "Factors Associated with Households' Movement into and out of Poverty in Kenya: The Rising Importance of Livestock." International Development Working Paper 90, Michigan State University, East Lansing.

Chaudhuri, Shubham. 2003. "Assessing Vulnerability to Poverty: Concepts, Empirical Methods, and Illustrative Examples." Columbia University, Department of Economics, New York, June.

Christiansen, Luc, and Kalanidhi Subbarao. 2005. "Towards an Understanding of Vulnerability in Rural Kenya." *Journal of African Economies* 14 (4): 529–58.

Coady, David, Margaret Grosh, and John Hoddinott. 2004. *Targeting of Transfers in Developing Countries: Review of Lessons and Experience*. Washington, DC: World Bank.

Deaton, Angus. 1992. *Understanding Consumption*. Oxford: Oxford University Press.

Dercon, Stefan. 2002. "Income Risk, Coping Strategies, and Safety Nets." *World Bank Research Observer* 17 (2): 141–66.

Fafchamps Marcel, Christopher Udry, and Katherine Czukas. 1998. "Drought and Savings in West Africa: Are Livestock a Buffer Stock?" *Journal of Development Economics* 55 (2): 273–305.

Glewwe, Paul, and Gillette Hall. 1998. "Are Some Groups More Vulnerable to Macroeconomic Shocks Than Others? Hypothesis Tests Based on Panel Data from Peru." *Journal of Development Economics* 56 (1): 181–206.

Government of Kenya. 2008. *Kenya Vision 2030: A Globally Competitive and Prosperous Kenya*. Nairobi.

———. 2009. "Budget Outlook Paper (BOPA)." Ministry of Finance, Nairobi.

Hall, Gillette. 2005. *Identifying the Vulnerable: New Evidence from Peru*. A joint publication of the Policy Research and Poverty and Social Policy Departments of the World Bank 6. Washington, DC: World Bank.

Hurrell, Alex, Patrick Ward, and Fred Merttens. 2008. "Kenya OVC-CT Programme Operational and Impact Evaluation: Baseline Report." Oxford Policy Management, Oxford.

IMF (International Monetary Fund). 2011. *Regional Economic Outlook: Sub-Saharan Africa, Sustaining the Expansion*. Washington, DC: IMF.

Kenya National Bureau of Statistics. 2007. *Kenya Integrated Household and Budget Survey 2005/06*. Nairobi: Government of Kenya, Ministry of Planning and National Development.

Kinsey, Bill, Kees Burger, and Jan Gunning. 1998. "Coping with Drought in Zimbambwe: Survey Evidence on Responses of Rural Households to Risk." *World Development* 26 (1): 89–110.

Ndirangu, Lydia. 2007. *Household's Responses to Shocks: Evidence from Central Kenya.* PhD diss. Netherlands: Wageningen University.

———. 2010. "Addressing the Food Price Situation in COMESA with Reference to Kenya." Paper presented at the Association for the Strengthening of Agricultural Research in Eastern and Central Africa (ASARECA), Kigali, Rwanda, May 4–5.

Schultz, Theodore. 1975. "The Value of the Ability to Deal with Disequilibria." *Journal of Economic Literature* 13 (3): 827–46.

Suri, Tavneet, David Tschirley, Charity Irungu, Raphael Gitau, and Daniel Kariuki. 2009. "Poverty, Inequality, and Income Dynamic in Kenya, 1997–2007." Tegemeo Institute Working Paper 030/2008, Egerton University, Tegemeo Institute of Agricultural Policy and Development, Nairobi.

World Bank. 2009. "Kenya Poverty and Inequality Assessment (KPIA): Executive Summary and Synthesis Report." World Bank, Washington, DC. http://hdl.handle.net/10986/3081.

———. 2011. "Kenya Economic Update, December 2011." World Bank, Washington, DC. www.worldbank.org/kenya/keu.

———. 2012. "Kenya Social Protection Review." World Bank, Washington, DC.

———. 2013. *World Development Report 2013: Jobs.* New York: Oxford University Press.

Chapter 6

Targeting Methods to Identify the Poorest in Malawi

Rodica Cnobloch and Kalanidhi Subbarao

Estimates suggest that in 2009, 15 percent of the population in Malawi were extremely poor and 40 percent were poor (IFPRI 2011). The incidence of poverty in Malawi fell from 52 percent in 2004/05 to 40 percent in 2009/10. Notwithstanding this decline, which was largely due to growth in labor demand, the need to reach out to the poor with safety net programs cannot be overemphasized for several reasons.[1] For one thing, in Malawi as elsewhere, the poorest households (the bottom 10 percent of income distribution) need support in all situations. For another, even during periods of reasonable economic growth, some households will always fall between the cracks, often hit by unpredictable and unforeseen shocks. Unless protected by timely and effective safety net programs, these households would be seriously hurt, and the human capital of their children would be at particular risk of being eroded. Given these considerations, safety net programs play an important role in Malawi and indeed in much of Sub-Saharan Africa.

At present, the social assistance system in Malawi, as a whole, is fragmented among different programs, is weak, and is ill-prepared to play an effective role in times of need when poor households experience shocks. In addition, limited funding and poor coordination between implementing agencies raise questions about the adequacy, impact, and scalability of existing programs. Responding to the need for systemic reform, the draft Social Protection Policy envisions a mixture of interventions to reach the differing strata of the poor (figure 6.1). What is needed now are clear criteria with which to identify beneficiaries consistently across the country. This case study fills that gap.

Even though the schematic framework of the social protection system delineated in figure 6.1 is well conceived and responds to multiple vulnerabilities confronted by the poor, there is a need to ensure that program coverage is adequate, program implementation is efficient, and targeting is effective. To accomplish these goals, three tasks need to be performed: (a) adopt a common

Figure 6.1 Draft Outline Social Protection Program

Draft outline social protection programme

40% Malawi poverty line	Categories and their social protection needs	Potential social protection programs or interventions

Moderately poor (25%)

- Employment
- Skill building
- Capital
- Productive assets
- Protection from asset or capital erosion

Protection and promotion
* **Inputs subsidy**
* **Public works programs**
- Insurance programs (social, crop and livestock)
- Village savings loans
- Micro-credit or Micro-finance
- School feeding

15%
Extreme poor

Extreme poor with labor capacity (5%)

- Survival
- Productive assets
- Employment

Promotion
* **Public works programs**
* **School feeding**
- Cash and food for assets combined with skills building and cash for consumption or adult literacy training

Extreme poor and incapacitated (10%)

- Survival
- Investment in human capital

Provision
* **Social cash transfers**
* **School feeding**

* To be funded out of the Government of Malawi Basket Fund for Social protection

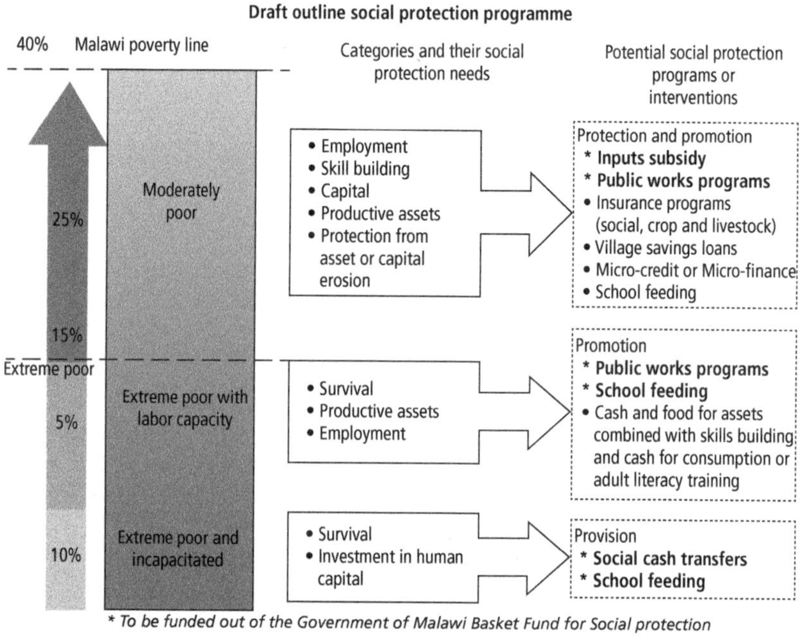

Source: UNICEF 2011.
Note: Households with inadequate labor capacity (or with labor constraints) are households that do not have an adult (19–64 years old) who is fit for labor. They include households headed by the elderly, children, the chronically ill, or the disabled. Inadequate labor also can apply to households that have an adult 19–64 years old but also a high dependency ratio (three or more dependents).

definition of target groups (the poor and extreme poor) that can be used across all programs, (b) adopt common criteria for identifying target groups, and (c) develop a unified data system. It is clear from figure 6.1 that various target groups have different social needs and that different social protection programs are needed to fulfill them. Even if these social protection programs employ different targeting methods, coordination of their targeting criteria is needed to ensure adequate coverage, avoid duplication, and prevent double dipping by beneficiaries. A common registry can be useful for understanding these gaps and overlaps, but a common targeting mechanism is not necessary.

In order to determine the path of reform, we first need to know the targeting effectiveness of current programs. The most recent data, however, are more than a decade old, providing information for 2003 (see table 6.1 or table 6A.1 in the annex to this chapter for more details).[2] Overall, in 2003 all social assistance programs covered half of the population; the main program, Starter Pack of

Table 6.1 Coverage, Exclusion, and Inclusion Rates of Social Assistance Programs in Malawi
% of the poor

Program	Coverage	Extreme poor		Poor	
		Exclusion	Inclusion	Exclusion	Inclusion
All social assistance	50.9	44.0	73.2	44.4	44.1
Free Food Program	13.3	86.3	75.2	86.2	47.1
Inputs for Work Program	0.6	99.0	59.4	99.1	25.3
Food- or Cash-for-Work Program	3.9	94.9	69.0	95.2	37.7
Targeted Nutrition Program	4.3	96.5	80.4	96.2	55.3
Supplementary Feeding Program	0.9	98.6	64.0	98.8	34.8
Agricultural Inputs	0.6	99.5	78.6	99.3	40.1
Starter Pack of Agricultural Inputs	44.3	51.0	73.5	50.8	43.5
Scholarships and GABLE Support for Girls	0.2	99.8	76.6	99.8	61.4

Agricultural Inputs, covered about 44.3 percent of the population, and the Free Food Program reached 13.3 percent of the population. The coverage of all other programs was relatively low, ranging from 0.2 to 4.3 percent of the population. The overall percentage of the extreme poor and the poor who did not receive transfers was around 44 percent. The best-performing programs were the Starter Pack of Agricultural Inputs (51 percent exclusion rate) and, to a lesser extent, the Free Food Program (86 percent exclusion rate); all of the other programs barely reached the poor at all (with exclusion rates higher than 95 percent). Among the beneficiaries, the percentage of nonpoor individuals decreased considerably from 73 percent of the extreme poor to 44 percent of the poor.

As shown in table 6.1, regardless of the targeting mechanism used, Malawi's safety net programs fared poorly in 2003 in terms of inclusion and exclusion errors. It is therefore essential to identify a targeting approach that would rank, with reasonable accuracy, the individuals or households who apply for social support by their poverty status. Bearing this need in mind, this chapter develops an objective measure for identifying potential beneficiaries for safety net programs. The main objective is to lay out the challenges in using a proxy means test (PMT) formula for targeting the poorest (bottom 10 percent) and the extreme poor (bottom 25 percent) of the consumption distribution.

Development of a PMT for Safety Net Programs

In order to devise a targeting mechanism for social support programs that improves the identification of poor and vulnerable households, we developed a model for a proxy means test.[3] The PMT model objectively links various easily observable household characteristics with household income or poverty status using an ordinary least squares (OLS) regression model. A stepwise specification was used for all the models tested, retaining only the set of predictors whose statistical significance is above 90 percent.[4] As our welfare measure,[5] we employed the logarithm of per capita annual consumption to reflect a household's income or poverty status, given our objective of improving the targeting of safety net programs to those with the lowest per capita annual consumption.[6]

We used data from the Malawi Integrated Household Survey (MHIS) because it is a nationally representative survey designed specifically to provide district-level estimates of welfare indicators. The most recent MHIS available at the time of writing this chapter was carried out by the National Statistical Office between March 2004 and March 2005 and included 11,280 households.

Selecting the Variables

The development of a PMT model involves the selection of certain (nonincome) indicators to predict household income or poverty status. We used four main criteria to select variables: (a) correlation with the selected indicator (the higher the better, as this determines the power and precision of the prediction); (b) easy to measure (readily collected and updated using a simple questionnaire); (c) verifiable (easily observed by the targeting team or by community observers, depending on the implementation arrangements); and (d) not easily manipulated by potential beneficiaries. An additional criterion—that predictors should not lead to political discontent—is also discussed, but was not strongly enforced in this case study. For example, variables that include specific local characteristics can be highly predictive of poverty, but they may also be associated with partisan targeting on behalf of certain politicians or parties. Moreover, if the locations are not clearly delineated (for example, rural-urban status or lower administrative units), field teams will have a hard time deciding which data to collect or which formula to apply.

In our case, there are six household and individual indicators in the base set:

1. *Household demographic composition:* household size, number of elders (65 years old or older), number of children 0–4 years old, 5–12 years old, and 13–18 years old; whether the household has an impaired member (for example, mentally or physically disabled, self-reported chronically ill, or with difficulty performing daily activities, such as sweeping or walking for 5 kilometers); whether the household has a mother only, has a father only, or is missing both parents and has orphans in the age groups of 0–12 and 13–18 years old

2. *Characteristics of the household head:* gender, marital status, education, whether the household head is impaired in any way (disabled, chronically ill,

or with difficulty performing daily activities), and whether the household head is employed in the formal sector

3. *Characteristics of the dwelling:* owned or rented, has electricity, number of rooms per capita, type of floor, roof, and walls

4. *Ownership of durables:*[7] fan, air conditioning, television, sewing machine, washing machine, refrigerator, kerosene stove, gas stove, bicycle, motorcycle, car, or boat

5. *Ownership of productive assets, especially land and livestock:* amount of cultivated[8] rain-fed and *dimba* land; whether the household cultivates tobacco; whether the household owns cattle or oxen, goats or sheep, or pigs

6. *Location variables:* in addition to the variables mentioned above, we introduced location variables by accounting for possible unobservable characteristics of poverty that are location specific. We ran a model in which location was introduced using the 26 administrative districts and a second one in which location was introduced as eight agricultural development districts.[9] We also ran separate models for rural and urban areas. We did not, however, attempt to estimate separate models by location mainly because the sample size used to estimate PMT was too small to allow for location-specific weighting.

We did not include hard-to-verify indicators (such as self-employment in agriculture or in the nonagriculture sector) or easy-to-conceal indicators (such as ownership of a radio or mobile phone). Some of the variables that we initially thought might be correlated with the level of per capita consumption (such as having a member who is disabled or has difficulty performing activities of daily living in the household, having a household head who is impaired or employed in a business outside of the household) were dropped because they were found not to be statistically significant.

Furthermore, when estimating a nationwide model, we found that the coverage of the target population (be it the poorest, the extreme poor, or the poor) in urban, better-off areas is lower than in rural, poorer, areas of the country. This uneven coverage of the poor as well as the different characteristics of poverty in urban and rural areas can be managed by (1) using a combination of regional models in order to derive the PMT formula or by (2) using one PMT model but different cutoff points for urban and rural areas. Of these models, the one calibrated separately for urban and rural areas performed marginally better and is the one used in this study. However, one has to bear in mind that (a) we selected the model involving the least amount of information (while losing some efficiency), (b) the combination models (urban-rural, with different cutoff points) might be more difficult to implement, and (c) the gains in achieving horizontal equity might not justify the undercoverage or leakage trade-offs (especially if the implementation is only undertaken in rural areas, for example). The government of Malawi ultimately will have to determine the primary goals of a new social support program and choose the appropriate approach.

Evaluating the Targeting Performance of PMT

Under PMTs, individuals are classified in four groups, according to their true and predicted poverty levels. Those whose true poverty level falls under a certain cutoff point constitute the target population (the poor), and those whose predicted poverty falls below an eligibility threshold represent the population found eligible for support. Based on this typology, the targeting errors most commonly used in evaluating a formula are (a) exclusion errors (or undercoverage), which is the percentage of the target group that is missed by the program (or E1/N1 in table 6.2), and (b) inclusion errors (or leakage), which is the percentage of eligible individuals who are not in the target group (or E2/N3 in table 6.2).[10]

In general, the formula that minimizes both inclusion and exclusion errors should be implemented. In practice, there are trade-offs between the minimization of these two types of errors. If the policy objective is to raise the income level of the extreme poor, minimizing the number of exclusion errors is more important than minimizing the number of inclusion errors. If there is a budget constraint, it is more important to minimize the inclusion errors than the exclusion errors and, in this way, to increase the amount available for transfers to those who are eligible. In general when targeting the extreme poor, for any formula, exclusion errors are considered a more serious—and unacceptable—problem than inclusion errors.

Besides analyzing the inclusion and exclusion errors, two other measures are used to describe a model's performance: (a) the proportion of the variation in per capita expenditures explained by the selected regression model (adjusted R^2, where higher R^2 means a better fit) and (b) the allocation of potential beneficiaries across the income-expenditure distribution (incidence of targeting,

Table 6.2 Measurement of PMT Performance

Eligibility predicted by the PMT	Target group	Nontarget group	Total
Eligible	Correctly identified: targeting success (S1)	Inclusion error (E2)	Total eligible population according to the PMT (N3)
Ineligible	Exclusion error (E1)	Correctly identified: targeting success (S2)	Total ineligible population according to the PMT (N4)
Total	Total population in the target group (N1)	Total population in the nontarget group (N2)	N

where the higher the proportion of eligible individuals at the bottom of the distribution, the better). In other words, the extent to which the program is contributing to a reduction in the poverty gap ratio (that is, disproportionately reaching the extreme poor at the bottom end of the income-expenditure distribution) is as important as (and possibly more important than) a simple reduction in the headcount poverty ratio (reaching households below the poverty threshold).

Final PMT Model and Other Targeting Mechanisms

We tested various models and selected a PMT model that has a separate calibration for rural and urban areas. Consistent with the standard literature on poverty diagnostics, the number of dependents, dwelling characteristics, and land cultivated remain in the final model. Table 6A.2 in the annex lists the regression coefficients and their statistical levels for the selected model. Associated scores are developed by multiplying the coefficients from the particular models by 100 and rounding to the first decimal. The values of the variables directly influence the logarithm of per capita consumption and hence the PMT score. PMT scores, in turn, influence program eligibility if used as eligibility criteria. For example, if a certain variable is negatively correlated with consumption, it will negatively influence the PMT score and therefore increase the likelihood of eligibility. The discussion that follows refers to the influence of different variables on (logarithm of per capita) consumption.

The results show that large households, households with elders, children, or both, crowded households, and female-headed households have lower consumption levels, as expected. Generally, households living in dwellings with better construction materials for the floors and roof and those living in dwellings with working electricity have higher per capita consumption. Households in dwellings in urban areas with anything other than a flush toilet are associated with lower consumption levels, while households in dwellings in rural areas with a flush toilet or a traditional latrine (with or without a roof) are associated with higher consumption. All sources of drinking water except water piped into the dwelling are related to a decrease in consumption levels. The effects of both the type of toilet and the source of drinking water are larger in urban than in rural areas. In line with the common belief that tobacco crops are an important source of income, having cultivated tobacco in the most recent growing season increases the consumption of a household and therefore decreases the chances of that household being eligible. This finding is not altogether surprising, because tobacco growers in Malawi are generally better off than subsistence farmers. The amount of cultivated land in the most recent cropping season (rain-fed cultivation) is strongly positively correlated with consumption in urban areas (where only having cultivated 2 or more acres matters), but it is negatively correlated in rural areas. Having cultivated *dimba* plots is only relevant in rural areas, and it is positively correlated with consumption. Lastly, households living in districts other than the central districts of Dedza, Dowa, Kasungu, Lilongwe, Nkhotakota, Ntcheu, and Ntchisi or in the northern districts of Mzimba–Mzuzu City and Karonga have lower consumption levels and therefore increased chances of enrollment.

The targeting performance of this model in terms of exclusion and inclusion improves as the target group shifts from the poorest 10 percent to the poorest 50 percent of the population (table 6.3). If policy makers want to target

Table 6.3 Targeting Effectiveness of Model 3 and Its Variants in Malawi
% of the poor

| Geographic focus and target population | Type of error | National model | | Rural-urban model |
		One cutoff, model 3	Separate cutoffs, model 3_1	Separate cutoffs, model 3_2
National				
Poorest 10%	Exclusion	48.3	45.5	48.7
	Inclusion	68.4	68.6	68.1
Extreme poor	Exclusion	31.6	30.5	31.6
	Inclusion	52.6	54.1	52.2
Poor	Exclusion	13.9	13.7	13.9
	Inclusion	29.3	30.6	29.1
Urban				
Poorest 10%	Exclusion	80.3	83.1	62.0
	Inclusion	78.4	40.9	74.2
Extreme poor	Exclusion	52.5	88.7	44.2
	Inclusion	51.3	55.9	56.8
Poor	Exclusion	40.3	74.9	27.8
	Inclusion	36.1	21.1	40.5
Rural				
Poorest 10%	Exclusion	47.2	44.2	48.2
	Inclusion	68.2	68.8	67.9
Extreme poor	Exclusion	30.7	28.2	31.1
	Inclusion	52.7	54.1	52.0
Poor	Exclusion	12.3	10.1	13.0
	Inclusion	29.0	30.7	28.5

the extreme poor, the exclusion rate would be 32 percent and the inclusion rate would be 52 percent. This means that one-third of the extreme poor would be excluded from receiving social assistance based on the PMT, while half of the beneficiaries would not be the extreme poor. However, most recipients benefiting from the reported inclusion errors are in the population that is vulnerable to poverty, though not currently poor.

Figure 6.2 provides a disaggregated picture of the program incidence (based on the PMT): basically, if the extreme poor are the intended target group, only 13 percent of the benficiaries are strictly nonpoor (in the upper half of the consumption distribution). Furthermore, those excluded are far more likely to belong to the upper deciles of expenditure, while 8 out of 10 individuals belonging to the poorest 10 percent of the population (or 14 out of 20 individuals belonging to the extreme poor, representing 25 percent of the population) are correctly identified by the PMT formula. It also shows that most inclusion goes to a population that is vulnerable to falling into poverty with a small income shock (the bulk of unintended beneficiaries come from the third, fourth, and fifth deciles, whose monthly household expenditure per adult equivalent is less than the official poverty line). In other words, the results are encouraging inasmuch as the model performs quite well in excluding the nonpoor from program benefits, while including the poorest disproportionately.

Adding additional layers of targeting might improve the performance of the PMT model further. For example, adding a community layer to the targeting process might reduce the inclusion rates by reducing the incentive to misreport

Figure 6.2 Program Incidence and Coverage in Malawi, by Expenditure Decile

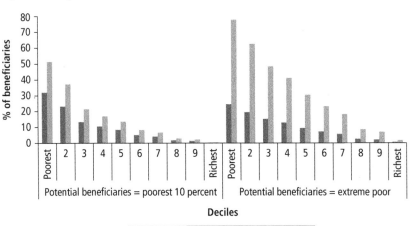

different indicators on the targeting forms. However, it is difficult to quantify the impact of such an additional layer without conducting a controlled experiment.

Alternative Model: PMT and Geographic Targeting

In a study of three African countries, Handa et al. (2012) study the extent to which a mix of demographic, geographic, and community-based targeting is able to identify direct beneficiaries of cash transfer programs effectively. Their paper emphasizes the role of employing multiple targeting mechanisms in order to minimize inclusion and exclusion errors.

The budgetary constraints and the localization of poverty in Malawi (concentrated mostly in rural and southern districts; see World Bank 2007) make it worthwhile to combine the model based on PMT targeting with the one based on geographic targeting. In this section, we briefly discuss differences in the effectiveness of the PMT formula in three situations.

First, we focus on the six districts with the largest incidence (rates) of the poorest 10 percent of the population, the extreme poor, and the poor. In this case, the program's coverage as well as exclusion and inclusion rates change dramatically. For example, if the program were implemented in the districts with the highest rates of the extreme poor (Balaka, Chikwawa, Machinga, Nsanje, Thyolo, and Zomba–Zomba City), it would cover more than half of the population of these districts. Only 17.8 percent of the extreme poor from these districts would not be covered, while less than half of the beneficiaries would not be extremely poor. Almost two-thirds of the inclusion would be of individuals who are poor but not extremely poor. Depending on the available budget, the number of districts can be adjusted accordingly.

Another alternative is to focus our attention on the top six districts with most of the poorest 10 percent of the population (in absolute numbers, as opposed to the "rate" or incidence in the above simulation), the extreme poor, and the poor.[11] This time, while the coverage and exclusion in the six districts are still higher than the nationwide rates, the inclusion rate improves only by a small percentage. The performance of the PMT model applied in these six districts is visibly lower than the performance of the model in the districts discussed above.

A third alternative is for the program to focus on the eight districts with the highest concentration of households with poor food consumption.[12] When doing so, the gains in performance, when compared to the national model, are minimal. The district-level effectiveness of the PMT model in predicting the poorest 10 percent and the extreme poor populations is shown in table 6A.3.

The strengths and weaknesses of using geographic targeting should be weighed carefully before deciding whether and how to use it: political opposition, stigma, migration, easy administration, and efficiency in allocating scarce resources. This analysis shows that mixed methods, especially targeting districts with a high incidence of poverty or vulnerability, will most likely improve the coverage, reduce the number of targeting errors, and, by its scale, generate savings. However, alternative mixed methods may also be implemented—for example, by combining a PMT with a census approach in high-poverty areas or a self-targeting approach in low-poverty areas.

Expected Coverage of Vulnerable Groups (Categorical Targeting)

Four of the main vulnerable groups identified in Malawi are households with (1) small landholdings, (2) female heads, (3) children 0–5 years old, (4) orphans 0–18 years old, and (5) labor constraints (see Makoka 2011). The PMT model is expected to improve the targeting of vulnerable groups, which helps other safety net programs to reach their own target groups.

Table 6.4 illustrates that all of the vulnerable groups listed above, except the individuals living in households with orphans, have higher rates of poverty, and their distribution across the deciles is skewed toward the lower end.

We find that, when the intended target group is the extreme poor, the program performs much better for the vulnerable groups, mostly due to the fact that some of the vulnerability criteria are accounted for in the PMT model. Nonetheless, the expected coverage within the vulnerable groups considered above lies between 35 and 45 percent; only 20–30 percent of the extreme poor and the vulnerable are not reached by the program, while about half of the potential beneficiaries are not extremely poor.

Table 6.4 shows that the exclusion among these potentially vulnerable categories of households is, in fact, much lower than the rate among the general population. Exclusion is particularly low among female-headed and labor-constrained households. This is evidence that the proposed targeting mechanism covers the main vulnerable groups as well as, or even better than, it does the poor in general. The inclusion rates are lower than in the general case for households with small landholdings, female heads, or labor constraints.

Exposure to Shocks and Targeting Performance of PMT

The vast majority (95 percent) of Malawi's households reported having experienced at least one shock in the last five years.[13] In general, Malawians are affected by both covariate and idiosyncratic shocks (table 6.5). The most prevalent shocks, which are also highly correlated, are related to crop yields and increases in food prices: 62.5 percent reported having had lower crop yields due to droughts or floods, and 77 percent reported having been affected by large rises in the price of food. The next most reported shocks were related to health or death: 45.7 percent of households were subject to an illness or

Table 6.4 Expected Performance of PMT Model with Respect to Vulnerable Groups in Malawi
% of the poor

Indicator	Small landholdings[a]		Female-headed[b]		With children 0–4 years old		With orphans 0–18 years old[c]		With labor constraints[d]		All households
	No	Yes	No	Yes	No	Yes	No	Yes	No	Yes	
Total % of individuals living in households with the following:	59.4	40.6	80.9	19.1	33.9	66.1	70.9	29.2	66.3	33.7	
Extreme poverty incidence	18.5	28.0	21.3	26.7	16.1	25.5	22.4	22.2	19.2	28.5	22.3
Poverty incidence	47.9	59.0	51.0	58.5	43.2	57.1	53.1	50.8	48.0	61.1	52.4
Distribution of individuals, by deciles											
Poorest	7.6	13.6	9.2	13.3	6.8	11.7	9.8	10.6	7.9	14.2	
2nd	8.7	11.9	9.8	10.8	7.2	11.4	10.5	8.8	9.2	11.6	
3rd	9.5	10.7	9.8	10.7	8.1	11.0	10.2	9.6	9.3	11.5	
4th	9.9	10.2	9.9	10.6	9.2	10.4	10.1	9.7	9.7	10.5	
5th	9.8	10.3	9.8	10.8	9.7	10.2	10.2	9.6	9.5	10.9	
6th	10.4	9.4	10.1	9.6	9.4	10.3	10.1	9.7	10.1	9.9	
7th	10.2	9.7	10.0	10.0	10.2	9.9	9.8	10.6	10.5	9.0	
8th	10.5	9.2	10.2	9.1	11.3	9.4	9.9	10.3	10.4	9.2	
9th	11.4	8.0	10.6	7.6	12.7	8.6	9.7	10.7	11.3	7.4	
Richest	12.1	7.0	10.6	7.5	15.5	7.2	9.8	10.5	12.1	5.9	
Expected coverage	27.1	38.9	29.7	41.0	18.7	38.6	30.7	34.6	25.1	45.1	31.9
Expected exclusion	36.8	26.6	34.7	21.2	45.6	27.1	32.9	28.5	39.9	20.7	31.6
Expected inclusion	57.1	47.1	53.3	48.5	53.1	51.9	51.2	54.2	54.4	49.7	52.2

a. Small landholdings are defined as households having cultivated rain-fed plots smaller than or equal to 2 acres.
b. Orphans refer to both-parent orphans, meaning that both parents are either dead or not living in the household.
c. Labor-constrained households are households with no adults (19–64 years old) fit for labor or households with fit-for-labor adults and a dependency ratio greater than or equal to 3:1.

Table 6.5 Self-Reported Shocks in Past Five Years in Malawi, by Quintile
% of households reporting

Indicator	Poorest	2nd	3rd	4th	Richest	Total	Most severe
Lower crop yields due to droughts or floods	71.4	68.1	67.1	62.5	50.8	62.5	23.3
Crop disease or crop pests	20.9	24.7	26.2	26.4	20.9	23.7	1.6
Livestock died or were stolen	29.9	35.2	35.5	36.1	30.1	33.3	1.9
Household business failure, nonagricultural	13.5	19.0	21.1	24.8	26.7	21.9	3.4
Loss of salaried employment or nonpayment of salaries	4.7	8.0	8.2	9.4	10.6	8.5	2.1
End of regular assistance, aid, or remittances	5.8	6.9	6.8	7.7	7.8	7.2	0.7
Large fall in sale prices for crops	33.7	37.8	40.5	41.3	36.1	38.0	4.3
Large rise in prices of food	74.3	75.5	79.7	78.6	76.1	77.0	19.4
Illness or accident of household member	41.8	46.3	47.1	49.0	43.7	45.7	8.5
Birth in the household	11.1	12.9	13.0	11.8	7.7	11.0	0.5
Death of household head	4.8	5.0	4.7	4.6	4.8	4.8	3.6
Death of working member of household	7.9	9.9	9.6	8.4	8.0	8.7	4.1
Death of other family member	35.5	39.3	43.4	41.8	41.1	40.6	12.7
Break-up of the household	10.1	10.2	9.9	8.9	10.3	9.9	2.4
Theft	13.2	17.6	17.8	21.7	22.9	19.3	3.0

Source: World Bank 2007.
Note: "Most severe" refers to the percentage of households reporting the shock as the most severe.

accident of a household member, and 54.1 percent experienced a death in the household (be it of the household head, a working member, or another household member). These shocks, as reported by the households, are not only the most widespread but also the most severe. The incidence of shocks experienced by households during the last five years by residence is shown in figure 6A.1.

Both the incidence and severity of shocks differ by household location. The large fall in prices is the most common major shock in both rural and urban areas. Thereafter, rural households reported having experienced a diversity of agricultural shocks, while urban households reported death of a family member. Furthermore, urban households reported having experienced fewer shocks overall, with 60 percent of urban households reporting that they had experienced three or fewer shocks. In contrast, more than 75 percent of rural households experienced four or more shocks in the last five years.

Even though the association between specific household characteristics and a shock depends on the type of shock, some patterns do emerge. For example, rural households with more education, larger landholdings, and higher expenditures are more likely to experience several shock events. With the exception of deaths and thefts, wealthier urban households are not more likely to have had an economic shock in the past five years. At the same time, both rural and urban households with a chronically ill household member are more likely to have experienced a shock.

Given this relative disconnect between the exposure to a shock and its possible correlation with poverty (visible from table 6.5, which shows the spread of shocks across all quintiles), it is useful to know the extent to which the PMT formula correctly identifies households exposed to a shock. The performance of the PMT formula among the households exposed to a shock is comparable to the performance of the formula among the general population. Among the households exposed to at least one shock during the last 12 months, 75 percent are correctly identified[14] as either eligible or not eligible by the PMT formula; the exclusion rate is about 31 percent, and the inclusion rate is 52 percent. For the households exposed to at least one shock during the last six months, these percentages are 73, 30, and 56 percent, respectively.

If used exclusively, the PMT formula will fail to incorporate into the program households where a shock has affected consumption levels but not (yet) affected the factors influencing the PMT score. This is reflected in the exclusion rates: the percentage of those who were affected by a shock and are currently considered as extremely poor but are not eligible under the PMT is around 30 percent. As mentioned, this performance is slightly better than the actual performance of the formula in a general setting.

We now focus only on the principal shocks affecting households in the last 12 months (31.8 percent of households)—namely, illness or death of a household member (18.9 percent of households), loss of crops due to droughts or floods (8.9 percent), and crop disease or livestock loss (7.7 percent). Of these,

- For the illness or death of a household member, the PMT formula correctly identifies households as eligible or not eligible in 77 percent of cases; the exclusion rate is 29 percent, and the inclusion rate is 51 percent.

- For the loss of crops due to droughts or floods, the PMT formula correctly identifies households as eligible or not eligible in 74 percent of cases; the exclusion rate is 19 percent, and the inclusion rate is 41 percent.

- For the loss of crops or livestock, the PMT formula correctly identifies households as eligible or not eligible in 74 percent of cases; the exclusion rate is 33 percent, and the inclusion rate is 56 percent.

By using a geographic approach to targeting, where only districts with more than 32 percent of households affected by one of the shocks in the last 12 months are selected (10 out of 26 districts), the indicators improve targeting, but not by much:

- For the illness or death of a household member, the percentages are 75, 29, and 46, respectively.
- For the loss of crops due to droughts or floods, the percentages are 75, 21, and 41, respectively.
- For the loss of crops or livestock, the percentages are 72, 30, and 48, respectively.

Therefore, the existing PMT model (combined with geographic targeting) should be applied with caution when rapid interventions are needed to address different needs of the vulnerable population.

Implementation of the PMT Model

Implementation of the PMT model has three components: (a) targeting strategy or arrangements, (b) application form, and (c) scoring (weighting). In the following section, we touch briefly on each of these steps.

Targeting Arrangements

If the PMT is combined with geographic targeting, then the implementing agency first has to identify the geographic regions where the program will be implemented. Once these regions are identified and clearly delimited in the field, the attention will turn to the targeting and enrollment processes for the households.

Regardless of the targeting method employed (through door-to-door targeting or through targeting centers), the next step is to register households using the targeting form. If the additional layer of community targeting is desired in order to minimize inclusion and improve coverage, this can be added either before or after registration. Each method has strengths and weaknesses, which require careful assessment and revision in order to determine the preferred course of action. If the community carries out the preliminary identification, there is opportunity for fraud and corruption as well as the possibility that households wrongly omitted at this stage might not apply in the future. If the identification is done after the registration, the chances of misreporting are minimized, and the chances of rent seeking are increased.

Potential beneficiaries are then selected based on the PMT formula. First the data collection team fills in the application forms based on information provided by household representatives, and the data are eventually entered into an automated data registry. Further, all of the variables collected through the application form and having a correspondent in the formula are weighted, and each household is assigned a score. Based on this score and the cutoff point (decided by government), households are declared eligible or not eligible to receive benefits. The enrollment process should then follow, with the selected households receiving enrollment cards together with information about their entitlements and payment methods.

Application Form

The application or targeting form should include at a minimum all of the variables needed to compute the PMT score, as well as variables that uniquely identify the applicants or recipients (national identification card). The following 11 variables are needed for the final model discussed in this case study:

- Age of the household members
- Gender and marital status of the household head
- Materials used in the construction of the floor, roof, and walls
- Number of rooms
- Availability of "working electricity"
- Type of toilet
- Source of drinking water
- Amount of land cultivated in the last cropping season (rain-fed cultivation, including both owned and rented land)
- Cultivation of tobacco in the last cropping season
- Amount of land cultivated in the last completed dry season (*dimba* cultivation, including both owned and rented land)
- District location.

The MIHS has all of the questions and definitions used for building this model. In addition to these, the national registration number of each applicant should be collected to lower the chances of duplication. An important source of fraud in this setting is that applications could be filed by different household members (as representing different households). Still, this problem can be solved with good administrative and community supervision.

Given the intended use of these data across different social support programs, the targeting form should not be reduced only to the 11 indicators used to compute the PMT formula. At the same time, it is desirable to avoid increased length or complexity. Before putting together the targeting form, the different stakeholders (the government and donors) should be consulted in order to decide what other information should be collected in order to make the process relevant for a range of programs and for future use.

The following principles or recommendations may be useful for designing the final questionnaire:

- For the variables used as proxy indicators, use the same questions as in the MIHS, which were used to derive the PMT formula. For new variables or indicators, use questions that already exist in censuses and national surveys. Such an approach may prove helpful for data validation and for subsequent program evaluation.

- Coordinate with the National Statistical Office when designing the targeting form and accompanying guidelines in order to ensure that the definition of indicators is perfectly aligned.

- Include a comprehensive household roster beyond the indicators used to build the PMT formula (include gender and education questions at a minimum), but try to avoid complex specialized modules (for example, on health or disability) that will create difficulties during data collection and may not be useful for purposes of the common targeting mechanism.

- Include a section on the possession of household assets, as they can be used to refine the formula.

- Include a short section with a few questions about the community (for example, the availability of infrastructure), as these variables could play an important role in refining the PMT and reducing the targeting errors.

Scoring

Even though we used the regression coefficients to compute the PMT formula (see table 6A.2), they can be rescaled in order to ease implementation. The current cutoff points for urban and rural areas are at the (a) 2.9 and 10.9 percentiles, respectively, of the predicted (log) consumption if the intended target population is the poorest 10 percent of the population and at the (b) 7.5 and 24.2 percentiles, respectively, if the intended target population is the extreme poor (22.4 percent of the total population). These cutoff points can be tweaked further depending on the needs of a specific program to be implemented and the available budget.

In order to account for (specified) indicators that we could not take into account (for example, remittances and employment) but which the communities might find important for determining welfare status, the community leaders could eventually be allowed to add or subtract approximately 15 percent of the cutoff point from the total score of a household. Nonetheless, there should be precise instructions on how to use discretion and the additional recommended indicators to be considered. Moreover, the persons making this choice should be instructed to keep track of the reasons for using these discretionary points.

Conclusion

The main objective of this case study has been to lay out a targeting mechanism that could be adopted as a common targeting tool in Malawi. After briefly introducing the various targeting mechanisms used, it presented the rationale for developing a PMT formula as a possible base targeting mechanism and extended the discussion to focus on the challenges in using a PMT formula for targeting the bottom 10 percent and the bottom 25 percent (the extreme poor) of the consumption distribution.[15]

After examining a variety of PMT models, the case study focused on a simple model based on 11 indicators. While this model is the best choice for the purpose of this case study, inasmuch as it performs extremely well in identifying the extreme poor and the poorest, correctly identifying poor and nonpoor households is still not easy. We selected the final model because (a) it involves less information (while losing some efficiency); (b) the combined models (urban-rural, with different cutoff points) might be more difficult to implement; and (c) the gains in achieving horizontal equity might not justify the exclusion-inclusion trade-offs (especially if the implementation is desired only in rural areas, for example). In the ultimate analysis, in Malawi (as in other countries), the goals of a new social support program will drive the choice of a PMT model.

Simulations also show that, when used alongside geographic targeting (covering the six districts where the incidence of the extreme poor and the poorest 10 percent is highest), the performance and predictive power of the selected model improves dramatically. Combining a PMT with geographic targeting seems eminently desirable.

In addition, we also tested the performance of PMT in identifying households exposed to different types of shocks. Given the pervasive nature of shocks experienced by the very poor in Malawi, this simulation is important. Notwithstanding the observed disconnect between exposure to shocks and poverty, it is noteworthy that the selected model correctly identifies as eligible or not eligible 75 percent of households exposed to shocks during the last 12 months, with an exclusion rate of 31 percent and an inclusion rate of 52 percent. When only principal shocks (illness or loss of breadwinner, crop loss, or livestock loss) are considered, the PMT correctly identifies 74–77 percent of households for different shocks, with exclusion rates ranging from 19 to 33 percent, and inclusion rates ranging from 41 to 56 percent.

Given the high levels of exclusion and inclusion rates, these findings suggest that the general PMT model (combined with geographic targeting) needs to be applied with caution in order to target the vulnerable population exposed to different types of shocks or to address the needs of the vulnerable population exposed to other types of risks and shocks. While improvements in the performance of the PMT can be realized under a variety of circumstances, in the ultimate analysis, it is best to incorporate community insights as much as possible to refine (or correct) the targeting efficiency accomplished with PMT models.

The case study also reviewed the implementation arrangements for the PMT and delineated various steps to be taken or decisions to be made. Once the target group has been identified, the eligibility cutoff point has to be determined. In doing so, the trade-offs between exclusion and inclusion rates need to be considered: as the eligibility cutoff point increases (that is, the eligible group expands), the exclusion rate decreases, while the inclusion rate increases. The opposite is true when the cutoff point is decreased.

Another decision facing policy makers is whether it is worth enlarging the eligible group at the same time as the target group (for example, if the target group is adjusted from the poorest 10 percent to the poorest 25 percent of the population). The trade-off in this case is that both the exclusion and inclusion rates will fall but, if the budget allocated to the program remains constant, this will come at the expense of a lower level of benefits for the beneficiaries. It is difficult to assess a priori the impact that a reduction of transfers and expansion of eligibility thresholds will have on poverty without knowing the distribution of household consumption and the distribution of consumption measurement errors. However, if the poorest are progressively targeted and not subject to measurement errors, they likely stand to be negatively affected by an expansion of eligibility thresholds and a contraction of benefit levels.

A few other challenges for policy makers include (a) updating the formula over time, (b) developing a data collection system that is both effective and cost-efficient, (c) developing a database that is updated easily and regularly, and (d) developing a credible monitoring, verification, and fraud control mechanism.

Some of the limitations of the PMT developed in this study are worth mentioning:

- Having a limited number of verifiable variables, which are mostly time-insensitive (because we are using such an old data set for current computations and implementation), implies a bias toward the chronically poor. Thus in these situations additional vulnerability indicators could be added for targeting groups vulnerable to different shocks or a combination of targeting methodologies could be employed (for example, PMT could be combined with categorical targeting, geographic targeting, or both).

- This particular PMT formula was developed using 2003 data, and the distribution of some of the variables over the population could have changed, implying that their weights or scores also could have changed. As new household expenditure survey data become available, it would be useful to redo this exercise to see whether the results based on 2003 data stand robust or need to be adjusted.

- Finally, while there is significant improvement in the performance of the PMT model when compared with the current targeting performance of ongoing programs (table 6.1), it is very difficult to target the bottom 10 percent of the population or the extreme poor (and it is more difficult with a limited budget). Moreover, the PMT model does not seem to be appropriate for identifying households exposed to other types of risks and vulnerabilities, except when these risks are correlated with poverty. However, some fine-tuning of methods, such as including rural community variables and at the same time calibrating separate regressions for rural and urban areas, can improve the targeting efficiency. Yet the PMT alone, like any other targeting mechanism, is not a silver bullet when it comes to reaching the poorest households. Combining PMT with information gathered directly from communities will help to correct errors, prevent fraud, and address dimensions of poverty that are not captured in the current model.

Annex 6A Detailed Results

Table 6A.1 Coverage, Exclusion, and Inclusion Rates of Social Assistance Programs in Malawi, Including Direct and Indirect Beneficiaries

% of population

Program	Coverage	Extreme poor 1		Extreme poor 2		Extreme poor		Poor	
		Exclusion	Inclusion	Exclusion	Inclusion	Exclusion	Inclusion	Exclusion	Inclusion
All social assistance	50.9	34.3	99.1	42.8	85.7	44.0	73.2	44.4	44.1
Free Food Program	13.3	71.3	98.6	85.4	86.1	86.3	75.2	86.2	47.1
Inputs for Work Program	0.6	100.0	100.0	99.1	81.2	99.0	59.4	99.1	25.3
Food or Cash for Work Program	3.9	92.8	98.8	95.3	84.7	94.9	69.0	95.2	37.7
Targeted Nutrition Program	4.3	94.4	99.1	96.6	90.0	96.5	80.4	96.2	55.3
Supplementary Feeding Program	0.9	93.2	95.2	98.6	81.8	98.6	64.0	98.8	34.8
Agricultural Inputs Program	0.6	100.0	100.0	99.5	90.0	99.5	78.6	99.3	40.1
Starter Pack of Agricultural Inputs	44.3	40.3	99.1	49.9	85.6	51.0	73.5	50.8	43.5
Scholarships and GABLE Support for Girls	0.2	100.0	100.0	99.8	89.6	99.8	76.6	99.8	61.4

Source: National Statistical Office 2005.

Note: Extreme poor 1 are those individuals whose per capita consumption is lower than a quarter of the median consumption. *Extreme poor 2* are those individuals whose per capita consumption is lower than half of the median consumption. *Coverage* is the portion of population in each group who receives the transfer. Specifically, coverage is (Number of individuals in the group who live in a household where at least one member receives the transfer)/ (Number of individuals in the group). *Exclusion* is the percentage of poor individuals who do not receive transfers. *Inclusion* is the percentage of individuals who receive transfers and are not poor.

Table 6A.2 Regression Coefficients for Model 3_2 for Malawi

Indicator	Urban	Rural
Household demographics		
Household size (preconstructed)		−0.067
		(8.99)***
Number of elders (65 years old or more)	−0.265	−0.11
	(5.59)***	(9.21)***
Number of children		
0–4 years old	−0.145	−0.07
	(7.73)***	(6.56)***
5–12 years old	−0.125	−0.073
	(9.89)***	(8.66)***
13–18 years old	−0.13	−0.024
	(7.71)***	(2.49)**
Characteristics of the household head		
Female household head	−0.206	−0.219
	(4.42)***	(11.20)***
Household head currently married	−0.157	−0.153
	(3.04)***	(7.31)***
Housing		
Floor materials		
Smoothed cement	0.213	0.226
	(6.23)***	(9.37)***
Sand, other	0.407	−0.122
	(2.59)**	(2.98)***
Roof materials		
Iron sheets, other	0.152	0.172
	(4.35)***	(8.85)***
Wall materials		
Burnt brick		0.031
		(1.95)*
Compacted earth	−0.173	
	(2.50)**	
Number of rooms per capita (no bathroom, no kitchen)	0.468	0.249
	(10.39)***	(17.00)***
Household has working electricity in dwelling	0.413	0.612
	(9.64)***	(11.77)***
Type of toilet		
Ventilated improved pit latrine	−0.447	0.115
	(4.63)***	(1.87)*
Traditional latrine with roof	−0.567	0.088
	(6.41)***	(5.18)***

(continued next page)

Table 6A.2 (continued)

Indicator	Urban	Rural
Traditional latrine without roof	−0.54 (5.59)***	0.059 (3.45)***
None, other	−0.799 (7.28)***	
Source of drinking water		
Other personal sources	−0.231 (2.75)***	
Communal standpipe	−0.101 (2.10)**	−0.088 (2.13)**
Communal hand pipe	−0.261 (4.38)***	−0.132 (3.57)***
Communal open well	−0.269 (4.10)***	−0.128 (3.47)***
Other open sources		−0.163 (3.63)***
Agricultural assets		
Cultivated land in last completed cropping season (rain-fed cultivation)		
Household cultivated more than 0 but less than or equal to 0.5 acres		−0.14 (5.42)***
Household cultivated more than 0.5 but less than or equal to 1 acres		−0.112 (6.41)***
Household cultivated more than 1 but less than or equal to 2 acres		−0.104 (7.22)***
Household cultivated more than 2 but less than or equal to 10 acres	0.175 (3.38)***	
Household cultivated more than 10 acres	0.225 (3.57)***	−0.045 (1.97)**
Household cultivated tobacco in the last cropping season		0.106 (4.95)***
Cultivated land in last completed dry season (*dimba* cultivation)		
Household cultivated more than 0 but less than or equal to 0.5 acres		0.064 (3.52)***
Household cultivated more than 0.5 but less than or equal to 2 acres		0.143 (6.44)***
Household cultivated more than 2 acres		0.069 (3.45)***
Location (district)		
Chitipa		−0.238 (2.90)***
Nkhata Bay		−0.284 (2.59)***

(continued next page)

Table 6A.2 (continued)

Indicator	Urban	Rural
Rumphi		−0.303
		(2.98)***
Salima		−0.105
		(1.83)*
Mchinji		−0.201
		(3.31)***
Mangochi		−0.175
		(3.17)***
Machinga		−0.337
		(7.98)***
Zomba–Zomba City	−0.33	−0.371
	(6.29)***	(5.67)***
Chiradzulu		−0.264
		(4.51)***
Blantyre–Blantyre City	−0.103	−0.127
	(1.92)*	(2.14)**
Mwanza		−0.137
		(2.01)**
Thyolo		−0.415
		(8.55)***
Mulanje		−0.428
		(11.35)***
Phalombe		−0.267
		(5.58)***
Chikwawa		−0.229
		(3.34)***
Nsanje		−0.133
		(2.48)**
Balaka		−0.185
		(3.17)***
Constant	10.731	10.377
	(105.35)***	(208.26)***
Number of observations	1,436	9,809
R^2	0.71	0.48

Note: Numbers in parentheses are robust *t*-statistics.
*** $p < .01$, ** $p < .05$,   * $p < .10$

Table 6A.3 Effectiveness of PMT Model for Malawi, by District

District	% of population	Poverty distribution			Poverty incidence			Effectiveness of the PMT formula in the district								
								Poorest 10 percent			Extreme poor			Poor		
		Poorest 10%	Extreme poor	Poor	Poorest 10%	Extreme poor	Poverty	Coverage	Under-coverage	Leakage	Coverage	Under-coverage	Leakage	Coverage	Under-coverage	Leakage
Nsanje	2.3	5.5	4.5	3.3	24.4	44.3	76.0	39.6	25.5	54.1	59.2	18.0	38.6	88.5	4.5	18.0
Machinga	3.6	6.1	6.2	5.1	16.9	38.3	73.7	33.2	33.0	65.8	60.1	18.9	48.2	90.2	2.8	20.7
Zomba–Zomba City	5.7	12.2	9.3	6.9	21.6	36.9	64.2	34.9	25.4	54.2	53.7	16.4	43.3	80.0	4.7	23.7
Balaka	2.5	4.8	3.8	3.2	18.9	33.5	66.8	30.4	26.4	54.3	48.4	19.4	44.0	78.0	8.8	21.8
Thyolo	5.3	6.9	7.8	6.6	13.0	33.0	64.9	33.6	30.1	72.9	56.0	14.7	49.6	76.4	8.5	21.9
Chikwawa	3.6	5.9	5.2	4.6	16.3	31.9	65.8	31.8	32.9	65.9	53.1	22.4	53.6	82.7	9.7	28.2
Mulanje	1.3	1.9	1.8	1.7	14.9	30.6	68.6	29.8	34.7	67.3	50.4	14.9	48.2	78.5	6.6	18.4
Chitipa	1.3	1.2	1.7	1.6	9.9	30.4	67.2	26.5	52.6	82.4	50.7	26.0	55.5	82.3	10.1	26.7
Mchinji	3.4	3.9	4.6	3.9	11.5	30.4	59.6	15.7	72.2	79.4	37.3	35.9	47.6	72.8	10.9	27.3
Nkhata Bay	1.4	2.8	1.9	1.7	19.4	30.3	63.0	29.6	29.1	53.7	47.2	21.3	49.5	76.5	8.4	24.6
Mangochi	6.4	9.1	8.3	7.4	14.4	29.3	60.7	19.9	54.1	66.8	42.9	31.5	53.2	77.6	9.3	28.9
Karonga	1.9	2.6	2.4	2.0	13.9	28.3	54.9	12.9	60.7	60.4	28.6	45.8	47.7	63.1	17.9	29.2
Chiradzulu	2.5	2.4	3.1	3.1	9.6	27.5	63.5	19.1	41.0	70.2	42.7	18.0	47.2	76.3	10.1	25.1
Phalombe	2.3	2.7	2.8	2.7	11.7	26.9	61.9	17.0	55.5	69.4	36.1	25.7	44.5	68.8	11.0	19.9
Salima	2.6	3.5	2.9	2.8	13.6	25.0	57.3	17.4	46.5	57.5	36.6	17.3	44.3	69.0	15.5	30.3
Rumphi	1.0	1.1	1.1	1.2	10.9	24.2	61.6	21.9	44.4	72.5	38.5	24.1	52.2	70.1	15.5	25.8
Ntcheu	4.0	3.5	3.7	3.9	8.7	21.1	51.6	7.9	84.4	82.8	23.6	47.1	52.5	62.9	16.6	31.8
Dedza	5.3	3.7	5.0	5.5	7.0	20.9	54.6	7.5	87.4	88.2	22.5	55.3	58.8	66.0	16.7	31.2
Mzimba–Mzuzu City	5.7	4.0	5.2	5.2	6.9	20.3	47.5	8.3	75.6	80.2	20.6	49.8	50.9	51.1	25.6	31.1

(continued next page)

Table 6A.3 (continued)

District	% of population	Poverty distribution			Poverty incidence			Effectiveness of the PMT formula in the district								
								Poorest 10 percent			Extreme poor			Poor		
		Poorest 10%	Extreme poor	Poor	Poorest 10%	Extreme poor	Poverty	Coverage	Under-coverage	Leakage	Coverage	Under-coverage	Leakage	Coverage	Under-coverage	Leakage
Mwanza	3.0	2.8	2.6	3.2	9.4	19.7	55.6	5.9	74.0	58.3	21.9	54.5	58.9	56.7	24.3	25.7
Kasungu	5.1	2.8	3.5	4.4	5.4	15.1	44.9	8.6	92.6	95.3	18.4	56.5	65.6	53.5	25.7	38.0
Ntchisi	1.8	1.1	1.0	1.7	6.2	12.2	47.3	12.7	41.3	71.2	25.0	30.6	66.1	59.0	15.9	32.5
Nkhotakota	2.4	1.1	1.2	2.2	4.5	11.4	48.0	10.4	100.0	100.0	23.6	60.0	80.6	63.1	16.7	36.5
Lilongwe–Lilongwe City	14.2	5.9	6.8	9.0	4.2	10.7	33.0	5.4	66.6	74.0	13.2	53.9	62.7	44.5	22.4	42.6
Blantyre	7.3	2.6	3.0	4.5	3.6	9.2	32.4	4.5	60.9	69.1	12.9	46.3	62.0	37.0	23.0	32.4
Dowa	4.1	0.0	0.6	2.9	0.0	3.3	36.6	4.7	0.0	100.0	16.7	0.0	79.9	51.1	13.5	38.1
Total (poorest 6 districts)								33.5	28.3	58.4	55.1	17.8	46.7	84.3	6.6	22.6
Total (6 districts with the highest concentration of poor households)[a]								30.0	35.0	64.6	43.2	22.7	50.1	68.5	10.2	26.3
Total (8 districts with the highest concentration of households with poor food consumption)[b]								17.3	46.3	65.1	35.6	28.1	50.6	66.0	11.8	25.3
Total	10.0		22.4	52.4				16.1	48.7	68.1	31.8	31.6	52.1	63.6	13.9	29.1

Note: When studying the targeting effectiveness by combining the PMT and geographic targeting, the formula and cutoff points are the same as for the overall model.
a. Lilongwe–Lilongwe City is excluded from these rankings.
b. See WFP (2010).The eight districts are Balaka, Blantyre, Chiradzulu, Machinga, Mangochi, Mulanje, Mwanza, and Phalombe, roughly corresponding to Lake Chirwa–Phalombe Plain, Shire Highlands, Phirilongwe Hills, and Middle Shire Valley.

Figure 6A.1 Incidence of Shocks in Last Five Years in Malawi, by Area of Residence

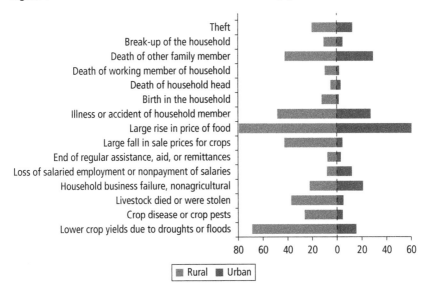

Source: National Statistical Office 2005.

Notes

1. The term "safety nets" is used to cover all social assistance programs.
2. The Malawi Integrated Household Survey 2004/05 has a separate module on safety nets. For this module, the household head provides information on whether any of the household members received benefits from specific programs in 2001, 2002, and 2003 separately. For those households benefiting from a specific program in 2003, the household head provides further information on the amount. Only the 2003 beneficiaries were taken into account in computing the rates in table 6.1. While the amount of benefits might include an additional source of errors (especially if the respondent was not the beneficiary), it is not likely that the respondents would not know or report whether their households were beneficiaries of specific programs.
3. Several examples of poverty scorecards have been constructed for Malawi, a review of which is found in Schreiner (2011) and Phiri (2011). Some use principal component analysis or factor analysis in order to derive "asset indexes," while others use different data sources. The most recent poverty scorecard based on the data set used in this case study is constructed by Schreiner (2011). The approaches are similar, and the reasons for choosing different specifications are not discussed here.
4. The significance of the coefficients is based on *t*-statistics, which measure whether the coefficient of a particular variable is statistically relevant for predicting

household expenditure. The variables for which the value of the t-statistic is too low are usually dropped. The values of the t-statistic are based on the values of the standard errors, which in this case study are computed by considering the sample design. However, step-wise regressions have limitations, in particular, sets of correlated variables that are jointly statistically significant but individually insignificant may be dropped from the specification (Grosh and Baker 1995).

5. In addition, the National Statistical Office uses this welfare measure to compute the official poverty rates in Malawi.

6. Broadly speaking, the consumption expenditures categories considered for the analysis are food; nonfood, nonconsumer durables; consumer durable goods; and actual or self-estimated rental cost of housing. The expenditures included in each category are only those related to household consumption; all expenditures related to business activities were excluded. The use-value of assets and durables related to income generation were also excluded. The consumption expenditures constructed as such are not net of any social support benefit.

7. Durable goods can be introduced in the model through an ownership variable ("Does your household own [ITEM]?") or through the number of items the household owns ("How many [ITEM] does your household own?"). We ran models using both the ownership and the number of assets owned. The explanatory power of the models using the number of assets owned did not differ significantly from the models using ownership only. Given that ownership requires less information to be collected and is harder to fake than asking the number of a certain durable good, we prefer the models using ownership of durables.

8. Cultivated land can be granted by local leaders, inherited, acquired through a spouse's family, purchased with or without a title, leased, rented short term, farmed as a tenant, or other.

9. The agricultural development districts are basically a higher level of aggregation than the districts. The eight agricultural development districts and their corresponding districts are Karonga (Chitipa, Karonga), Mzuzu (Nkhata Bay, Rumphi, Mzimba–Mzuzu City), Kasungu (Kasungu, Ntchisi, Dowa), Salima (Nkhotakota, Salima, part of Dedza), Lilongwe (Lilongwe–Lilongwe City, Mchinji, Dedza, Ntcheu), Machinga (Mangochi, Machinga, Zomba–Zomba City, Balaka), Blantyre (Chiradzulu, Blantyre–Blantyre City, Mwanza, Thyolo, Mulanje, Phalombe), and Ngabu (Chikwawa, Nsanje).

10. In this context, the literature also refers to type I and type II errors. An individual incorrectly excluded by the PMT is a case of type I error, while an individual incorrectly included by the PMT is a case of type II error.

11. Given the poverty rates in Lilongwe–Lilongwe City district, we excluded this district from the analysis.

12. See WFP (2010). The eight districts are Balaka, Blantyre, Chiradzulu, Machinga, Mangochi, Mulanje, Mwanza, and Phalombe, roughly corresponding to Lake Chirwa–Phalombe Plain, Shire Highlands, Phirilongwe Hills, and Middle Shire Valley.

13. The first part of this section draws from World Bank (2007).

14. "Correctly identifies" in this context means that those who suffered a certain shock are either consumption poor and eligible according to the PMT formula or consumption nonpoor and not eligible according to the PMT formula.
15. These percentages correspond largely to the extreme poor with labor constraints (10 percent) and the extreme poor (25 percent).

References

Grosh, Margaret, and Judy Baker. 1995. "Proxy Means Tests for Targeting Social Programs: Simulations and Speculation." LSMS Working Paper 118, World Bank, Washington, DC.

Handa, Sudhandshu, Carolyn Huang, Nicola Hypher, Clarissa Teixeira, Fabio V. Soares, and Benjamin Davis. 2012. "Targeting Effectiveness of Social Cash Transfer Programmes in Three African Countries." *Journal of Development Effectiveness* 4 (1): 78–108.

IFPRI (International Food Policy Research Institute). 2011. "Poverty in Malawi: Current Status and Knowledge Gaps." Policy Note 9, International Food Policy Research Institute, Washington DC.

Makoka, D. 2011. "Identification of Key Vulnerable Groups in Malawi." Background paper for the "Effective and Inclusive Targeting Mechanisms for Formal Social Support Programs in Malawi." World Bank, Washington, DC.

National Statistical Office. 2005. *Malawi Integrated Household Survey 2004–2005.* Zomba: Government of Malawi.

Phiri, A. 2011. "Review of Targeting Tools Employed by Existing Social Support Programs in Malawi." Background paper for the "Effective and Inclusive Targeting Mechanisms for Formal Social Support Programs in Malawi." World Bank, Washington, DC.

Schreiner, Mark. 2011. "A Simple Poverty Scorecard for Malawi." Microfinance Risk Management, Kansas City, KS. www.microfinance.com.

UNICEF (United Nations Children's Fund). 2011. "Malawi National Social Support Program Update." Briefing by UNICEF to Heads of Cooperation, May.

WFP (World Food Program). 2010. *Rural Malawi Comprehensive Food Security and Vulnerability Analysis.* Rome: WFP.

World Bank. 2007. "Poverty and Vulnerability Assessment." World Bank, Washington, DC.

Chapter 7

Climatic Shocks and Poverty Dynamics in Mozambique

Kimberly Groover, Bradford Mills, and Carlo del Ninno

Poverty reduction continues to be at the forefront of economic development efforts in low-income countries, particularly in Sub-Saharan Africa, where poverty rates remain high. Research on poverty dynamics documents that some households are transient poor, in that they move in and out of poverty due to internal and external changes in their environments, while others are chronically poor (Datt and Hoogeveen 1999; Günther and Harttgen 2009). Traditional static poverty estimates do not differentiate between the chronic and transient poor (Dercon and Krishnan 2000), and the factors that give rise to chronic and transient poverty differ (Jalan and Ravallion 2000). Interventions that target households based solely on the characteristics of the current poor are likely to leave some groups unprotected in the face of negative shocks affecting their economic well-being.

Climatic shocks, such as droughts, floods, and agricultural pests, are covariate risks, meaning that exposure to the shock is correlated spatially across households. Exposure to climatic shocks may push individual households into transient poverty and, in aggregate, significantly increase local poverty rates. However, even with covariate shocks, considerable variation in household exposure occurs due to variations in local geography and conditions (del Ninno et al. 2001). A shock's impact on household well-being is also likely to depend on the individual assets and conditions of the household (Devereux et al. 2006; Dorward and Kydd 2004; Devereux 2002). Some households may be forced to rely on transfers from social networks or public programs to smooth consumption, while others may have accumulated sufficient assets to withstand shocks without assistance. Households without adequate resources and transfers may resort to negative coping mechanisms, including the depletion of assets and the withdrawal of their children from school. As a result, shocks can have a significant effect not only on immediate consumption but also on long-term expected consumption as households reduce their investments in human and physical capital. Continual exposure to shocks can have a particularly pernicious impact on the ability of poor and vulnerable households to maintain adequate levels of consumption and buffer against future shocks (Dercon and Krishnan 2000). Thus understanding the impact of covariate climatic shocks on household well-being is particularly crucial for efforts to identify the transient poor and address their social assistance needs.

Increasingly, the designers of social assistance programs are recognizing the need to target the chronic and transient poor separately. Programs targeted toward households that are permanently, or chronically, poor usually seek to provide long-term assistance and to augment household assets in order to remove "poverty traps." Efforts to increase household assets include incentives for households to invest in human capital, regional infrastructure, and sustainable income-generating activities. Programs targeting households that are vulnerable to shorter spells of poverty provide a temporary safety net to secure immediate well-being and to prevent households from resorting to negative coping mechanisms that deplete the household asset base in the long term. Interventions may focus on mitigating exposure to, or impacts from, short- and medium-term negative shocks. During emergency situations, households vulnerable to transient poverty must be identified quickly in order for social protection programs to respond rapidly to the crisis and to provide alternatives to coping mechanisms with negative long-term implications.

This case study presents a method for identifying chronic and transient poverty in the face of exposure to climatic shocks and tests the method in the Mozambican context. An endogenous treatment effects (ETE) model is employed to identify households likely to be poor without exposure to climatic shocks (the chronic poor) and with exposure to climatic shocks (the transient poor), both ex ante and ex post. The next section provides an overview of the poverty and social assistance programs in Mozambique, followed by the conceptual framework and empirical model. The model specification and description of the data are then presented, followed by the results of the ETE model. The chapter concludes with a discussion and policy implications.

Mozambique's Poverty and Climatic Shocks

The need to identify households vulnerable to transient poverty effectively is urgent in Mozambique, which faces high poverty rates, frequent exposure to climatic shocks, and severely constrained financial, institutional, and managerial resources for social assistance. The national poverty rate is 54.7 percent, with considerable regional variation in the distribution of poverty—ranging from 31.9 percent in fertile, northern Niassa to 70.5 percent in central, coastal Zambézia (MPD 2010). Disparities also exist between urban and rural areas, with poverty rates of 56.9 and 49.6 percent, respectively (MPD 2010). Many Mozambican households continue to be heavily dependent on rain-fed agriculture and are frequently exposed to weather-related shocks. Mozambique has one of the highest occurrences of natural disasters and hazards among African nations, making national poverty rates vulnerable to sudden increases. A 2007 report by the Food and Agriculture Organization labeled 20 of the 128 districts in Mozambique as "highly prone to drought," 30 as prone to flooding, and 7 as prone to both climatic shocks (FAO 2007). The country's climate is significantly drier in the southern provinces, which experience recurrent periods of drought. The northern region is exposed to annual flooding of the Zambezi River, and the coast suffers a five-month cyclone season. Exposure to agricultural pests is also prevalent in the heavily agricultural regions in the north and center of the country. The link between poverty and exposure to natural disasters is apparent, yet there is a lack of data analyzing the magnitude and frequency of climatic shocks and their impact on household poverty (Shendy, Nucifora, and Thomas 2009). The 2011 Disaster Risk Assessment compiled by Mozambique's National Institute for Disaster Management cites the lack of risk assessment and vulnerability data, as well as their poor integration and dissemination among relevant agencies, as a challenge to implementing a National Risk Assessment Program (GRIP 2010). In this context, enhancing capacity to provide rapid relief to near-poor households in emergency situations is an important component of Mozambique's poverty reduction strategy.

Mitigation of Risk through Social Assistance Programs and Insurance

Cash transfer programs are often initiated during an emergency to lessen the long-term impacts of natural disasters. While mitigation programs, such as Food-For-Work and input transfer programs, help to alleviate the impact of natural disasters, a large number of affected households are continually left out of these programs (Hodges and Pellerano 2010). Further, such programs are often reactive and provide too little assistance too late. Social assistance programs can increase their impact on transient poverty by using an accurate, ex ante identification of who is in need, where they are, and how much assistance is required.

Programs that target chronic poverty, rather than transient poverty, typically employ multiple targeting mechanisms to identify eligible households.

Handa et al. (2012) analyze the ability of social cash transfer programs to select direct beneficiaries effectively in three African countries: Kenya, Malawi, and Mozambique. All three programs use a combination of demographic, geographic, and community-based targeting mechanisms to identify recipient households. In Mozambique, the Food Subsidy Program (PSA) is the nation's largest cash transfer program in terms of the number of beneficiaries. The PSA targets the elderly, the disabled and chronically ill who are unable to work, heads of destitute households, and persons who live alone. However, the elderly constitute 93 percent of PSA direct beneficiaries (Handa et al. 2012). As expected, the number of eligible households in the PSA, as well as the Kenyan and Malawi programs, greatly surpasses the amount of program resources, and additional ranking of households is required to select beneficiaries.

When comparing households eligible to receive benefits under the "elderly" criteria to all other households, Handa et al. (2012) find that elderly households are only slightly poorer than all households and there is some evidence of leakage to the nonpoor. They suggest that using better geographic targeting methods, specifically the selection of participating villages, could increase the effectiveness of the PSA. Handa et al. also emphasize the importance of employing multiple targeting mechanisms for effective selection of beneficiaries. When considering these conclusions with respect to programs seeking to stabilize poverty rates following exposure to a covariate shock, developing effective and accurate targeting criteria to minimize the inclusion of ineligible households or the exclusion of eligible households most in need is clearly important.

Another key consideration is the ability of households to secure their own protection against losses resulting from natural disasters. Mozambique's disaster relief and recovery objectives, as well as overall poverty reduction goals, include the development and uptake of insurance programs targeting low-income households. According to the Global Facility for Disaster Reduction and Recovery, only 5.1 percent of Mozambicans are covered under any insurance program (GFDRR 2011). Only a portion of this figure has coverage for losses resulting from climatic catastrophes, where current coverage is included in property and agricultural insurance programs (GFDRR 2011). Insurance programs, such as microinsurance and index insurance, are only recently being developed for Mozambican markets. Thus households have limited ability to use insurance programs to offset potential losses resulting from future exposure to climatic shocks.

Current research addresses the gap in knowledge about effective methods of program targeting by identifying and developing targeting indicators for chronically poor households and households that become poor with exposure to weather-related shocks. A conceptual framework for modeling the impact of climatic shocks on household food expenditures using cross-sectional data follows, based on recent research on household poverty and vulnerability.

Applying Cross-Sectional Data to Identify the Chronic and Transient Poor

Transient poverty is best detected using panel data sets to identify temporary spells of poverty. but panel data are not available in most Sub-Saharan African countries. However, cross-sectional data are increasingly available through National Living Standards Measurement Surveys and can be used to identify empirically households with short- and long-term assistance needs. To date, cross-sectional analyses of transient poverty have focused on determining the mean and variance of household expenditures (Chaudhuri, Jalan, and Suryahadi 2002; Christiaensen and Subbarao 2005; Dercon and Krishnan 2000; Günther and Harttgen 2009). Yet factors that cause a variation in household expenditures, like climatic shocks, can sometimes be observed and used by social assistance programs to identify households likely to be poor in the face of shocks.

The impact of negative events on household expenditures can be estimated by including exposure to shocks and other household and community characteristics in the household expenditures equation (Datt and Hoogeveen 1999; del Ninno and Marini 2005). However, unobserved heterogeneity may generate biased parameter estimates in a regression of this type. For example, in the case of covariate shocks, exposure may not depend on observed household characteristics or levels of well-being. However, unobserved factors that influence both exposure to shocks and household expenditures may bias parameter estimates of the impact of the shock. The bias associated with this type of unobserved heterogeneity can be controlled for by jointly estimating equations for household exposure to a shock and household expenditures. The endogenous treatment effects model outlined below follows this strategy with respect to climatic shocks. Unbiased estimates of the impact of shocks and expenditures are then used to identify the expected (chronic) poor and those who are likely to be poor only after a shock (transient poor).

Empirical Model

The food expenditure equation is defined as follows:

$$C_i = X_i B + S_i \alpha + u_i, \tag{7.1}$$

where C_i is food expenditures per person per day of household i adjusted for temporal differences in prices. X_i is the vector of variables for household demographics, human capital, physical assets, and the interview month. S_i is a binary indicator of exposure to a climatic shock, and u_i is a household-specific error term. Further, observed S_i arises from a latent intensity of exposure, S_{ij}^*:

$$S_i^* = Z_i\gamma + v_i, \tag{7.2}$$

where S_i^* is estimated as $S_i = \begin{cases} 0 \text{ if } S_i^* \leq 0 \\ 1 \text{ if } S_i^* > 0 \end{cases}$,

and Z_i is a vector of observed climatic, geographic, and household variables. α is unbiased if exposure to a climatic shock is orthogonal to the error term; $cov[S_i, u_i] = 0$. The expenditure equation is identified by a variable (or variables) that appears in row vector Z_i and does not appear in the expenditures equation. Further, the unique variable(s) in Z_i influence(s) expenditures only through the impact on household exposure to the shock.[1] In the case of climatic shocks, community rates of exposure and several meteorological station rainfall variables are likely to be highly correlated with household exposure to climatic shocks, but not related to household food expenditures—except through their impact on exposure to climatic shock. Thus these variables are included as identifying variables in the household expenditure equation.

The ETE model is estimated by a two-step procedure. The first step is to predict household exposure to a shock, S_i^*, with a probit model. The latent variable, S_i^*, is then included in the household food expenditure equation. The parameters β and α are estimated by the ordinary least squares (OLS) method. The inverse Mills ratio is also included in the food expenditure equation to control for potential bias arising from correlation between error terms in the food expenditure equation and the treatment equation.[2]

Households are categorized as nonpoor, transient poor, or chronic poor based on their estimated food expenditures. To begin, household food expenditures are predicted from model results with the assumption that the household has not been exposed to any shock (S_i is set equal to 0). The chronic poor are then defined as households whose food expenditures fall below the national food poverty line in the absence of a shock based on this prediction. Alternatively, the transient poor are defined as households whose predicted food expenditures are above the chronic poverty line in the absence of a shock, but are expected to fall below the national food poverty line with exposure to a shock or shocks as outlined in the simulations discussed below.

Three simulations are employed to estimate the magnitude of the impact of shocks. The first approach is an ex post simulation that identifies transient households based on their reported exposure to shocks. Specifically, the shock indicator S_i is set equal to 1 for households that reported a shock in the last year. Household predicted food expenditures are, thus, adjusted by the shock's coefficient. Transient households are identified as those whose food expenditures fall below the poverty threshold after being adjusted by the impact of reported exposure.

The second simulation is an ex ante simulation that multiplies the estimated probability of exposure to a shock S_i^* by the shock's food expenditure equation coefficient to yield an estimate of the *expected* impact of the shock on the household's food expenditures in a given year. The transient poor are identified as those households whose food expenditures fall below the poverty line when adjusted for the expected impact of a shock in a given year.

A frequent method of selecting beneficiaries is geographic targeting. So a third simulation geographically targets households by selecting all households within districts that experienced a high, negative deviation from historical rainfall in the survey year. Geographic targeting results are then compared with transient poverty estimates from the ex ante simulation for droughts.

Model Specification and Data

Three climate-related shocks are modeled: droughts, floods and cyclones, and agricultural pests. For each shock model, a common set of variables is used in the food expenditure equation. Regional disparities in poverty levels are accounted for with binary indicators for household residence in the northern and central provinces and rural areas. Characteristics of the household head, the share of household members who are children and elderly, level of education of adult household members, employment sector of the head of household, percentage of adult members who are unemployed, agricultural assets of the household, and wealth quintile of the household are also included as variables in the expenditure equation.

For the treatment equation, climatic shocks are more likely to affect farm households than nonfarm households and indicators for rural households and nonagriculture-based households are included in all of the shock specifications. The household's use of irrigation and its cultivated land quintile within the sample distribution of cultivated land are included to control for household assets. As part of the model identification strategy, rates of community exposure to the shock are included in each of the shock equations but not the food expenditure equation. Each shock equation also includes rainfall variables. For droughts, the average daily rainfall and the percentage deviation from historic average weekly rainfall (during the regional rainy seasons) are used as exclusion restrictions. Low rainfall is assumed to affect exposure to a drought directly, but only to affect household food expenditures indirectly through its impact on drought.

In modeling exposure to flooding and cyclones, a variable for the number of weeks that received more than 25 millimeters of rain during the rainy and cyclone seasons is included as an exclusion restriction. This climatic variable accounts for short periods of time in the agricultural season when households are subject to exceptionally high rainfall. In modeling exposure to agricultural pests, both high and low amounts of rain can induce exposure. Thus the daily rainfall average and the deviation from the long-term mean during the rainy season are included as exclusion restrictions in the agricultural pest specification.

Description of Data

Household and community variables are constructed from Mozambique's 2008/09 *Inquérito Sobre Orçamento Familiar* (IOF) or Household Budget Survey. The IOF is a nationwide survey administered by Mozambique's National Institute of Statistics (NIS 2009). The sample size is rather large, with 10,832 households surveyed from 1,040 enumeration areas (EAs) in 144 districts in all 10 provinces as well as the capital city.

Food expenditures per person per day were calculated based on 2008/09 IOF survey data. In the model estimation, expenditures are expressed in logarithmic form. The national food poverty line was obtained by taking the national poverty line multiplied by the average food share (0.5851) to arrive at the national food poverty line (Mt 10.8).[3] Nonpoor households are defined as those with food expenditures above the national food poverty line.

The model only considers shocks that were reported to have occurred in the year before the interview. This has a significant implication for estimating the impact of shocks: as the number of months since exposure increases, households have more time to employ coping mechanisms and to smooth consumption, and the observed impact of the shock is likely to lessen. However, a year-long period is necessary because the percentage of households in the survey that report exposure to each of the three covariate shocks at a subyear period is very small.

Daily rainfall data were obtained from the National Aeronautical and Space Administration's Climatology Resource for Agroclimatology for the period January 1, 1997 to April 31, 2009 (NASA 2009). Point data were collected for 204 cells from 10.5°S to 26.5°S and 30.5°E to 41.5°E, where the point refers to the center of the cell (NASA 2009). The rainfall data were matched to the district point locations by interpolating the point rainfall data using the inverse distance-weighted (IDW) method in the ArcGIS Editor program.[4] Average daily rainfall, weekly rainfall (millimeters), and the percent deviation from the historical weekly average (millimeters) were computed for Mozambique's distinct regional rainy and cyclone seasons, with region-specific season durations identified through USAID's Famine and Early Warning Systems Network reports from September 2007 to June 2009 (USAID 2007, 2008, 2009a, 2009b).[5]

Community rates of exposure to shocks were used as identifying restrictions in the specifications for each covariate shock. The rate of community exposure was generated from reports of exposure to the shock in the past year by other households in the same EA, excluding the observed household *i*.

Results and Discussion

All of the climatic shocks considered have significant negative impacts on food. Coefficients and confidence intervals for key variables in the food expenditure equation are presented in figure 7.1.[6] Among the three shocks (treatments),

Figure 7.1 Key Coefficients and Confidence Intervals for the Food Expenditure Equation for Mozambique

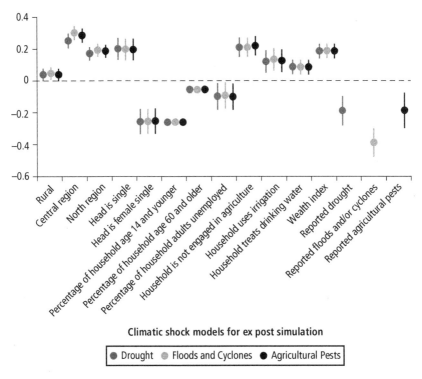

Climatic shock models for ex post simulation

● Drought ● Floods and Cyclones ● Agricultural Pests

Note: The two-step endogenous treatment effects model cannot be estimated using weights, and thus the results are unweighted. Coefficients for the share of the household 14 years of age and younger and 60 years of age and older have been rescaled to reflect a 25 percent increase.

floods and cyclones have the strongest impact on household food expenditures, reducing them 32.2 percent. Agricultural pests and drought reduce food expenditures approximately 17 percent. Droughts may have a lower impact than floods and cyclones due to the more gradual onset of the shock, leaving households with more time to develop coping mechanisms to deal with the effects. Similarly, farmers typically employ some form of pest control and adjust agricultural production as a means to prevent or offset losses due to agricultural pests.

The other variables specified in the food expenditure equations are common across shocks, and their parameter estimates are fairly consistent across the models. Food expenditures are estimated to be notably lower in households with single, female heads, in households with higher shares of children (14 years of age or younger), and in households with higher shares of elderly members (60 years and older).

Household demographics that have a significant, positive relationship with household food expenditures include regional indicators for the northern and southern provinces, residence in rural areas, employment of the household head outside of agriculture, and wealth quintile of the household. Physical assets also have a significant impact on household food expenditures. While few Mozambican households can afford irrigation, its use is associated with a 12.9 percent increase in food expenditures. An important indicator of investment in household health—treating drinking water—is associated with 9 percent higher expenditures.

Table 7.1 presents the parameter estimates for the treatment equations. Droughts are less likely to be reported among rural households than urban households. However, households not involved in agriculture have a significantly lower probability of reporting exposure to a drought. Thus agricultural households (which are more predominant in rural areas) are most susceptible to a drought. The probability of indicating exposure also decreases for households with more cultivated land, suggesting that households can diversify the risk of exposure with larger crop areas. Irrigation does not have a significant impact on the probability of reporting exposure in the drought model, but, as noted, irrigation is rather rare. Higher rates of community exposure to drought significantly increase the likelihood of an individual household in the community being exposed to a drought, highlighting the covariate nature of the shock. The probability of exposure to a drought increases with the district's average daily rainfall during the rainy season, but it is not influenced by the deviation from the historical average weekly rainfall during the rainy season prior to the shock. This result suggests that agricultural systems in areas with higher average rainfall are more dependent on rainfall and, thus, more susceptible to a drought.

A similar set of household control variables was employed in the treatment equations for floods and cyclones. The probability of indicating exposure to

Table 7.1 Treatment Equation Coefficients for Each Shock Model for Mozambique

Indicator	Droughts	Floods and cyclones	Agricultural pests
Household resides in a rural area	−0.114**	−0.059	−0.131**
	(0.050)	(0.086)	(0.057)
Household head is employed outside of agriculture	−0.746***	−0.226*	−1.280***
	(0.092)	(0.133)	(0.181)
Household's quintile of cultivated land	−0.035**	−0.064**	−0.048***
	(0.016)	(0.027)	(0.018)
Household uses irrigation	0.084	0.463***	0.140
	(0.095)	(0.131)	(0.112)
% of households in the same EA that responded yes to drought as a top three negative event in the last year	**3.636*****		
	(0.091)		
Average millimeters of rainfall for the region's rainy season	**0.045*****		
	(0.010)		
% deviation in millimeters of rainfall for the region's rainy season based on a historical average from 1997 to season before drought	**−0.002**		
	(0.002)		
% of households in the same EA that responded yes to flood as a top three negative event in the last year		**3.081*****	
		(0.217)	
% of households in the same EA that responded yes to cyclone as a top three negative event in the last year		**2.766*****	
		(0.163)	
Number of weeks when rainfall was over 25 millimeters during the region's rainy season		**0.116*****	
		(0.007)	
Number of weeks when rainfall was over 25 millimeters during the region's cyclone season		**0.103*****	
		(0.007)	
% of households in the same EA that responded yes to agricultural pests as a top three negative event in the last year			**3.489*****
			(0.111)
Average millimeters of rainfall for the region's rainy season			**0.078*****
			(0.010)
% deviation in rainfall (millimeters) for the region's rainy season based on a historical average from 1997 to season before shock			**−0.032*****
			(0.003)
Constant	−1.851***	−2.462***	−1.855***
	(0.059)	(0.093)	(0.069)

Note: Numbers in parentheses are standard deviations. Instrumental variables used in the treatment equations are in bold.
*** $p < .01$, ** $p < .05$, * $p < .1$

floods and cyclones is lower for households whose primary employment sector is not agriculture and for households in the higher quintiles of the distribution of cultivated land. The irrigation indicator is significant and increases the likelihood of reporting exposure, suggesting that irrigated fields are particularly susceptible to high-rainfall events. As expected, variables for community rates of exposure to floods and cyclones and the number of weeks with 25 millimeters or more of rain during the rainy and cyclone seasons are strong predictors of household-reported exposure to flooding and cyclones.

As in the drought model, households in rural areas are less likely to report exposure to agricultural pests. However, households engaged primarily in agricultural activities are significantly more likely to report exposure to pests. Households with more cultivated land are less likely to report exposure to pests, and larger landholders may have more resources to devote to pest management practices. Again, there is a significant positive relationship between the community rate of exposure to agricultural pests and household reported exposure. Higher average rainfall for the district increases the likelihood of reporting exposure, while deviations from last year's rainfall decrease the likelihood of reporting exposure to agricultural pests. Simulations were employed to understand the impacts that shocks have on chronic and transient poverty in Mozambique.

Chronic Poverty Simulation

Estimates of chronic poverty were developed by comparing predicted household food expenditures without exposure to any shock to the national food poverty line (S_i is set equal to 0).[7] While a common set of variables was used to estimate food expenditures for each shock, food expenditure parameter estimates vary slightly for different shocks, and there is a small variation in estimates of chronic poverty across models (figure 7.2). However, in every model chronic poverty is clearly the driving force in total poverty in Mozambique. The national chronic poverty rate is approximately 50 percent. Regional chronic poverty estimates are highest in the center of the country (57.1 percent).

Transient Poverty: Ex Post Simulation

Transient poor households are those whose estimated expenditures fall below the food poverty line when adjusted by the estimated impact of covariate shocks reported in the last year (S_i is set equal to the observed value). Estimates in the ex post simulation illuminate the impact that covariate shocks have on current poverty estimates, with their combined impact increasing the national poverty rate by 4.6 percentage points. Floods and cyclones were reported less frequently,

Figure 7.2 Reported Exposure to Climatic Shocks and Poverty Rates (Ex Post Simulation) in Mozambique

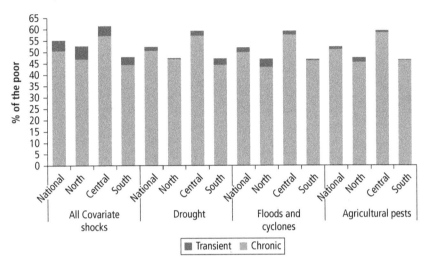

Note: Transient poverty is estimated with the ex post simulation, where household expenditures are adjusted by the estimated impact of shocks reported by the household. Chronic poverty is defined as households below the national food poverty line without exposure to a shock. Based on observed food expenditures, 45.2 percent of the households in the model fall below the national food poverty line. Data are weighted.

yet they have the largest individual contribution to national transient poverty rates, at 2.0 percentage points, due to the large estimated impact of the shock. Regionally, estimates of transient poverty follow expected patterns. Droughts generate transient poverty mostly in the south and central regions (2.1 and 2.7 percentage points, respectively). Floods and cyclones have a noticeably larger impact in the north (3.5 percentage points). Exposure to agricultural pests also generates the largest rates of transient poverty in the fertile, agriculture-dependent northern provinces, at 2.0 percentage points.

Transient Poverty: Ex Ante Simulation
The ex ante simulation predicts transient poverty arising from expected household exposure to climatic shocks, derived as the product of the household's probability of exposure to the shock and the estimated impact on expenditures of the shock obtained from the food expenditure equation (figure 7.3). Floods and cyclones, droughts, and agricultural pests increase the expected national poverty rate by 2.3, 2.0, and 1.2 percentage points, respectively. The estimated transient poverty rate when the three shocks are combined is 5.1 percent. Regionally, estimates of transient poverty follow expected patterns. Droughts affect transient poverty rates most notably in the southern and central regions

Figure 7.3 Estimated Exposure to Climatic Shocks and Transient Poverty Rates (Ex Ante Simulation) in Mozambique

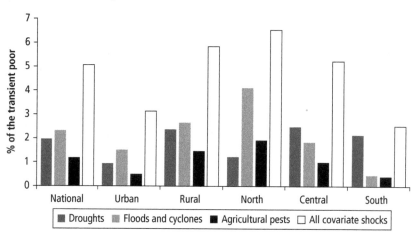

Note: Transiently poor households are households that are below the food poverty line when multiplying the probability of exposure by the coefficient for the shock. Data are weighted.

(2.1 and 2.7 percentage points, respectively). Floods and cyclones have a noticeably larger impact in the north (3.5 percentage points). Exposure to agricultural pests also has the largest estimated impact on transient poverty rates in the fertile, agriculture-dependent northern provinces, at 2.0 percentage points.

A final simulation evaluated targeting estimates for households eligible for social assistance benefits in response to a period of drought. Figure 7.4 compares the percentage of households identified using two targeting methods: a geographic targeting method identifying all households in areas with below-average rainfall and an ex ante targeting method for droughts, described in simulation 2 above. The geographic targeting simulation selects provinces that have districts in the bottom fifth percentile for deviation of annual rainfall from the historical mean (large negative deviation from the mean). All households in these districts are selected for social assistance benefits. The ex ante targeting method uses the drought model described above and identifies households vulnerable to transient poverty through household food expenditures adjusted for the expected impact of drought. With geographic targeting, 17.2 percent of households in Niassa, 2.9 percent of households in Zambezia, 13.1 percent of households in Tete, and 4.1 percent of households in Manica are identified for assistance. In comparison, 1.0 percent of households in Niassa, 2.4 percent of households in Zambezia, 0.5 percent of households in Tete, and 2.8 percent of households in Manica are identified as vulnerable

Figure 7.4 Geographic Targeting and Selection of Households Vulnerable to Transient Poverty in Mozambique

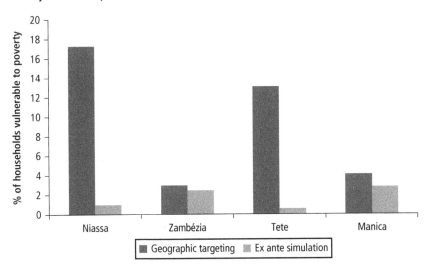

to transient poverty and thus in need of temporary social assistance, following drought in the ex ante simulation. We expect that programs targeting households vulnerable to transient poverty due to exposure to a drought would be operated in conjunction with existing programs targeting chronically poor households and that these program benefits probably would increase with exposure to a drought. The findings suggest that geographic targeting alone casts a broad net and does not offer a means to identify the unique group of households vulnerable to transient poverty when exposed to a shock.

Alternative Specifications

The food expenditure equation was also run as an OLS model to examine the robustness of the results to the exclusion restrictions in the shock models. Rainfall station variables replace the jointly estimated exposure to climatic shock indicators in the expenditure equation, and the food expenditure equation is estimated as:

$$C_i = X_i B + R_i \rho + u_i, \tag{7.3}$$

where R_i is the vector of rainfall station variables.

The parameter estimates obtained are similar to those obtained using the ETE model in figure 7.1. Thus we conclude that the impact of reported exposure to a shock strongly reflects variability in the exogenous difference in rainfall

Table 7.2 Transient Poverty Rates and Rainfall Fluctuations in Mozambique
% of households in transient poverty

Indicator	Droughts	Floods and cyclones	Agricultural pests
Transient poverty rates with observed rainfall data	3.21	2.31	3.2
Transient poverty rates with an increase in rainfall data by 1 standard deviation	8.18	10.22	11.2
Change in transient poverty rates	4.97	7.91	8.01

exposure. The result also suggests that social assistance programs can use regional rainfall data to predict household exposure to transient poverty.

The sensitivity of transient poverty estimates to changes in rainfall was then simulated by increasing rainfall variables by 1 standard deviation (table 7.2). When both observed average rainfall and deviation from the historical rainfall average increase by 1 standard deviation, transient poverty rates increase to 8.2 and 11.2 percent for droughts and agricultural pests, respectively. In the flood and cyclone model, the number of weeks with rainfall over 25 millimeters is increased by 1 standard deviation, increasing the transient poverty rate to 10.2 percent. The OLS simulations highlight the vulnerability of Mozambican households to changes in rainfall and the resulting increase in poverty rates.

Conclusions

Households that are poor today may not be the same households that are poor in the future, as households move in and out of poverty in response to shocks to their external environment. An analysis of the impact of common covariate shocks on household well-being has allowed us to distinguish between the two components of total poverty: chronic poverty and transient poverty. Poverty reduction programs that focus on social protection and target the chronically poor seek to improve their ability to obtain a basic level of well-being. Alternative, or concurrent, social assistance and insurance programs can be designed to provide safety nets to vulnerable households to prevent or shorten temporary lapses into poverty. Ex post simulations find that household well-being varies strongly with exposure to climatic shocks and that climatic shocks generate a national transient poverty rate of 4.6 percentage points. Ex ante simulations estimate a national transient poverty rate of 5.1 percentage points. A comparison of targeting methods in response to exposure to shock suggests that geographic targeting of areas strongly affected by lower than average rainfall alone selects a much higher percentage of households and does not uniquely select households vulnerable to transient poverty with exposure to climatic shocks. Further, rainfall is a strong predictor of exposure to covariate shocks and can be incorporated directly into social assistance targeting procedures to identify households that are vulnerable to transient poverty.

A long-term reduction in Mozambique's poverty rate requires a political commitment to programs that address the determinants of chronic poverty in addition to short-term initiatives that enable near-poor households to maintain adequate levels of well-being even when exposed to a climatic shock. Developing programs that offer temporary aid to households vulnerable to transient poverty may be politically more difficult to implement than programs targeting chronic poverty and providing sustained support, such as the PSA. This challenge highlights the importance of selecting transparent indicators and dedicating program resources to communicate the eligibility and enrollment process to potential beneficiaries. Additional research on household coping mechanisms employed in response to climatic shocks and on the impact of the coping mechanism on the severity and duration of reduced household consumption can offer guidance in selecting strong targeting indicators. Further, social assistance programs can use a combination of targeting mechanisms, such as demographic, geographic, and community indicators, to mitigate the negative impacts of covariate shocks on household well-being. However, political factors often influence the selection of targeting criterion, preventing the poorest and most vulnerable households from receiving aid. In the case of geographic targeting, climatic data may offer an objective criterion for identifying and selecting program districts and regions, but many nonvulnerable households will also be targeted. Rainfall index-based insurance programs offer a promising alternative mechanism for identifying household exposure to climatic risk in developing countries (Barnett, Barrett, and Skees 2008). However, such programs still have issues in terms of implementation, economic sustainability, accessibility, and use by poor and near-poor households. Thus social assistance programs offering timely disaster relief aid to near-poor households remain necessary to prevent short-term and long-term increases in poverty rates.

Notes

1. Formally, $\text{Cov}[S, Z] \neq 0$, $\text{Cov}[u, Z] = 0$, $\text{Cov}[u, X] = 0$, $\text{Cov}[v, Z] = 0$.
2. See Maddala (1983, 120–22) for a complete derivation of the two-step estimator.
3. Mozambique's currency is the meticais. A national food poverty lines was used for all households because reliable spatial and temporal price indexes were not available.
4. The IDW method estimates cell values by averaging the values of sample data points near the cell, giving closer points larger weights.
5. Region-specific seasons are available from the authors.

6. The coefficients for all binary variables are interpreted as a percentage shift in food expenditures, calculated by taking the exponent of the coefficient and subtracting 1.

7. All shock variables are set equal to 0 in this simulation.

References

Barnett, Barry J., Christopher B. Barrett, and Jerry R. Skees. 2008. "Poverty Traps and Index-Based Risk Transfer Products." *World Development* 36 (10): 1766–85.

Chaudhuri, Shubham, Jyotsna Jalan, and Asep Suryahadi. 2002. *Assessing Household Vulnerability to Poverty from Cross-sectional Data: A Methodology and Estimates from Indonesia*. Discussion Paper 0102-52. New York: Columbia University, Department of Economics, April.

Christiaensen, Luc, and Kalanidhi Subbarao. 2005. "Towards an Understanding of Vulnerability in Rural Kenya." *Journal of African Economies* 14 (4): 529–58.

Datt, Gaurav, and Hans Hoogeveen. 1999. "El Niño or El Peso? Crisis, Poverty, and Income Distribution in the Philippines." Policy Research Working Paper 2466, World Bank, Washington, DC, November.

del Ninno, Carlo, Paul A. Dorosh, Lisa C. Smith, Dilip K. Roy. 2001. "The 1998 Floods in Bangladesh: Disaster Impacts, Household Coping Strategies, and Response." Research Report 122, International Food Policy Research Institute, Washington, DC.

del Ninno, Carlo, and Alessandra Marini. 2005. "Households' Vulnerability to Shocks in Zambia." World Bank, Washington, DC, September.

Dercon, Stefan, and Pramila Krishnan. 2000. "Vulnerability, Seasonality, and Poverty in Ethiopia." *Journal of Development Studies* 36 (6): 25–53.

Devereux, Stephen. 2002. "The Malawi Famine of 2002." *IDS Bulletin* 33 (4): 70–78.

Devereux, Stephen, Bob Baulch, Ian Macauslan, Alexander Phiri, and Rachel Sabates-Wheeler. 2006. *Vulnerability and Social Protection in Malawi*. Discussion Paper 387. Institute of Development Studies at the University of Sussex Brighton, November.

Dorward, Andrew, and Jonathan Kydd. 2004. "The Malawi 2002 Food Crisis: The Rural Development Challenge." *Journal of Modern African Studies* 42 (3): 343–61.

FAO (Food and Agriculture Organization). 2007. *Promoting Integrated and Diversified Horticulture Production in Maputo Green Zones: Towards a Stable Food Security System*. Maputo, Mozambique, July.

GFDRR (Global Facility for Disaster Reduction and Recovery). 2012. "Mozambique: Disaster Risk Financing and Insurance Country Note." GFDRR, June. http://www.gfdrr.org/sites/gfdrr.org/files/DRFICountryNote_Mozambique_Jan072013_Final.pdf.

GRIP (Global Risk Identification Programme). 2010. "Disaster Risk Assessment in Mozambique: A Comprehensive Country Situation Analysis." GRIP, National Institute of Disaster Management, and United Nations Development Programme Mozambique. http://www.gripweb.org/gripweb/sites/default/files/disaster_risk_profiles/mozambique_CSA_black_0.pdf.

Günther, Isabel, and Kenneth Harttgen. 2009. "Estimating Households' Vulnerability to Idiosyncratic and Covariate Shocks: A Novel Method Applied in Madagascar." *World Development* 37 (7): 1222–34.

Handa, Sudhandshu, Carolyn Huang, Nicola Hypher, Clarissa Teixeira, Fabio V. Soares, and Benjamin Davis. 2012. "Targeting Effectiveness of Social Cash Transfer Programmes in Three African Countries." *Journal of Development Effectiveness* 4 (1): 78–108.

Hodges, Anthony, and Luca Pellerano. 2010. "Development of Social Protection: Strategic Review for UNICEF Mozambique." Unpublished, Oxford Policy Management.

Jalan, Jyotsna, and Martin Ravallion. 2000. "Is Transient Poverty Different? Evidence for Rural China." *Journal of Development Studies* 36 (6): 82–99.

Maddala, G. S. 1983. *Limited-Dependent and Qualitative Variables in Econometrics.* Cambridge, U.K.: Cambridge University Press.

MPD (Ministry of Planning and Development). 2010. *Poverty and Well-Being in Mozambique: The Third National Assessment.* Maputo: MPD.

NASA (National Aeronautics and Space Administration). 2009. "NASA Climatology Resource of Agroclimatology, Daily Average Data." NASA, Washington, DC. http://earth-www.larc.nasa.gov/cgi-bin/cgiwrap/solar/agro.cgi?email=agroclim@larc.nasa.gov.

NIS (National Institute of Statistics). 2009. *Household Budget Survey, 2008/09.* Maputo: NIS.

Shendy, Riham, Antonio Nucifora, and C. J. Thomas. 2009. "A Brief Note on the State of Social Protection in Mozambique." World Bank, Social Protection Unit, Human Development Network, Africa Region, Washington, DC.

USAID (U.S. Agency for International Development). 2007. "Mozambique Food Security Update: September 2007." Famine and Early Warning Systems Network, Washington, DC.

———. 2008. "Mozambique Food Security Update May 2008." Famine and Early Warning Systems Network, Washington, DC.

———. 2009a. "Mozambique Food Security Update March 2009." Famine and Early Warning Systems Network, Washington, DC.

———. 2009b. "Mozambique Food Security Update June 2009." Famine and Early Warning Systems Network, Washington, DC.

Chapter 8

Evaluation of Targeting Methods and Impact of the Cash Transfer Pilot in Niger

Linden McBride

Since achieving independence from France in 1960, the landlocked West African country of Niger has endured four droughts, four coups d'état, two armed conflicts, and several food crises ranging from localized incidences of severe acute malnutrition to widespread famine. According to available data, Niger has realized a significant reduction in poverty rates since the 1990s: poverty fell 40 percent between 1992 and 2008 based on the US$1.25 poverty line and 17.4 percent based on the US$2 poverty line. However, the prevalence of the effects of chronic hunger rose over a similar time period. Among children, chronic malnutrition, or stunting, rose 13.5 percent between 1992 and 2006. Meanwhile, acute malnutrition, or wasting, decreased only 2.7 percent (figure 8.1). More recent analyses find that more than 50 percent of the Nigerien population suffer from some form of food insecurity, whether transitory or seasonal, and that at least 20 percent of the population are severely, chronically food insecure each year (World Bank 2009). Following the food crises in 2005 and 2010, hunger hit the region again in 2012.

Such growing and persistent malnutrition both exacerbates and is exacerbated by the effects of climate and economic shocks. The structural nature of this problem as well as the overall vulnerability of the population to food insecurity are well established.[1]

A 2009 World Bank report identifies safety net strengthening as one of the key policy recommendations for alleviating both chronic and seasonal food insecurity in Niger. According to the report, despite the fact that at least 20 percent of the population are severely, chronically food insecure even in years without negative shocks, most safety net programs are deployed only in times of crisis (World Bank 2009). Consequently, Niger lacks a sustainable safety net system.

Figure 8.1 Poverty Rates and Prevalence of Malnutrition in Niger, 1992–2008

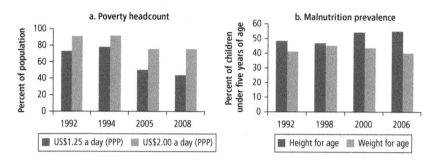

Source: World Bank 2012.
Note: PPP = purchasing power parity.

In response to these concerns, the government of Niger and the World Bank have developed a safety net cash transfer program, *Filets Sociaux par le Cash Transfert* (FS-CT), to address the country's chronic and transitory poverty and food insecurity. Two critical questions are whether the targeting mechanism employed to identify project beneficiaries has successfully identified food-insecure households and whether project assistance has had an impact on the welfare and food security of those households. This case study answers these questions in the context of the FS-CT Pilot Project (PPFS-CT).

The targeting mechanism employed in the PPFS-CT—geographic targeting combined with proxy means tests (PMTs)—selected beneficiaries in two food-insecure regions of the country based on a weighted index of household characteristics that are highly correlated with household expenditures collected in a nationally representative survey in 2007. However, it is unknown whether this mechanism, commonly used to target the chronic poor, has succeeded in identifying the most food-insecure households. Targeting of program beneficiaries and evaluation of the success of the program are complicated by the fact that, while household income and expenditure aggregates (that is, means tests) and proxy means tests are established methodologies for estimating household welfare, methodologies for measuring food security are still being developed, tested, and debated. This case study constructs household-level food security indicators in an attempt to provide a robust picture of the food security status of beneficiary and nonbeneficiary households, while also assessing the performance of such indicators vis-à-vis available household-level, expenditure-based indicators of welfare. Correlations between the PMT score and a basket of food security indicators are examined to evaluate the targeting of the pilot project. In addition, the impact of the pilot project—using both welfare and food security indicators—is assessed.

PPFS-CT Targeting Methods

The FS-CT has as its global objective to improve the quality of life of chronically poor households in Niger. To pilot the safety net, the PPFS-CT selected 2,500 households in two regions[2] of Niger—Tillabéri and Tahoua—to receive unconditional monthly cash transfers of CFAF 10,000[3] for a period of 18 months (Comité de PPFS-CT 2010).

Following the selection of target villages via geographic targeting,[4] the PPFS-CT team used data collected from the nationally representative 2007 household expenditure survey, the *Enquête Nationale sur le Budget et la Consommation des Ménages Niger* (ENBC) for 2007, to identify observable household characteristics highly correlated with per capita expenditure. Such household characteristics include location, household size, gender of the head of household, household construction materials, fuel source, water source, and household possessions, including furniture, electronics, and livestock. The correlation between per capita household expenditure and these household characteristics was estimated through ordinary least squares (OLS) regression of logged per capita household expenditure on variables for each of the household characteristics.[5] Through this process, the PPFS-CT team identified a set of variables that explained a significant portion of the variation in household per capita expenditures ($R^2 = 0.48$) with inclusion and exclusion errors of 12.4 and 13.6 percent, respectively (Katayama 2010). The coefficients from this regression were then applied as weights to each of these same variables in the pilot study data, and a PMT score was generated for each household, allowing the PPFS-CT team to rank households based on the PMT score.

The PPFS-CT team selected the lowest 30 percent of PMT scorers within each village as beneficiaries; village authorities validated this selection. Due to cross-village variation in average welfare as proxied by the PMT score, beneficiary status within the project greatly depended on the relative deprivation of a household within its village. That is, households with relatively low PMT scores in villages with overall high mean PMT scores were selected as beneficiaries despite being better off than nonbeneficiary households in villages with overall low mean PMT scores.

Methods and Analysis

This evaluation assesses the extent to which food-insecure households in the region have been targeted and the effect that the PPFS-CT transfer may have had on household-level welfare in terms of expenditure-based measures and food security indicators. The data, methods, and analysis are described below.

Data

Two data sets were used for this analysis. The first, referred to here as the 2010 data set, was collected in September 2010 in 51 rural villages of the Tahoua and Tillabéri regions of Niger. The main module includes PMT data for 7,315 households, of which 2,223, or 30 percent, were selected as beneficiaries of the pilot study. An additional food security module was administered to households in the Tahoua region; this module includes food security data on 3,948 households, of which 1,195, or 34.2 percent of the total, were selected as beneficiaries for the pilot study.

The second data set, referred to here as the 2011 data set, was collected in October 2011 in 31 villages in the Tahoua and Tillabéri regions of Niger. These data are a representative random selection of the households surveyed in the 2010 data and include 1,395 households, of which 30 percent were beneficiaries of the pilot study. At the time of the 2011 survey, beneficiary households had been receiving monthly cash transfers of CFAF 10,000 for 12 months. The 2011 data include food security modules identical to those in the 2010 data; in addition, the 2011 data include a household expenditure module. A complete PMT module was not administered in the 2011 survey.

Food Security Indicators

Food security is an elusive, multifaceted, and ultimately unobservable concept (Barrett 2002, 2010). Despite these challenges, various proxies for measuring food security have proliferated over the past decade; however, there is still no consensus in the literature about how best to implement or interpret them. Given the difficulty of measurement and interpretation, this evaluation takes as broad an approach as possible to proxy food security. A basket of the four most commonly used food security indicators, plus several adaptations or variations of the standard indicators, is applied to the available data. These indicators are intended to capture food security by measuring the households' ability to access food, meaning that they do not account for food availability or use, nor do they measure nutritional outcomes or account for the intrahousehold allocation of food. Combinations or "suites of indicators" are commonly used for geographic targeting and have been validated in the literature as sound proxies for household-level food security for the purpose of evaluating and assessing the impact of food security interventions (Maxwell and Caldwell 2008; Hoddinott and Yohannes 2002).

The basket of food security indicators considered here contains the following: the food consumption score (FCS) as well as a nontruncated adaptation of the food consumption score (FCSnt); the household dietary diversity score (HDDS); the food consumption and dietary diversity score (FCDD), which is an adaptation of the FCS and HDDS combined; the household hunger scale (HHS); and several versions of the coping strategies index (CSI).

These indicators can be split into two groups: (a) the FCS, HDDS, and FCDD indicators, which measure the frequency, quality, and diversity of food consumption, and (b) the HHS and CSI indicators, which record the frequency and severity of households' behavioral responses to food insecurity. Table 8.1 highlights the data set–specific construction of each indicator; an extensive

Table 8.1 Construction and Validation of the Food Security Indicators for Niger

Indicator and acronym	Construction	Validation
Frequency or diversity indicator		
Food consumption score (FCS) and food consumption score, nontruncated (FCSnt)	Consumed food items were regrouped into 9 categories, the consumption frequencies were summed, and, in the case of the FCS, any value above 7 was recoded as 7. For the FCSnt, the frequencies were not altered. The resulting food group consumption frequencies were multiplied by their respective weights (see WFP 2008 for the standard weighting scheme) and summed.	Wiesmann et al. (2009)
Household dietary diversity score (HDDS)	Consumed foods were regrouped into 12 categories, the consumption frequencies were truncated at 1, and the values were summed to construct the composite HDDS score.	Hoddinott and Yohannes (2002)
Food consumption and dietary diversity score (FCDD)	The FCDD was calculated from the same module as the FCS and HDDS by placing 7-day recall data into the 12 HDDS food group categories, as above, and then truncating at 7. The consumption frequencies for each group were summed for the composite FCDD score. No weights were applied.	This indicator has not undergone validation testing; support is drawn from Wiesmann et al. (2009), where an unweighted food frequency indicator aggregated from the 12 HDDS food groups is shown to "perform slightly better than the FCS" in terms of correlation with the benchmark calorie consumption per capita.
Household hunger scale (HHS)	HHS modules were not included in the available surveys; three questions from the CSI module were close enough (see table 8A.1) to the standard HHS to accommodate the calculation of an indicator similar to the HHS with the available data. The calculation involved summing the responses to the three questions.	Deitchler et al. (2010)
Coping strategies index, including reduced (redCSI), full (full CSI), and weighted (weiCSI) indexes	The full CSI is the sum of all 16 CSI frequency responses available in the data. The reduced CSI includes only the 5 standard reduced CSI questions with the appropriate weights (see Maxwell and Caldwell 2008 for details). The weighted CSI is the full CSI module weighted by the average of the weights in Maxwell, Caldwell, and Langworthy (2008).	Maxwell (1995, 1999); Maxwell, Caldwell, and Langworthy (2008)

discussion of the features of each indicator as well as their distribution in the 2010 and 2011 data sets is available in the annex to this chapter.

As FCS, HDDS, and FCDD (measures of food *security*) rise, HHS and CSI (measures of food *insecurity*) fall, and vice versa. Sample means from both the 2010 and 2011 data follow this pattern. Whereas the mean HDDS and FCS indicators are higher in October 2011 than in September 2010, indicating greater quantity, quality, and diversity of food consumption in 2011, the mean HHS and CSI indicators are higher in September 2010 than in October 2011, indicating greater behavioral response to food insecurity and deprivation in 2010. These data are for the Tahoua region only, as food security data were not collected in Tillabéri in the 2010 survey (table 8.2).

The substantial differences in the food security indicators between the two samples are likely due to the year and season during which each sample was collected. The 2010 data were collected in September during a year of food crisis, while the 2011 data were collected in October during a year of no crisis (and following 12 months of cash transfer to 30 percent of the sample). According to FEWSNET, the difference between the months of September and October in Niger is the difference between the hunger season and the

Table 8.2 Food Security Indicator Means for the Tahoua Region, Niger, 2010 and 2011

Variable, month, and year	Number of observations	Mean[a]	Standard deviation or standard error[b]	Minimum	Maximum
FCS					
September 2010	3,944	21.98	13.13	0	100.5
October 2011	717	38.56	1.27	9	97.5
FCSnt					
September 2010	3,944	25.10	15.88	0	138.5
October 2011	717	43.69	1.37	9	123
HDDS					
September 2010	3,944	3.54	1.70	1	12
October 2011	717	4.50	0.09	1	11
FCDD					
September 2010	3,944	16.32	7.76	1	57
October 2011	717	21.20	0.58	5	56
HHS					
September 2010	3,944	4.18	3.28	0	21
October 2011	717	1.50	0.12	0	14

(continued next page)

Table 8.2 (continued)

Variable, month, and year	Number of observations	Mean[a]	Standard deviation or standard error[b]	Minimum	Maximum
redCSI					
September 2010	3,944	15.86	14.44	0	56
October 2011	717	6.53	0.49	0	45
fullCSI					
September 2010	3,944	20.50	14.80	0	73
October 2011	717	7.84	0.52	0	51
weiCSI					
September 2010	3,944	37.31	28.87	0	165.7
October 2011	717	15.29	1.14	0	109.5

a. The October 2011 observation means are weighted to be representative of the September 2010 survey population.
b. Standard deviation is reported for the 2010 data, while the standard linearized error is reported for the weighted 2011 data.

main harvest season. In this respect, the increase (decrease) in the average food security (insecurity) indicator values from the 2010 to the 2011 data is expected.

Expenditure-Based Welfare Indicators

Following Deaton and Zaidi (2002) and available information from the Niger National Institute of Statistics (NIS; personal correspondence), total household expenditures for the 2011 data were estimated via aggregation of food and non-food consumption, the flow of services from consumer durables, and the estimated value of housing consumption.

Because the NIS uses per capita as opposed to per adult-equivalence scales to estimate household welfare and poverty lines, per capita values were also used to calculate household food and total expenditure variables. The resulting mean total expenditures are shown in table 8.3. These values are substantially lower than those estimated in the last national expenditure survey, the ENBC 2007; in the case of Tahoua, 2011 expenditures are less than half the value of those in 2007.

From food and total household expenditures, a variable for the share of food expenditures in total expenditures, *foodsh*, was also generated. Both the mean and median shares of food in total expenditures for the 2011 data are greater than 80 percent. The 2010 PMT indicator was calculated by the PPFS-CT team, as indicated above. It was not possible to generate a comparable 2011 PMT due to data limitations.

Table 8.3 Mean Household per Capita Expenditures in
Niger, by Region, 2007 and 2011
CFAF, constant 2011

Region	2011 data	2007 NIS data
Tahoua	89,454	192,072
Tillabéri	101,267	156,589

The PPFS-CT cash transfer, CFAF 10,000 per month, represents approximately 18.3 (23.7) percent of the average (median) household total expenditure, 23.5 percent of the average household total expenditure in Tahoua, and 14.3 percent of the average household total expenditure in Tillabéri in the 2011 data. Shares are higher for beneficiary households that lie on the poorer end of the distribution. Consistent with the calculated values for food share, PPFS-CT beneficiary households report spending most of the monthly cash transfer on food (table 8A.2).

Relationship between Food Security Indicators and Welfare Indicators

Correlation coefficients for each of the food security indicators and PMT welfare indicators for the Tahoua region in 2010 are shown in table 8.4. Significant and moderate correlations are observed between the PMT and the behavioral measures of food insecurity—the CSI and the HHS indicators. The weighted CSI, which estimates the frequency and severity of household coping strategies, shows the greatest numerical correlation with the PMT, with a value of −0.1597. No significant correlations are observed between the PMT and the frequency and diversity measures—the FCS, HDDS, and FCDD.

Notably, however, correlations are observed between the different types of food security indicators.[6] Specifically, the HHS is weakly correlated with the FCS, FCDD, and HDDS indicators. While there are no significant relationships between the FCS and CSI indicators, significant and moderate correlations are seen between the indicators that account for dietary diversity—the HDDS and the FCDD—and the CSI indicators. The magnitude of correlation is generally stronger between the FCDD and the CSIs than between the HDDS and the CSIs, with the slight exception of the reduced CSI.

Behavioral food security indicators—CSI and HHS—are correlated most strongly with the PMT in the 2010 data. However, in the 2011 data the frequency-diversity food security indicators—FCSnt, HDDS, and FCDD— show a higher correlation with expenditure-based welfare indicators (table 8.5).

Correlations between the different types of food security indicators in the 2011 data follow a pattern similar to that seen in the 2010 data, with the FCDD

Table 8.4 Pearson's *r* Correlation Coefficient Matrix for the Tahoua Region in Niger, 2010

	HHS	redCSI	fullCSI	weiCSI	FCSnt	FCS	HDDS	FCDD	PMT
HHS	1.00								
redCSI	0.4489*	1.00							
fullCSI	0.7041*	0.8386*	1.00						
weiCSI	0.6289*	0.8710*	0.9676*	1.00					
FCSnt	−0.0954*	−0.0365	−0.0253	0.0068	1.00				
FCS	−0.0873*	−0.0418	−0.0235	0.0079	0.9437*	1.00			
HDDS	−0.0881*	−0.1242*	−0.0799*	−0.0684*	0.6346*	0.6209*	1.00		
FCDD	−0.1392*	−0.1144*	−0.1405*	−0.1142*	0.8088*	0.8016*	0.7767*	1.00	
PMT	−0.1230*	−0.0910*	−0.1545*	−0.1597*	0.0067	0.0021	−0.0364	0.0413	1.00

Note: N = 3,948 households. HHS is a subset of the CSI values, HDDS is a reaggregation of the FCS values, and FCDD is a composite of the HDDS and FCS values; therefore, correlations between these values are by design and should not be considered in this evaluation (and are therefore not presented in bold on the table).
* $p < .01$ after Bonferonni correction for multiple comparisons.

showing higher correlation with the HHS and with each of the CSIs (with the exception again of the reduced CSI) than either the FCS indicators or the HDDS indicator.

Keeping in mind the general lack of consensus regarding food security indicators and what they measure, one might cautiously tease out some conclusions about the observed patterns among the various indicators. The various correlations between the two types of food security indicators—behavioral and frequency or diversity—and the welfare proxies in 2010 and 2011 data may indicate that they are measuring different components of food security and perform better or worse as indicators at different levels and durations of household deprivation. Indicators such as food consumption scores and dietary diversity scores do not reflect the full extent of household food insecurity because they do not capture portions, intrahousehold allocation, or frequency of daily consumption and they do not reveal whether a household has had to make other adaptations so as to continue to eat at a given frequency and diversity. For example, if a household resorts to the coping strategies included in, for instance, the reduced CSI—consuming less preferred foods, borrowing foods, limiting portion size, restricting adult portions in favor of children's diets, and reducing the number of meals eaten in a day—none of these changes would *necessarily* register in an FCS or HDDS so long as the number of food groups from which the household eats and the number of times those food groups are consumed by at least one member of the household remain the same. It is possible that changes in frequency and diversity will only take place, and therefore register on a frequency or diversity indicator, after many other coping strategies have been exhausted.

Table 8.5 Pearson's *r* Correlation Coefficient Matrix for the Tahoua and Tillabéri Regions, Malawi, 2011

	HHS	redCSI	fullCSI	weiCSI	FCSnt	FCS	HDDS	FCDD	lnPCexp	lnPCFexp	foodsh
HHS	1										
redCSI	0.3837*	1									
fullCSI	0.6319*	0.8849*	1								
weiCSI	0.4741*	0.9184*	0.9682*	1							
FCSnt	**-0.2006***	**-0.1666***	**-0.1909***	**-0.1504***	1						
FCS	**-0.1884***	**-0.1847***	**-0.1946***	**-0.1558***	0.9145*	1					
HDDS	**-0.1791***	**-0.2033***	**-0.2092***	**-0.1903***	0.6837*	0.6587*	1				
FCDD	**-0.2367***	**-0.1941***	**-0.2337***	**-0.1932***	0.7956*	0.7561*	0.8103*	1			
lnPCexp	-0.0889	0.0247	-0.0339	-0.003	**0.1653***	0.0392	**0.1734***	**0.1876***	1		
lnPCFexp	-0.0696	0.0407	-0.001	0.022	**0.1678***	0.0297	**0.1412***	**0.1586***	0.9309*	1	
foodsh	0.0532	-0.0219	-0.0134	-0.0207	-0.0321	-0.098	-0.0663	-0.0669	0.2918*	0.4791*	1

Note: N = 1,375 households. HHS is a subset of the CSI values. HDDS is a reaggregation of the FCS values, and FCDD is a composite of the HDDS and FCS values; therefore, correlations between these values are by design and should not be considered in this evaluation (and are therefore not presented in bold on the table).
* p < .01 after Bonferroni correction for multiple comparisons.

It is likewise plausible that adjustments in household dietary diversity and frequency (for example, dropping meat and fish from the diet) are some of the first coping strategies used by a household in time of food insecurity or a shock and that the more severe coping strategies come later, in which case the adaptations would register first on the frequency-diversity indicators and then on the behavioral indicators. This appears to be the case in the 2010 data. At the time of data collection (in the height of the lean season during a period of regional food crisis), food frequency and diversity had already been significantly reduced: more than 80 percent of the sample were consuming at an FCS considered either poor or borderline and more than 70 percent of the sample were consuming from four or fewer unique food groups a day (see the annex to this chapter for graphs and details). Overall, there was relatively little variation in diet and consumption frequency across the sample. Therefore, the variable that best correlated with household welfare in the 2010 data set was the extent to which the household was making other sacrifices to consume at the level indicated in the FCS and HDDS. The reverse was the case in the 2011 data: at the time of data collection (the first month following the harvest, when food was plentiful), household welfare was best correlated with the frequency or diversity of consumption and not with behavioral responses to food insecurity. Thus correlations between different food security measures and between food security measures and other welfare measures appear to be relatively context specific.

Impact Evaluation

Comparison of means across beneficiary and nonbeneficiary households in Tahoua 2010 (see table 8A.3 for details) suggests that the PMT generally targeted households that have higher average food insecurity according to behavioral indicators such as the HHS and each of the CSI indicators. However, there is little to no statistical difference in the means of beneficiary and nonbeneficiary households in the frequency or diversity indicators such as the FCS and FCDD.[7] In the 2011 data set, the beneficiary household means show either greater dietary diversity (HDDS, FCDD) or lower food insecurity (HHS), or they are statistically indistinguishable from the means of the nonbeneficiaries (FCS, FCSnt, fullCSI, redCSI, weiCSI).

Options for evaluating the causal impact of the cash transfer project on household welfare are limited by the data. Because of the nature of beneficiary targeting (the households selected for the cash transfer are observably different from those who did not receive the transfer; for instance, they are poorer according to their household assets and characteristics), there was not enough common support between treated and untreated groups along the PMT variables—the observables on which selection was made—to justify the use of propensity score matching and reweighting methods. Another familiar estimation technique for impact evaluation—difference in differences estimation—has limited applicability here. Food security indicators in the 2010 data set are available for households only in the Tahoua region (about half the original sample), and other outcome variables such as total and food expenditures are available in the 2011 data set only.

Due to these data limitations, the most appropriate method of impact evaluation that might be applied is regression discontinuity, a method that estimates the local average treatment effect of the treatment on the treated. Evaluating impact using regression discontinuity requires using the 2011 cross-section only, meaning that food security and expenditure-based welfare indicators for both the Tahoua and Tillabéri regions can be used in the analysis; this is an advantage, given the limitations of the 2010 data.

Regression discontinuity methods exploit a discontinuity in treatment as a function of a continuous assignment variable. The crucial assumption is the interchangeability of households at the treatment cutoff point, meaning that households with a few CFAF more are assumed to be effectively the same as households with a few CFAF less, on average. This may not be true where a treatment cutoff is known to respondents, because respondents can manipulate the survey response in order to receive treatment; however, in this setting potential beneficiaries did not know the cutoff for treatment. Because the arbitrary cutoff of the 30 percent lowest PMT scores per village was used, households clustered around the cutoff should be nearly identical with the exception of their selection for treatment. In this respect, they serve as randomly assigned treatment and control groups around the cutoff, and any discontinuity in the outcome variables can be ascribed to the treatment effect (Imbens and Lemieux 2007).

Sharp regression discontinuity estimates of the form

$$y_i = \alpha + \beta B_i + \delta(PMT_i) + \varepsilon_i \qquad (8.1)$$

are estimated in the 2011 data using the Stata rd 2.0 program developed by Nichols (2011); y_i are the food security and expenditure outcomes (each estimated in separate regressions) for household i, B_i is a binary indicating the household's beneficiary status, and PMT_i is the forcing variable, the PMT score of household i in 2010. The coefficient β captures the effect of treatment on the outcome variable, estimated at various bandwidths close to the treatment cutoff point. The rd 2.0 program selects a default bandwidth that prioritizes minimizing the mean squared error following Imbens and Kalyanaraman (2009) and then estimates two additional bandwidths—one that is half the size of the default and one that is twice the size of the default. All three bandwidths are reported in table 8.6 with results of the regression discontinuity model.

To maintain an acceptable error rate in a multiple regression framework, we have to adjust the p-values at which we reject the null hypothesis that the resulting

Table 8.6 Regression Discontinuity Wald Estimates in the Tahoua and Tillabéri Regions of Niger, 2011

Bandwidth	HHS (1)	redCSI (2)	fullCSI (3)	weiCSI (4)	FCSnt (5)	FCS (6)	HDDS (7)	FCDD (8)	Intot_pc (9)	lnfood_pc (10)	foodsh (11)
Default	-0.317	-5.788	-4.105	-6.379	-7.331	-3.760	0.462	3.923	0.145	-0.0930	-0.180
	(0.736)	(0.078)	(0.262)	(0.342)	(0.487)	(0.686)	(0.658)	(0.208)	(0.736)	(0.840)	(0.016)
	[10.89]	[15.46]	[14.96]	[20.10]	[19.49]	[18.75]	[10.20]	[13.54]	[7.61]	[8.77]	[5.15]
Half default	0.0380	-2.566	-1.903	-5.706	-7.853	-6.087	3.384***	9.389	0.691	0.326	-0.292*
	(0.979)	(0.558)	(0.697)	(0.480)	(0.507)	(0.540)	(0.000052)	(0.006)	(0.147)	(0.495)	(0.001)
	[5.45]	[7.73]	[7.48]	[10.05]	[9.75]	[9.37]	[5.10]	[6.77]	[3.80]	[4.38]	[2.58]
Twice default	0.485	-2.015	0.0344	1.671	-2.796	-0.751	-0.0332	1.810	0.0367	-0.140	-0.128
	(0.593)	(0.505)	(0.992)	(0.819)	(0.729)	(0.916)	(0.967)	(0.524)	(0.923)	(0.726)	(0.038)
	[21.78]	[30.91]	[29.92]	[40.20]	[38.98]	[37.50]	[20.41]	[27.08]	[15.21]	[17.54]	[10.30]

Note: N = 1,289. Numbers in parentheses are p-values; numbers in brackets are bandwidths.
*** p < .000091, ** p < .00091, * p < .0045

191

coefficient is statistically equivalent to 0 with confidence. For a confidence level of 5 percent ($\alpha = .05$), the p-value below which we reject the null now becomes $p < 0.05/11 = 0.0045$. For a confidence level of 1 percent ($\alpha = .01$), the p-value below which we reject the null now becomes $p < 0.01/11 = 0.00091$. Finally, for a confidence level of .1 percent ($\alpha = .001$), the p-value below which we reject the null now becomes $p < 0.001/11 = 0.000091$.

Under these conditions, the estimates show a statistically significant and positive outcome for the HDDS indicator at the smallest estimated bandwidth and a statistically significant and negative outcome for the *foodsh* indicator at the smallest estimated bandwidth, where the statistical significance of these coefficients disappears at larger bandwidths. The direction and magnitude of the significant Wald estimates are consistent with an increase in food security and welfare among PPFS-CT beneficiaries. However, the nine other indicators do not show significant differences for PPFS-CT beneficiaries. Further, the results of a series of assumption and sensitivity tests weaken the findings for the two significant indicators.

Drawing causal inference from regression discontinuity design relies on the following assumptions (Nichols 2007): (a) the treatment exhibits a discontinuity at the assignment cutoff point; (b) the outcome and treatment variables are continuous in the assignment variable conditional on assignment status, which is tested by examining these variables for discontinuities away from the cutoff point; (c) observations are exchangeable at the cutoff in terms of potential confounders, tested by examining whether control variables show a discontinuity at the cutoff point; and (d) there is no manipulation of assignment, tested by confirming that the density of the forcing variable is continuous at the cutoff point. Testing each of these four assumptions for the outcome variables HDDS and *foodsh* yields the following:

- The data show a discontinuity in treatment at the smallest bandwidths for the HDDS and *foodsh* outcomes. For the HDDS outcome, assignment to treatment jumps at the treatment cutoff point only at a bandwidth of 5.1 (figure 8.2, panel a); however, assignment to treatment does not jump at larger bandwidths. For the *foodsh* outcome, assignment to treatment jumps at the treatment cutoff point only at a bandwidth of 2.6 (figure 8.2, panel b). See figures 8A.4 and 8A.5 for the complete set of discontinuity results.

- The data do not meet the assumption that the outcome and treatment variables are continuous in the assignment variable conditional on assignment status, as evidenced by apparent discontinuities away from the cutoff point. Following Imbens and Lemieux (2007), the test of this assumption was performed by looking for outcome discontinuities at the median of the forcing variable to the left and right of the cutoff and then repeating the process with the submedians. This process yielded statistically significant

Figure 8.2 Treatment Discontinuities Found in Niger for PMT Cutoffs at Low Bandwidths

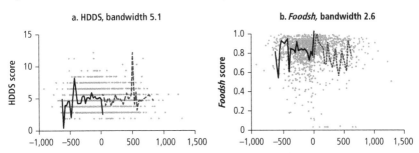

discontinuities in the outcome variables, HDDS and *foodsh*, at points other than the PMT cutoff. Of the 10 median points estimated, four statistically significant jumps in the outcome variables were observed both above and below the cutoff point (that is, in both beneficiary and nonbeneficiary groups). Failure to pass this test means the significance of the HDDS and *foodsh* outcomes at the PMT cutoff point may not be attributable to beneficiary status.

- Testing for the exchangeability of households at the cutoff in terms of potential confounders by examining whether control variables show a discontinuity reveals that households are generally statistically identical, with three significant exceptions. For the bandwidths at which significant jumps in the outcome variables, HDDS and *foodsh*, were estimated, three PMT variables also show significant discontinuities (table 8A.4): *eau_puitouvert* (water accessed from open well), *eau_surface* (water accessed from surface water), and *nchaise* (number of chairs owned). Therefore, the assumption of the random assignment of households to treatment at the PMT cutoff is only weakly supported, as there is a consistent difference in household characteristics in terms of access to water and number of chairs owned between the beneficiary and nonbeneficiary groups.

- The data do not exhibit evidence of manipulation in the distribution of the assignment variable around the cutoff. At the bandwidths for which significant discontinuities in outcome were estimated, the density of the forcing variable, PMT score, is continuous (figure 8A.6).

Finally, figures 8A.4, panel d, and 8A.5, panel d, show the dependence of the estimated effects on bandwidth size. In the case of the HDDS outcome, the significant results are very sensitive to the bandwidth 5.1; small bandwidths show positive and significant impacts, and large bandwidths show negligible and insignificant impacts (figure 8A.4, panel d). In the case of the *foodsh* outcome, the significant results are less sensitive to bandwidth size, as estimated effects change relatively little in magnitude or significance as the bandwidths grow larger (figure 8A.5, panel d). Smaller bandwidths typically have lower bias, since observations closer to the cutoff are more alike; however, they also have lower efficiency, as more of the data are discarded. These results are not driven by a lack of data at the cutoff point (see figures 8A.4, panels a–c, and 8A.5, panels a–c, for the estimates at each bandwidth overlaying a scatterplot of the data, which are well distributed).

The robustness checks for the HDDS outcome are consistent with small positive effects that disappear as the bandwidth is enlarged to include more disparate cases; however, the violations of the required assumptions discussed above cast doubt on the identifying assumptions at smaller bandwidths. The findings in the *foodsh* outcome are more robust to bandwidth size, but the data still violate the assumptions of continuity away from the cutoff point as well as the exchangeability of households at the cutoff. Therefore, the statistically significant results of each of these indicators should be viewed with caution. It is not clear that these outcomes are attributable to the cash transfer program. However, failure to demonstrate causality should not be interpreted as evidence that there was no program impact.

Conclusion

While it is not clear that the improved food security outcomes seen in 2011 are due to the PPFS-CT, it is clear that the program successfully targeted households exhibiting greater food insecurity in terms of behavioral food security indicators and that food security across all indicators was higher among beneficiaries than among nonbeneficiaries. The failure to show a robust statistically significant impact of the PPFS-CT on beneficiary households may be a consequence of the timing of the data collection or contamination of the control group. As noted, the data were collected immediately following the harvest, when food was at its most plentiful and variation in food security status among households was, thus, less discernible. In addition, the data and analysis do not account for the activities of informal safety nets that may be operating in the background and affecting the outcomes observed here. For example, if a beneficiary household shared food or income with a nonbeneficiary household as a result of the cash transfer, this would contaminate the "control" group and make it more difficult to observe the treatment effect.

The different correlation patterns between the behavioral and the frequency or diversity food security indicators with PMT score and expenditures in the 2010 and 2011 data sets, respectively, merit further investigation. If such patterns are observed in other data sets, they may shed light on the stages of food deprivation at the household level; they may also assist with the selection of indicators for future projects and analyses. Including anthropometrics in a random subsample of the total surveyed population might serve as a benchmark—albeit an imperfect one given that anthropometrics capture yet another dimension of food insecurity—against which to compare the food security indicators.

Overall, data constraints imposed substantial limitations on the analyses provided here. Investment in capacity building with national partners might assure better implementation and data collection. For example, implementation of identical PMT and expenditure modules across the 2010 and 2011 surveys would have greatly facilitated an evaluation of impact as well as a greater comprehension of the relationship between the two expenditure-based welfare measures and the basket of food security indicators. Going forward, incorporating random control trail design either in the project scale-up or among a random subsample of the target population also may provide better data for estimating program impact.

Annex 8A Food Security Indicators

This annex explains the methodology underlying each of the food security indicators and takes a closer look at their application to the two samples.

Food Consumption Score

The World Food Program (WFP) developed the food consumption score (FCS) to proxy household food security based on seven-day food consumption recall data (WFP 2008). In the calculation of the FCS, food consumption is scored not only by the frequency of consumption of foods from nine categories over the past seven days, but also by the quality—"nutrient density" (WFP 2008)—of the foods consumed. The latter is accomplished through the assignment of weights to the food groups.

The WFP FCS underwent validation testing in 2009. The validation study generally supports the use of FCS as a food security assessment tool (Wiesmann et al. 2009). Comparing the FCS with other indicators as well as testing it directly against household calorie consumption, Wiesmann et al. (2009) find that, in two out of three case studies, "food frequency scores are clearly superior to simpler measures of diet diversity." However, they also find that construction of the FCS could be improved. One of their suggestions—not to truncate food consumption frequencies at 7 so as not to lose the variation in frequency of staple consumption—was applied here.

To construct the FCS, the following steps, as outlined in the WFP Technical Guide (WFP 2008), were followed: from the seven-day recall data on consumption of food from 24 categories available in both the 2010 and 2011 data sets, consumed food items were regrouped into nine categories; the consumption frequencies were summed; and, in the case of the FCS, any value above 7 was recoded as 7. For the nontruncated FCS (FCSnt), the frequencies were not altered. The resulting food group consumption frequencies were multiplied by their respective weights (see WFP 2008 for the standard weighting scheme). Finally, the weighted food group consumption frequencies were summed to create the household FCS and FCSnt. The WFP standard *poor* and *borderline* food security cutoffs are an FCS of 21 and 35, respectively.

The contribution of the consumption frequency of each food group to the 2010 household FCS is shown in figure 8A.1. Because food group consumption has been truncated, consumption frequency of staples flattens at 7—the maximum. This plateau occurs after an FCS of 14, indicating that households with an FCS of 14 or greater consume staples at least once each day. Also following an FCS of 14, vegetables begin to play a larger role in household diet. Following the FCS *poor* food security cutoff point of 21, milk consumption rises. Consumption of pulses rises following the *borderline* food security cutoff point of 35. Sugar consumption is relatively consistent—consumed approximately 1.2 times a week—across all FCS scores, while meat consumption remains weak until an FCS of 57.5. Fruit played little to no role in household diets at the time of this survey. Extremely low-FCS households rely on condiment-quantity foods, oil, and sugar in addition to some staples.

Figure 8A.1 Contribution of Truncated Food Group Consumption Frequencies to the 2010 FCS in the Tahoua Region of Niger

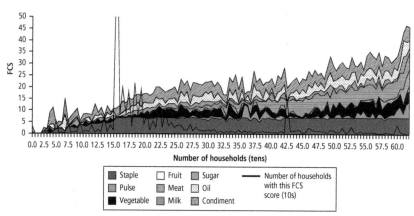

Note: Food group consumption frequencies are averaged for each FCS. For an FCS at 60, the averages are extended to all households with an FCS at 60–69. The same method is applied to households with an FCS at 70–79, 80–89, 90–99, and 100 and higher.

Overall, the FCS sample composition displayed in figure 8A.1 lends support to use of the standard WFP cutoff points in the sample in that sugar and oil do not appear to inflate scores[8] and the consumption of key dairy and protein increases following the cutoff points.

With the standard FCS construction, weighting, and cutoffs, 68.2 percent of households in the 2010 sample, which includes only Tahoua, are classified as having a *poor* FCS, 15.1 percent as a *borderline* FCS, and 16.7 percent as an *acceptable* FCS. In the case of the October 2011 full sample (Tahoua only), 39.1 (18.4) percent of households are classified as having a *poor* FCS, 21.6 (21.3) percent as a *borderline* FCS, and 39.3 (60.2) as an *acceptable* FCS. The high number of *poor* and *borderline* food-secure households in September 2010 as compared with October 2011 is consistent with the seasonal and annual shift in food security between the two data sets.

The FCS and FCSnt have some limitations as indicators of food security: the standard weighting scheme may not accurately reflect the quality of diets across cultures (SecureNutrition 2012; Wiesmann et al. 2009) and therefore may not be pertinent to the case of Niger; the seven-day recall period does not differentiate between long- and short-term food insecurity; and the aggregation of household food consumption into 9, as opposed to 12 or more, food categories may reduce the indicators' power to discern variation among household diets. Finally, practitioners note that the FCS can underestimate food insecurity when compared with other indicators of food security (SecureNutrition 2012).

Household Dietary Diversity Score

The household dietary diversity score (HDDS) was developed by FANTA (Food and Nutrition Technical Assistance) and is used by the FAO (Food and Agriculture Organization) to measure access to a variety of foods at the household level; the tool is also considered a "proxy for [the] nutrient adequacy of the diet of individuals" (Kennedy, Ballard, and Dop 2011). The HDDS includes more food groups than the FCS—12 for the HDDS and 9 for the FCS—but does not weight them. Validation studies have demonstrated that the HDDS is correlated with other measures of household welfare and food security. For example, Hoddinott and Yohannes (2002) find statistically significant positive relationships between measures of dietary diversity, which they define as the number of unique foods or food groups consumed over a reference period, and per capita consumption and daily caloric availability for 24 data sets from 10 different countries. Across the available data, they estimate that a 1 percent increase in dietary diversity is associated with a 0.65–1.11 percent increase in per capita consumption and a 0.37–0.73 percent increase in per capita caloric availability (with a 0.31–0.76 percent increase in caloric availability from staples and a 1.17–1.57 percent increase in caloric availability from nonstaples).

The FAO guidelines (Kennedy, Ballard, and Dop 2011) detail the following steps in constructing the HDDS: 24-hour recall data on all meals consumed by any member of the household are placed by the enumerator into 1 of 16 categories; the food items are then regrouped into 12 categories, each of which is truncated at 1. The HDDS is calculated as the total number of food categories consumed over the reference period. The maximum possible HDDS in the sample is 12; a score of 12 indicates that the household has consumed food from all 12 food groups over the past 24 hours and therefore has high dietary diversity.

An HDDS questionnaire was not administered in the two available surveys; therefore, the HDDS was constructed from the same module as that used to construct the FCS. Due to this limitation, the HDDS used here differs from the standard in one respect: the collected data were from a 7-day, as opposed to a 24-hour, recall. However, because Hoddinott and Yohannes (2002) find that associations between dietary diversity indicators and caloric availability hold whether 24-hour or 7-day recall data are used, the adapted HDDS values should meet the needs of this analysis. Working with the data available, the foods consumed by the household over the past week were aggregated into 12 categories, the consumption frequencies were truncated at 1, and the values were summed to construct the composite HDDS score.

It is not clear how respondents were prompted to indicate their food consumption. The HDDS guidelines recommend that the enumerator prompt the respondent to describe the foods consumed by any member of the household over the past 24 hours and suggest additional probes only for meals and snacks between the traditional breakfast, lunch, and dinner. It does not suggest prompting for particular food groups. In the case of the available data, the questionnaire modules do prompt for particular food groups and list items that belong in those food groups. Such prompts may bias the data toward those foods mentioned in the prompt, while other foods that are consumed but not prompted may be overlooked.

As seen in the graph of the 2010 HDDS, as HDDS rises, so do the number of food groups consumed over the course of the week (figure 8A.2). The weekly diet of the majority (the mean 2010 HDDS is 3.5) of the households in the sample consists of cereals and condiment-quantity meat, fish, or vegetables with some vegetables, oil, sugar, dairy, and very little tuber. Real gains in dietary diversity—beyond cereals, sugars, condiments, and oil—are seen around an HDDS of 4, where vegetable consumption increases, or after an HDDS of 5, where dairy, tubers, legumes, and meat start playing a greater role in the weekly diet. Food groups such as fish, eggs, and fruit do not make a strong showing until an HDDS of 9. Daily consumption of cereal and condiment-quantity foods is consistent across the dietary spectrum, reflecting the millet- and rice-based diet flavored with condiment-quantity meat, fish, or vegetables common in Niger.

Figure 8A.2 Contribution of Food Group Categories to 2010 HDDS in the Tahoua Region of Niger

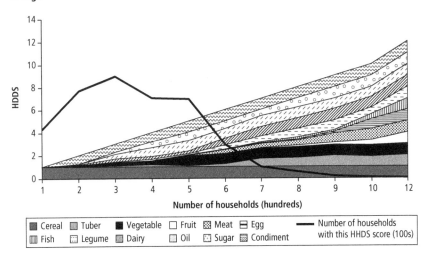

As discussed above, the 2011 HDDS is greater than that of 2010, with the mean 2011 household consuming at an HDDS of 4.3 (4.5 in Tahoua only).

Several limitations should be acknowledged in the use of the HDDS as a food security indicator. These limitations include the inability to account for frequency, quantity, or quality of consumption. For example, the consumption of one vegetable item once over the past week will contribute just as much to the HDDS as the consumption of many vegetables several times over the past week. Likewise, the addition of sugar to a diet will increase the score just as much as the addition of vegetables or meat. In addition, as with the FCS indicators, the HDDS does not discern long- from short-term food security.

Food Consumption and Dietary Diversity

Given the limitations of the HDDS and the FCS, an additional indicator was constructed that combines the food consumption frequency of the FCS and the diversity of the 12 food groups of the HDDS. This food consumption frequency and dietary diversity indicator (FCDD) combines the advantages of both of its parent indicators to reflect frequency and diversity simultaneously. Support for the construction of this indicator is drawn from Wiesmann et al. (2009), where it is shown that an unweighted food frequency indicator aggregated from the 12 HDDS food groups "performs slightly better than the FCS" in terms of correlation with the benchmark calorie consumption per capita.

The FCDD was calculated from the same module as the FCS and HDDS by placing 7-day recall data into the 12 HDDS food group categories, as above, and then truncating at 7. The consumption frequencies for each group were summed for the composite FCDD score. No weights were applied to the consumed food groups, because Wiesmann et al. (2009) demonstrate that weighting does not necessarily improve the accuracy of the indicator; in fact, they find that correlation with caloric intake per capita falls slightly when weights are applied to the standard FCS.

The FCDDs calculated from the 2010 PMT and 2011 consumption data sets show the same pattern of improvement from 2010 to 2011 as seen in the FCS and HDDS.

The limitations of the FCDD are the same as those of the FCS and HDDS. In addition, the FCDD does not account for the quality of foods consumed, is not established in the literature, and has not undergone validation testing beyond the correlations shown in Wiesmann et al. (2009).

Coping Strategies Index

The coping strategies index (CSI), developed by the WFP and Cooperative for Assistance and Relief Everywhere (CARE), offers a tool for measuring household-level behavioral response to food insecurity with regard to a lack of access to sufficient food. The behaviors measured by the CSI fall into four categories: changes in diet, short-term adaptations made by the household to increase the availability of food, short-term adaptations made by the household to reduce the number of people to feed, and rationing strategies. The CSI operates by measuring the frequency (via household-level responses) and severity (via application of severity weights) of such behavioral responses.

While built around a set of common coping strategies, it is recommended that the CSI be adapted to the local context (Maxwell and Caldwell 2008). The CSI Field Methods Manual emphasizes the importance of building the index questionnaire and weights out of local circumstances and with the participatory input of a community-level focus group. To construct the full CSI along these guidelines, the researcher must work with the community to generate a set of questions regarding relevant coping strategies as well as severity weights. The survey is then administered at the household level, and the index is composed as the sum of the frequency responses multiplied by the severity weights.

In addition to the full (original) CSI, a reduced CSI was developed by Maxwell, Caldwell, and Langworthy (2008). As compared with the context-specific full CSI, the reduced CSI entails five standard questions and severity weights that can be applied in any context. The reduced CSI has undergone testing to establish comparability with the full CSI. Findings indicate that the reduced CSI "reflects food insecurity nearly as well" as the full CSI, but it may do a poorer job of identifying the most food-insecure households because it does not capture or account for the more extreme coping strategies relied on in a given setting (Maxwell, Caldwell, and Langworthy 2008).

Because weights are not provided for the CSI module in either the 2010 data or the 2011 data and because it is not known whether or not the survey was designed for the local context, three versions of the CSI were calculated from the available data:

- The full CSI was calculated as the sum of all 16 CSI frequency responses available in the data. No weights were applied; therefore, this indicator does not account for severity.
- The reduced CSI includes only the five standard reduced CSI questions with the appropriate weights (see Maxwell and Caldwell 2008 for details).
- The weighted CSI is the full CSI module weighted by the average of the weights assigned by local communities across seven African countries or regions in a study conducted by Maxwell, Caldwell, and Langworthy (2008); questions in the CSI module of the 2010 and 2011 data sets that were not included in Maxwell, Caldwell, and Langworthy's study were given a weight of 0.

Across both the 2010 and 2011 data, the various CSIs are consistently higher in 2010 than in 2011, which is expected given the season (lean) and circumstances (food crisis) in 2010.

Maxwell (1995, 1999) examines correlations between the CSI and a variety of other indicators of food security and welfare for several case study data sets. He generally finds statistically significant correlations of varying magnitude, and Maxwell and Caldwell (2008) recommend using the full (context-specific) CSI to assess the accuracy of targeting for food-security interventions. While the variations of the CSI calculated here may capture dimensions of food insecurity in the Niger context, it is not clear that a context-specific CSI was developed, and so the indicators should be considered with that limitation in mind.

Household Hunger Scale

The FANTA II household hunger scale (HHS) is a three-question tool developed from the earlier, longer household food insecurity access scale (HFIAS). Like the CSI and the HFIAS, the HHS was developed to measure household behavioral response to food insecurity. The HHS loses the severity weighting components of the CSI but looks at frequency over a longer time period with less precision and is therefore less subject to short-term fluctuations in food security. The advantage of the HHS over the HFIAS is the cross-cultural comparability of the scale, which has been validated by Deitchler et al. (2010) for FANTA II. The validation study finds that the three HHS questions are cross-culturally comparable across the seven data sets considered (the seven data sets were collected in six settings, including Kenya, Malawi, Mozambique, South Africa, West Bank and Gaza, and Zimbabwe).

The standard HHS survey module asks three questions about access to food and food deprivation as well as frequency of the deprivation over the past 30 days. The frequency is categorized as either rarely or sometimes (1–10 times) or often (more than 10 times). In constructing the HHS, a frequency of "rarely or sometimes" is assigned a 1, and "often" is assigned a 2; the composite HHS is then calculated as the total of those frequency responses. Calculated in this way, the HHS ranges from 0 to 6, with a score of 0–1 indicating little to no hunger, a score of 2–3 indicating moderate hunger, and a score of 4–6 indicating a state of severe hunger.

While an HHS module was not included in either of the available surveys, three questions from the coping strategies module are close enough (table 8A.1) to the standard HHS questionnaire to accommodate the calculation of an indicator similar to the HHS with the available data. The HHS indicator used here also differs from the standard HHS in the length of reference period. The available data are for a 7-day rather than the HHS recommended 30-day reference period. Because of this difference in reference period, this tabulation does not categorize responses into the rarely, sometimes, and often categories. Consequently, this HHS is not comparable to the standard scale, and the categories of little, moderate, and severe hunger do not apply. The calculation used here involved simply summing the responses to the three HHS questions for an HHS that can range from 0 to 21, with 21 indicating that the household experienced each type of deprivation every day of the last 7 days.

The HHS survey module involves three questions that capture behavioral response to food deprivation; because these questions were not available in the 2010 and 2011 surveys, the substitutions indicated in table 8A.1 were made.

The HHS from the 2010 Tahoua households is shown in figure 8A.3. Frequency of response to the question, "Over the course of the past seven days, have there been moments when you did not have enough food or enough money with which to purchase food?" appears to be the greatest contributor to the overall score, with all households above an HHS of 0 responding yes for at least one of the past seven days. Having passed an entire day without food is the next most frequent contributor to the HHS, followed by going to bed hungry. More than 90 percent of the 2010 Tahoua sample have an HHS of 8 or below. Following the trends noted above, the mean HHS is greater in 2010 (4.18) than in 2011 (1.5 full sample, 1.5 Tahoua).

The HHS entails several limitations. Ballard et al. (2011) note that the HHS indicator captures the more extreme behavioral responses to the lack of access to sufficient food and therefore may not be sensitive to less severe, though still

Table 8A.1 Questions Available in the Standard Household Module and in the Survey Data for Niger

Standard HHS module	Questions available in the 2010 and 2011 survey data
In the past [4 weeks or 30 days], was there ever no food to eat of any kind your house because of lack of resources to get food?	In the past 7 days, have there been moments when there was not enough food or not enough money with which to purchase food?
In the past [4 weeks or 30 days], did you or any household member go to sleep at night hungry because there was not enough food?	In the past 7 days, have you or a member of your household gone to bed hungry because there wasn't enough to eat?
In the past [4 weeks or 30 days], did you or any household member go a whole day and night without eating anything at all because there was not enough food to eat?	In the past 7 days, has your household had to pass an entire day without eating?

Figure 8A.3 Contribution of Each Question to the 2010 HHS Score in the Tahoua Region of Niger

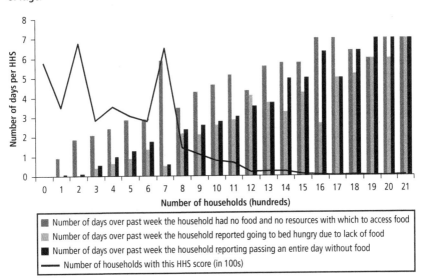

significant, types of deprivation. In addition to the limitations of the standard HHS indicator, this approximation of the HHS entails unique limitations due to the short reference period used in data collection: Ballard et al. (2011) caution against using a reference or recall period shorter than the past 30 days due to the common fluctuation of deprivation over time.

Table 8A.2 Beneficiary Reported Use of Cash Transfer in the Tahoua and Tillabéri Regions, Niger, 2011

Use of cash transfer	% of beneficiaries
Purchases of food for the household	96.4
Purchases of food for the children	82.3
Purchases of consumer products for the household	87.6
Purchases of consumer products for the children	78.3
Savings	74.7
Investments in agricultural activities	38.9
Investments in other economic activities	47.2
Investments in assets (livestock)	53.9
Transfers to other households	25.2
Other	11.8

Note: N = 1,980.44, weighted.

Table 8A.3 Comparison of Beneficiary and Nonbeneficiary Food Security and Welfare Indicator Means in the Tahoua Region, Niger, 2010 and 2011

Year of survey, indicator, and category of household	Mean	Standard deviation or linearized standard error	Number of observations	Test of equality of means
2010				
FCS				
0	22.13	13.27	2,751	
1	21.64	12.80	1,193	Prob > F = 0.2693
Total	21.98	13.13	3,944	
FCSnt				
0	25.15	16.07	2,751	
1	25.00	15.43	1,193	Prob > F = 0.7812
Total	25.10	15.87	3,944	
FCDD				
0	16.33	7.77	2,751	
1	16.31	7.74	1,193	Prob > F = 0.9378
Total	16.32	7.76	3,944	
HDDS	3.50	1.70	2,751	
0	3.65	1.67	1,193	Prob > F = 0.0086
1	3.54	1.69	3,944	
Total	3.50	1.70	2,751	

(continued next page)

Table 8A.3 (continued)

Year of survey, indicator, and category of household	Mean	Standard deviation or linearized standard error	Number of observations	Test of equality of means
HHS	4.02	3.25	2,751	
0	4.55	3.32	1,193	Prob > F = 0.0000
1	4.18	3.28	3,944	
Total	4.02	3.25	2,751	
fullCSI				
0	19.83	14.78	2,751	
1	22.04	14.75	1,193	Prob > F = 0.0000
Total	20.50	14.80	3,944	
redCSI				
0	15.43	14.45	2,751	
1	16.86	14.36	1,193	Prob > F = 0.0044
Total	15.86	14.44	3,944	
weiCSI				
0	35.95	28.78	2,751	
1	40.45	28.84	1,193	Prob > F = 0.0000
Total	37.31	28.87	3,944	
2011				
FCS				
0	38.70	1.10	2,472.05	
1	40.64	0.83	1,357.72	Prob > F = 0.1600
Total	39.39	0.77	3,829.77	
FCSnt				
0	43.43	1.24	2,472.05	
1	46.28	0.94	1,357.72	Prob > F = 0.0679
Total	44.44	0.87	3,829.77	
FCDD				
0	20.99	0.57	2,472.05	
1	22.61	0.40	1,357.72	Prob > F = 0.0200
Total	21.57	0.39	3,829.77	
HDDS				
0	4.30	0.12	2,472.05	
1	4.77	0.10	1,357.72	Prob > F = 0.0019
Total	4.47	0.08	3,829.77	

(continued next page)

Table 8A.3 (continued)

Year of survey, indicator, and category of household	Mean	Standard deviation or linearized standard error	Number of observations	Test of equality of means
HHS				
0	1.69	0.17	2,472.05	
1	1.18	0.10	1,357.72	Prob > F = 0.0105
Total	1.51	0.12	3,829.77	
fullCSI				
0	8.22	0.71	2,472.05	
1	7.75	0.55	1,357.72	Prob > F = 0.6011
Total	8.06	0.50	3,829.77	
redCSI				
0	6.59	0.67	2,472.05	
1	7.08	0.57	1,357.72	Prob > F = 0.5758
Total	6.76	0.48	3,829.77	
weiCSI				
0	15.82	1.54	2,472.05	
1	15.76	1.22	1,357.72	Prob > F = 0.9721
Total	15.80	1.10	3,829.77	
lnPCexp				
0	11.06	0.06	2,472.05	
1	11.23	0.04	1,357.72	Prob > F = 0.0231
Total	11.12	0.04	3,829.77	
lnPCFexp				
0	10.61	0.15	2,472.05	
1	10.98	0.05	1,357.72	Prob > F = 0.0158
Total	10.74	0.10	3,829.77	
foodsh				
0	0.81	0.01	2,472.05	
1	0.81	0.01	1,357.72	Prob > F = 0.8022
Total	0.81	0.01	3,829.77	

Figure 8A.4 HDDS Discontinuity at PMT Cutoff with Various Bandwidths and Bandwidth Dependence of Estimated Effects in Niger

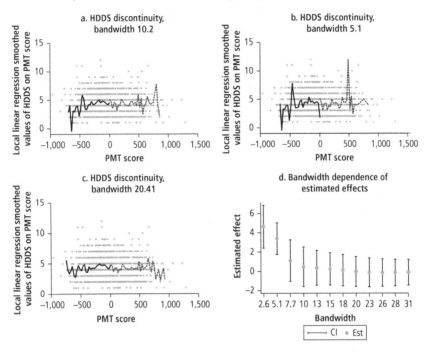

Figure 8A.5 *Foodsh* Discontinuity at PMT Cutoff with Various Bandwidths and Bandwidth Dependence of Estimated Effects in Niger

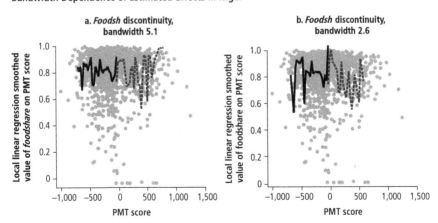

(continued next page)

Figure 8A.5 (continued)

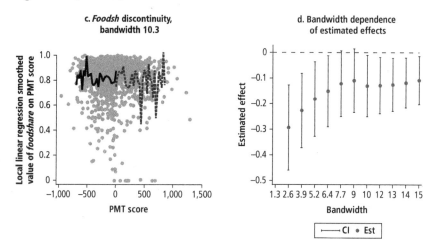

c. *Foodsh* discontinuity, bandwidth 10.3

d. Bandwidth dependence of estimated effects

Table 8A.4 Test of Discontinuity of PMT Variables across the Cutoff Point for Niger

Variable	HDDS (1)	foodsh (2)
eau_puitouvert (default bandwidth)	0.631**	0.700***
	(2.94)	(3.33)
eau_surface (default bandwidth)	−0.419	−0.954**
	(−1.50)	(−2.59)
nchaise (default bandwidth)	1.169*	1.751***
	(2.31)	(3.35)
lwald (default bandwidth)	0.650	−0.180*
	(0.59)	(−2.40)
eau_puitouvert (default bandwidth × 0.5)	0.728***	1.277***
	(3.55)	(3.99)
eau_surface (default bandwidth × 0.5)	−1.034**	−1.346**
	(−2.68)	(−2.83)
nchaise (default bandwidth × 0.5)	1.748***	1.522**
	(3.50)	(3.06)
lwald (default bandwidth × 0.5)	3.664***	−0.292***
	(4.70)	(−3.42)
eau_surface (default bandwidth ×2)	−0.254	−0.357
	(−1.64)	(−1.46)

(continued next page)

Table 8A.4 (continued)

Variable	HDDS (1)	foodsh (2)
eau_puitouvert (default bandwidth × 2)	0.760***	0.657**
	(4.42)	(3.25)
nchaise (default bandwidth × 2)	0.586	0.988*
	(1.28)	(2.02)
lwald (default bandwidth × 2)	0.0943	−0.128*
	(0.11)	(−2.07)
Number of observations	1,289	1,289

Note: Numbers in parentheses are t-statistics.
*** $p < .001$, ** $p < .01$, * $p < .05$

Figure 8A.6 Density of Assignment Variable, PMT Score, at Bandwidths Yielding Significant Discontinuities in the Outcome Variables in Niger

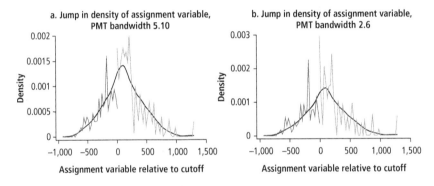

a. Jump in density of assignment variable, PMT bandwidth 5.10

b. Jump in density of assignment variable, PMT bandwidth 2.6

Notes

1. See, for example, the following reports on the four most recent food crises in Niger (2000, 2005, 2010, and 2012): a special report submitted to the Commission on Human Rights (Ziegler 2002), a special report for the Famine Early Warning System Network (FEWSNET) by Grobler-Tanner (2006), and monthly reports on the FEWSNET website (USAID 2010a, 2010b, 2010c, 2013d, 2012).
2. Niger has eight administrative regions, 36 *départements*, and 265 *communes*, of which 52 are urban and 213 are rural (NIS 2008).
3. Niger's currency in the CFA franc. This figure represents approximately US$20, depending on current exchange rates.
4. The geographic targeting of villages operated as follows. The *Dispositif National de Prévention et de Gestion des Crises Alimentaire* selected the *départements* Tillabéri and Ouallam in the Tillabéri region and Illéla and Bouza in the Tahoua region.

From the *départements* selected, *communes* and villages were selected based on the
following criteria: frequency of food crises, absence of similar programs, and access
to well-functioning food markets (Katayama 2010).

5. Separate models were developed for rural and urban households; however, only the
rural model is discussed here because food consumption scores are only available
for rural households.

6. See Maxwell, Vaitla, and Coates (2011) for an analysis of food security indicator
correlations. In general, the correlations observed here are slightly lower than those
recorded by them; however, the indicators considered here and by Maxwell, Vaitla,
and Coates were likely constructed in different ways.

7. The HDDS indicator shows an unexpected statistically significant difference, with
beneficiary households having a mean HDDS 4.6 percent higher than that of nonbeneficiary households.

8. In the case of an FCS of 6, reliance on oil may inflate the weighted FCS score.

References

Ballard, Terri, Jennifer Coates, Anne Swindale, and Megan Deitchler. 2011. *Household
Hunger Scale: Indicator Definition and Measurement Guide*. FHI 360. Washington, DC:
USAID, Food and Nutrition Technical Assistance (FANTA) II Project.

Barrett, Christopher. 2010. "Measuring Food Insecurity." *Science* 327 (5967): 825–28.

———. 2002. "Food Security and Food Assistance Programs." In *Handbook of Agricultural
Economics*. Vol. 2, edited by Bruce Gardener and Gordon Rausser. New York: Elsevier
Science B.V.

Comité de PPFS-CT (Pilotage Charge de la Coordination du PPFS-CT). 2010. "Projet
pilote des filets sociaux par le cash transfert (PPFS-CT)." Draft manuscript, Cabinet
du Premier Ministre, Republique du Niger, July.

Deaton, Angus, and Salman Zaidi. 2002. *Guidelines for Constructing Consumption
Aggregates for Welfare Analysis*. Washington, DC: World Bank.

Deitchler, Megan, Terri Ballard, Anne Swindale, and Jennifer Coates. 2010. *Validation of
a Measure of Household Hunger for Cross-Cultural Use*. Washington, DC: Food and
Nutrition Technical Assistance (FANTA) II Project, USAID.

FAO (Food and Agriculture Organization) and WFP (World Food Program). 2012.
"Food Security and Humanitarian Implications in West Africa and the Sahel." Joint
Note, FAO and WFP, Rome, April.

Grobler-Tanner, Caroline. 2006. *Understanding Nutrition Data and the Causes of
Malnutrition in Niger: A Special Report by the Famine Early Warning Systems Network
(FEWSNET)*. Washington, DC: USAID.

Hoddinott, John, and Yisehac Yohannes. 2002. *Dietary Diversity as a Food Security
Indicator*. FCND Discussion Paper 136. Washington, DC: International Food Policy
Institute.

Imbens, Guido, and Karthik Kalyanaraman. 2009. "Optimal Bandwidth Choice for the
Regression Discontinuity Estimator." Working Paper 14726, National Bureau of
Economic Research, Cambridge, MA.

Imbens, Guido, and Thomas Lemieux. 2007. "Regression Discontinuity Designs: A Guide to Practice." *Journal of Econometrics* 142 (2): 615–35.

Katayama, Roy. 2010. "Appui à l'equipe de gestion dans le cadre de la mise en œuvre du projet pilote des filets sociaux par le transfert de cash." Rapport de la Mission, 20 julliet 2010–18 aout 2010, World Bank, Niamey.

Kennedy, Gina, Terri Ballard, and Marie Claude Dop. 2011. *Guidelines for Measuring Household and Individual Dietary Diversity*. Rome: Food and Agriculture Organization of the United Nations.

Maxwell, Daniel. 1995. "Measuring Food Insecurity: The Frequency and Severity of 'Coping Strategies.'" International Food Policy Research Institute, Food Consumption and Nutrition Division, Washington, DC.

———. 1999. "Alternative Food Security Indicators: Revisiting the Frequency and Severity of Coping Strategies." *Food Policy* 24 (4): 411–29.

Maxwell, Daniel, and Richard Caldwell. 2008. *The Coping Strategies Index: Field Methods Manual*, 2d ed. Atlanta, GA: Cooperative for Assistance and Relief Everywhere (CARE).

Maxwell, Daniel, Richard Caldwell, and Mark Langworthy. 2008. "Measuring Food Insecurity: Can an Indicator Based on Localized Coping Behaviors Be Used to Compare across Contexts?" *Food Policy* 33 (6): 533–40.

Maxwell, Daniel, Bapu Vaitla, and Jennifer Coates. 2011. "Capturing the 'Access' Element of Food Security: Comparing Different Indicators." Presentation at FAO's International Scientific Symposium on Food and Nutrition Security Information, Rome, January 18. Slides available online at https://www.securenutritionplatform.org/Documents /D.Maxwell-Comparing%20Indicators%20to%20capture%20Access.pdf.

Nichols, Austin. 2007. "Causal Inference with Observational Data." *Stata Journal* 7 (4): 507–41.

———. 2011. "rd 2.0: Revised Stata Module for Regression Discontinuity Estimation." Boston College. http://ideas.repec.org/c/boc/bocode/s456888.html.

NIS (National Institute of Statistics). 2008. *Enquête nationale sur le budget et la consummation des ménages Niger 2007*. Niamey: NIS.

SecureNutrition. 2012. "World Bank Workshop on Food Security and Nutrition: From Measurement to Results." Workshop held at the World Bank, Washington, DC, March 22. Workshop materials available at https://www.securenutritionplatform.org/Lists /Events/DispForm.aspx?ID=35.

USAID (U.S. Agency for International Development). 2010a. "Niger." FEWSNET. http:// www.fews.net/pages/country.aspx?gb=ne.

———. 2010b. "Niger Food Security Outlook Update: February 2010." FEWSNET, February. http://www.fews.net/docs/Publications/Niger_2011_02_en.pdf.

———. 2010c. "Niger Food Security Outlook Update: July through December 2010." FEWSNET, July. http://www.fews.net/docs/Publications/Niger_Outlook_July_2010 _final_en.pdf.

———. 2010d. "Niger Food Security Outlook Update: September 2010." FEWSNET, September. http://www.fews.net/docs/Publications/Niger_OU_2010_Sept_en.pdf.

———. 2012. "Niger Food Security Outlook Update: April through September." FEWSNET, May. http://www.fews.net/sites/default/files/documents/reports /Niger_FSOU_2012_5_final_en.pdf.

WFP (World Food Program). 2008. "Food Consumption Analysis: Calculation and Use of the Food Consumption Score in Food Security Analysis." Technical Guidance Sheet. WFP, Geneva. http://documents.wfp.org/stellent/groups/public/documents /manual_guide_proced/wfp197216.pdf.

Wiesmann, Doris, Lucy Basset, Todd Benson, and John Hoddinott. 2009. "Validation of the World Food Programme's Food Consumption Score and Alternative Indicators of Household Food Security." Discussion Paper 00870. International Food Policy Research Institute, Washington, DC.

World Bank. 2009. "Niger Food Security and Safety Nets." Report 44072-NE, World Bank, Washington, DC.

———. 2012. World Development Indicators (database). Washington, DC: World Bank. http://data.worldbank.org/data-catalog/world-development-indicators.

Ziegler, Jean. 2002. "Economic, Social, and Cultural Rights: The Right to Food." Mission to Niger, United Nations Economic and Social Council, New York.

Chapter **9**

Targeting Effectiveness of Safety Net Programs in Senegal

Phillippe Leite, Quentin Stoeffler, and Adea Kryeziu

Following a decade of strong economic performance beginning in the mid-1990s, Senegal suffered from a succession of domestic and external shocks, many of which were exogenous. In the decade after 1995, Senegal enjoyed robust growth of per capita gross domestic product (GDP), averaging 5 percent annually in real terms. The sudden change in economic performance, however, exposed the country's vulnerabilities and the government's limited capacity to respond effectively to these shocks. First, the run-up in oil prices, starting in 2007, slowed the economy, increased inflation, and resulted in a significant deterioration in Senegal's external and fiscal positions. Second, unfavorable rains prompted a sharp decline in agricultural production for two successive years, reducing the availability of food. Further, weaknesses in fiscal policy hurt private growth, especially in the construction and public works sector, and the onset of the global recession produced further headwinds against a rapid rebound from previous shocks. Each of these successive crises had its own time frame, channels of transmission, economic scale, and social or regional targets; yet, taken together, they have accounted for much of Senegal's weak economic performance in recent years.

In response to these successive crises and the rising costs of fuel and food, the government introduced general tax breaks and subsidies on rice and other commodities in 2007. These measures proved to be very expensive (between 3 and 4 percent of GDP) and poorly targeted to the poor. By the end of 2008, the government, under severe budget constraints, lifted most of the general subsidies. This experience underscored the need for effective programs to protect the most vulnerable from shocks and destitution and generated interest in developing a national safety net system.

By the end of 2008, however, the government had accumulated domestic debts to the private sector equivalent to more than 3 percent of GDP, forcing a strong tightening of fiscal policy. The onset of the global financial crisis in 2008, its deepening in 2009, and continued electricity shortages further contributed to the general slowdown of the country's economic activity.

Poverty, Vulnerability, and Social Assistance Response

Poverty has remained elevated, with only slight progress made since 2005. Poverty rates in Senegal declined from 55.2 percent to 48.3 percent between 2001 and 2005, but barely fell during the five years after that, reaching 46.7 percent in 2011. Growth in GDP per capita has been less than 1 percent per year for the past five years, well below the average for Sub-Saharan Africa.

Despite small gains in poverty reduction overall, extreme poverty has risen significantly. Defined as the proportion of the population whose total consumption is less than the costs of a food basket that provides minimum calorie requirements, extreme poverty has more than doubled over the last 10 years, rising from 7 percent in 2001 to 15 percent in 2011.

Poverty remains concentrated in rural areas. In Senegal, 57 percent of the poor population is located in rural areas, and the poverty rate in rural areas is more than twice the rate in urban Dakar (26 percent). High rates of rural poverty are driven largely by low productivity in agriculture. About 62 percent of people living in households with a head whose main occupation is in agriculture are poor, compared with 33 percent for other occupations. Between 2001 and 2011, poverty rates fell fastest in the capital of Senegal, where it declined 12 percentage points, compared to a fall of 8 and 4 percentage points in rural areas and "other urban centers," respectively.

The main household characteristics associated with poverty are related to education, family size, and gender. About 83 percent of the poor live in households headed by a person with no education, a figure that has not changed over the past 10 years. Poverty rates among persons living in households whose head has completed a primary education declined from 43 percent in 2005 to 34 percent in 2011. Also, larger household size (usually headed by a male) remains strongly associated with higher poverty: 78 percent of households with 20 members or more are poor. Female-headed households are relatively better off and tend to be smaller. About a quarter of all Senegalese live in a household headed by a woman.

Vulnerability

Table 9.1 summarizes the distribution of the vulnerable population—defined as the disabled, the elderly, early marriage, and children not in school.

Poverty is higher among the disabled population and the elderly without family support. There are an estimated 181,500 disabled persons in the country,

Table 9.1 Number of Vulnerable Individuals and Households in Senegal, by Poverty Level

Characteristic	Individuals			Individuals in a household with a vulnerable person			Households		
	Poor	Nonpoor	Total	Poor	Nonpoor	Total	Poor	Nonpoor	Total
Disabled adults	9,260	10,214	19,474	128,705	104,574	233,279	7,809	9,407	17,216
Disabled children	79,224	82,751	161,974	772,140	630,322	1,402,461	56,166	63,687	119,853
Elderly	107,131	121,751	228,883	1,151,060	1,031,780	2,182,841	79,617	101,355	180,972
Early marriage	6,355	5,812	12,167	91,531	59,440	150,971	5,965	5,625	11,590
School-age children not in school	702,330	635,710	1,338,040	2,119,480	2,121,707	4,241,186	160,495	222,571	383,066

Source: Echevin 2012.

nearly half of whom are under the national poverty line. Similarly, almost half of the elderly are poor, and they tend to be highly reliant on family support.

Vulnerable children (defined as those with a disability, in early marriage, uneducated, and poor) are in highly precarious situations. Vulnerable children account for about 1.65 million poor, with almost 61 percent living in extreme poverty. In addition to these groups, 34 percent of orphans do not attend school, and, along with other vulnerable children, are often engaged in child labor. Among children 5–17 years of age, 72 percent are involved in labor activities. Many of these are engaged in family production, especially in rural areas.

Formal social security coverage remains limited, reaching only 13 percent of the population. This includes 6.2 percent covered by a formal pension, 3 percent receiving social security administration benefits, and 3 percent having some form of health insurance. In particular, the poor and informal sector workers have little or no access to health insurance. Even health *mutuals* overwhelmingly serve the nonpoor.

Food insecurity plays a crucial role in household vulnerability. Household data reveal a lack of means to satisfy minimum consumption needs. According to the Senegal Demographic Health Survey/Multiple Indicator Cluster Survey for 2010–11, 27 percent of children under five suffer from chronic malnutrition (which remains highest in rural areas) and 11 percent suffer from severe malnutrition (Measure DHS 2011). In terms of self-reported difficulty obtaining food, poor households "always" or "often" have difficulty satisfying household nutrition needs. The highest rate is among the urban poor, at 32.7 percent (table 9.2).

Rural households remain highly vulnerable to changing environmental conditions. Senegal is a Sahelian country in which 60 percent of the population is engaged in agriculture, with groundnuts as the principal product. Rural regions are highly vulnerable to variations in rainfall, with rainfall shortages causing significant reductions in agricultural harvests and rural incomes and at least

Table 9.2 Percentage of Households Satisfying Food Needs over Last 12 Months in Senegal, by Location

Frequency	Nonpoor			Poor		
	Urban	Rural	Total	Urban	Rural	Total
Never	42.6	27.1	36.2	18.6	18.1	18.3
Rarely	25.8	25.0	25.5	19.0	20.2	19.8
Sometimes	19.3	26.9	22.4	29.7	32.6	31.6
Often	11.1	18.3	14.1	24.2	24.1	24.1
Always	1.2	2.8	1.8	8.5	5.1	6.2
Total	100.0	100.0	100.0	100.0	100.0	100.0

Source: Diop 2012.

5 million families exposed to drought risk. Flooding also affects several regions, compromising production and infrastructure as well as damaging and destroying household assets. The risk of drought continues to be one of the main sources of vulnerability for rural households as well as one of the biggest internal risks.

Vulnerability to Shocks

Significant exogenous shocks frequently affect the Senegalese economy, with lasting consequences for economic growth. As demonstrated in the food, fuel, and financial crises of 2008–09, external shocks strike Senegal's small, open economy particularly hard. Senegal imports all of its oil (which powers most of its electricity), and 80 and 100 percent of its rice and wheat for consumption, respectively. In 2007–08, the price of rice in local markets tripled, while the price of grain increased 50 percent; the price of other staples like sugar, wheat, and milk products rose an average of 30 percent. Increases in the price of fuels were also significant, with particularly large increases for the types of fuel on which poor households rely, like butane gas.

The macroeconomic effects of these price increases were substantial. A widening current account deficit and fiscal slippages in 2008 led to a slowdown in private growth, especially in the construction sector. Real GDP growth fell to 2.2 percent in 2009. These price increases affected businesses, both directly through increased outlays on fuel, as well as indirectly through their general inflationary effects. With Senegal's dependence on petroleum products for electricity generation, these input price hikes placed a financial strain on the national electricity company, SENELEC. Senegal's GDP growth was hindered further by frequent electricity outages, which caused a slowdown of economic and manufacturing activities. According to local reports, the outages contributed to the closure of many small and medium-size enterprises in the food-processing, textile, and tourism sectors. Larger companies reported declines in output averaging 30 percent (U.S. Mission to Senegal 2009).

The national poverty rate rose 6 percentage points, from 51 percent in 2005/06 to 57 percent in 2008, affecting rural and urban households alike (Ivanic and Martin 2008). As a result of the sharp rise in food prices, living conditions of the poorest households deteriorated, with an increase in the level of household indebtedness and a reduction in the quality and frequency of meals—leading to more food insecurity and malnutrition (World Bank 2009).

Coping Mechanisms

Households employ a variety of coping mechanisms to address adverse economic shocks (table 9.3). Only 25 percent of households tap into their savings in response to a shock, mainly in cases of health shocks (illness or death) and business failure. Some households sell their assets, which can lock them into long-term poverty. Some rely on family support, whether from within the country or abroad. Only a few households receive aid from nongovernmental organizations or the government (2 and 1 percent, respectively).

More than half of households have no specific strategy for responding to shocks. This coping profile highlights the essential vulnerability of households. Even the few households that do have a formal coping strategy tend to rely heavily on assets and savings, which are less available to the poor.

Social Assistance Response

The last decade has shown how frequently large-scale shocks occur in the Senegalese economy and the limited range of government responses available to help households to cope. Historically, the government of Senegal has used financial support to farmers and general assistance to the poor as a direct response to droughts. A series of financial mechanisms were put in place in the late 1990s to mitigate and cope with the risks to agriculture as well as to ensure an adequate flow of credit following a drought.[1] The fiscal costs of these responses to agricultural shocks rose to 0.2 percent of GDP during this period. This type of support proved to be poorly targeted, with larger subsidies and write-offs for larger rural producers and those able to participate in the formal credit system.

More recently, in response to the triple wave of crises in 2008, the government introduced a series of fiscal measures, including subsidies on basic foodstuffs (rice, wheat, and milk), butane or natural gas, and electricity. Table 9.4 documents the magnitude of these subsidies over time. This response absorbed 2.4 percent of GDP, or one-tenth of all spending, in 2008. Additionally, the use of subsidies came with administrative difficulties and generated economic

Table 9.3 Household Responses to Reported Shocks in Senegal
% of households

Type of shock	Aid from government	Aid from a nongovernmental or community-based organization	Sale of assets	Savings	Loan	Aid from family in-country	Aid from family abroad	Aid from friends	No strategy
Death of family support	0.9	2.3	12.5	24.9	8.8	31.2	14.0	17.1	38.7
Serious illness or accident	1.2	3.4	25.9	36.3	12.5	27.7	16.4	15.8	18.9
Loss of employment	0.1	0.5	12.2	19.2	7.7	13.9	4.7	11.1	60.4
Failure of a family enterprise	0.0	0.0	26.8	30.7	27.5	1.5	0.4	6.2	36.3
Loss of harvest	0.7	0.8	7.0	6.3	7.5	5.2	2.3	2.2	77.6
Loss of livestock from a fire, flood, pests, theft	0.3	0.5	7.5	6.1	2.2	1.2	0.3	0.9	82.0
Significant loss of income (temporary layoff)	3.4	0.0	3.5	11.3	9.1	14.8	3.9	12.0	62.3
Partial or full loss of housing from fire, floods	2.1	3.0	8.3	12.5	2.9	3.7	1.7	2.7	66.4
Loss of main means of production	0.0	1.2	0.4	16.3	1.7	0.0	0.0	8.4	57.2

Source: Echevin 2012.

Table 9.4 Amount of Subsidies on Basic Goods and Utilities in Senegal, 2005–11
CFAF, billions

Indicator	2005	2006	2007	2008	2009	2011
Transfers and subsidies	165	308	287	333	286	331
Subsidies on basic consumer goods	26	152	76	145	63	139
Société Africaine de Raffinage and other producers of liquefied petroleum gas	14	66	55	69	33	15
SENELEC	12	86	0	30	30	124
Food subsidies	0	0	21	46	0	0
Total as % of GDP	0.6	3.1	1.4	2.4	1.0	2.1

Source: World Bank 2013.

disincentives, with the bulk of benefits going to the nonpoor. For example, 31 percent of households benefiting from electricity subsidies were poor and about 7 percent were in the poorest quintile. The strong majority of beneficiaries of both food and utility subsidies were urban dwellers.

The government as well as key international partners agree that the country needs to build a targeted safety net system rather than rely on general subsidies. In 2005, in analyzing the use of the agricultural security funds to respond to droughts, the International Monetary Fund concluded, "A more efficient safety net program would explicitly target poor farmers for compensation in response to a severe shock" (IMF 2005).

The social protection system has been strengthened, although progress has been insufficient to respond to the recent shocks. The National Social Protection Strategy, 2005–15 was developed in 2005 with strong support from the World Bank. Its principle objective was to adopt an integrated global vision of social protection that promotes access to risk management by vulnerable groups. The strategy foresaw the diversification and expansion of social protection instruments. It was, however, less specific on the exact nature of safety nets to be expanded, as there was little experience in the country at that time. There was little in the way of guidance on priority interventions, implementation structures, program harmonization, or institutional arrangements around safety nets. The Second Poverty Reduction Strategy Paper 2006–10, adopted by the government in mid-2006, made a strong case for strengthening Senegal's social protection system. While the second pillar of the strategy aims to promote access to basic social services by a growing share of the population, the third pillar emphasizes the need to improve the lives of vulnerable groups through targeted interventions and prescribes actions to ensure that these groups benefit from wealth creation and gain better access to social services.

A recent review of Senegal's safety net programs identified 12 programs currently under implementation by the government (table 9.5). These programs

Table 9.5 Objectives, Type of Benefit, and Geographic Distribution for Each Safety Net Program in Senegal

Program	Objective	Type of benefit	Geographic distribution
Sésame Plan	Access to health services	Fee waiver	National, all the territory
Programme de Réadaptation à Base Communautaire (PRBC): community-based readaptation program	Social integration	Grant, materials	National, all the territory
Projet d'Appui à la Promotion des Aînés (PAPA): old-age support program	Social integration	Loan	National, all the territory
Initiative de Protection Sociale des Enfants Vulnérables (IPSEV): social protection initiative for vulnerable children	Family integration	Cash	(Pilot) Kolda region, 2 cities: Coumbacara, Kolda; 35 rural and periurban communities
Programme d'Appui à la Mise en Oeuvre de la Stratégie de Réduction de la Pauvreté (PRP): poverty reduction program	Poverty reduction	Loan	3 regions: Matam, St. Louis, Louga (rural)
Nutrition Ciblée sur l'Enfant et Transferts Sociaux (NETS): pilot cash transfers for child nutrition program	Resistance to shocks	Cash	(Pilot) 6 regions (64 rural communities): Matam, Louga, Kaolack, Tambacounda, Sédhiou, Kédgougou (rural)
Bons d'Achat World Food Program (WFP CV): cash vouchers for food pilot program	Resistance to shocks	Cash	(Pilot) 2 regions (10 cities): Pikine, Ziguinchor, urban
Fond de Solidarité Nationale (FSN): national solidarity fund	Resistance to shocks	Cash, materials	National, rural and periurban
Commissariat à la Sécurité Alimentaire (CSA): food aid agency	Resistance to shocks	Food	National, all the territory
Bourses d'étude pour les orphelins et autres enfants vulnérables (OEV): educational support for vulnerable children	Access to education	Cash	National, all the territory
Programme d'Alimentation Scolaire (DCaS): national school lunch program	Access to education	Food	National, rural and periurban
Cantines Scolaires World Food Program: school lunches	Access to education	Food	All regions except St. Louis and Dakar, rural and periurban

serve a variety of objectives, including increasing school attainment, improving access to health services, maintaining children within families via the social protection initiative for vulnerable children, providing cash transfers in response to shocks, and promoting the social and economic integration of marginalized groups (such as the disabled and elderly). The majority of the programs are implemented by the Ministry of Family and the Ministry of Social Action and National Solidarity.

Despite the large number of poor and vulnerable individuals, the safety net programs in place have limited coverage. An estimated 4 million people receive some type of safety net assistance each year (table 9.6), which is

Table 9.6 Number of Safety Net Beneficiaries in Senegal, by Program and Year, 2009–11

Program	2009	2010	2011
PRBC	1,500	1,900	—
FSN	32,000	—	—
CSA	2,760,000	3,000,000	3,600,000
DCaS	700,414	761,439	780,000
Of which			
Cantines Scolaires World Food Program	567,185	565,560	596,253
NETS	2,982	21,986	26,294
PRP	1,274	1,440	700
WFP CV	n.a.	97,000	55,000
OEV	3,290	5,060	4,956
IPSEV	n.a.	n.a.	900
Total	3,501,460	3,888,825	4,467,850

Source: World Bank 2013.
Note: — = not known; n.a. = not applicable.

equivalent to a little under one-quarter of the national population. However, this grossly overestimates the number of people covered by an effective safety net. The CSA accounts for about 80 percent of these beneficiaries, and school lunches account for an additional 17 percent. *In particular, the CSA provides food aid assistance to vulnerable populations either in response to catastrophes or through the distribution of rice at public rallies and religious festivals.* Neither CSA nor school lunches screen beneficiaries based on their need. Considering only those programs that target and screen vulnerable beneficiaries, and for which data are available on the number of beneficiaries (that is, excluding the CSA and school lunches), only 100,000 people benefited last year (NETS and WFP CV).

With regard to safety net spending, the existing programs have averaged about CFAF 17 billion per year over the last three years, equivalent to 0.27 percent of GDP. Government spending can reach up to 4 percent of GDP for shock response interventions such as indirect tax cuts or subsidies. The school lunch programs account for more than 70 percent of safety net expenditures, reflecting large coverage.

In general, Senegalese safety net funding remains largely dependent on donor financing, and thus programs are fragmented and unsustainable. Out of the nine programs with funding information, donors finance 62 percent of costs, local governments account for 7 percent, the national budget accounts for 27 percent, and community contributions make up the remaining 4 percent.

In sum, Senegal has taken action to protect the poor and vulnerable in recent years; yet the scale, coverage, targeting mechanisms, targeting population, and delivery methods of these safety net programs differ. Greater coordination of programs is needed to create a coherent safety net and develop a more integrated national social protection system. A better-targeted, more efficient, and scaled-up national system of safety nets would contribute directly to poverty reduction among vulnerable populations.

Targeting Method Covered in the Case Study

Choosing the appropriate targeting mechanism is crucial in the Senegalese context, given the increasing need and constrained resources. It is necessary to concentrate limited resources on the most vulnerable populations with the aid of effective targeting mechanisms. Effective targeting mechanisms have several advantages, including reducing the errors of exclusion (eligible beneficiaries who do not benefit) and of inclusion (ineligible beneficiaries who do benefit) and promoting pro-poor public expenditures. One of the principal challenges, however, is to define target populations when half of the population is below the poverty line, and the differences between poor households are minimal.

Safety nets in Senegal use a variety of targeting mechanisms, with a predominance of categorical targeting. Categorical targeting is often reinforced by prioritizing certain geographic areas and confirmed through community-based mechanisms. However, it typically requires some further eligibility screening to ensure that the poorest and most vulnerable benefit in the end. To date, in Senegal, no proxy means test (PMT) methodology has been used to screen beneficiaries at the household level. Geographic targeting may use different poverty maps, yet none systematically identifies poorer communities below the region or *departement* level. Table 9.7 provides an overview of the targeting systems used by existing programs.

Several programs rely on geographic targeting to determine eligibility for benefits. That is, all people who live in the designated areas (particularly areas with high levels of poverty, food insecurity, malnutrition, or exposure to natural disasters) are identified as eligible and those who live elsewhere are not. In the literature on targeting, geographic targeting is used frequently as a first tool to identify areas with a high prevalence of potential beneficiaries (see Grosh et al. 2008; Coady, Grosh, and Hoddinott 2004). Geographic targeting is also employed frequently as a social assistance budgetary allocation tool, where areas with high levels of poverty receive larger budgets than other areas.

As a stand-alone tool, geographic targeting treats all individuals in a given area equally. It does not allow policy makers to disentangle the most affected or

Table 9.7 Targeting Methods, Criteria, and Source of Information in Senegal, by Program

Program	Method	Criteria	Sources
Sésame Plan: elderly health fee waiver	Categorical	Age	Identification card
PRBC: support to disabled	Categorical	Disability	Candidate dossier
PAPA: support to elderly	Categorical	Age and vulnerability	Candidate dossier
FSN: solidarity fund	Categorical	Victim of a disaster	Candidate dossier
CSA: food aid agency	Categorical	Food insecure	Candidate dossier
IPSEV: support to vulnerable families	Geographic	Vulnerable children at risk of family separation	Reports
	Categorical	Age and vulnerability	Social worker survey
OEV: HIV/AIDS vulnerable child grants	Geographic	Epidemiological situation	Epidemiological data or surveys
	Categorical	Orphans and vulnerable children	Social worker survey
DCaS: school lunches	Geographic	Rural food insecurity	Poverty surveys
	Categorical	School enrollment lists	School reports
WFP: school lunches	Geographic	Food-insecure rural areas	Poverty surveys
	Categorical	School enrollment lists	School reports
PRP: poverty reduction program	Geographic	Poverty	Local development plans
	Categorical	Women, disability, HIV/AIDS	Neighborhood reports
	Community-based	Prioritized at community level	Community information
CLM: cash transfer	Geographic	Zones with high malnutrition	Nutritional surveys
	Categorical	Vulnerable children	Reports
	Community-based	Prioritized at community level	Community information
WFP CV: food voucher	Geographic	Vulnerable areas	Poverty surveys
	Categorical	Food insecure	Reports
	Community-based	Prioritized at community level	Community information

Source: World Bank 2013.
Note: HIV-AIDS = human immunodeficiency virus/acquired immunodeficiency syndrome.

the actual affected population in an area hit by a given type of shock. Moreover, to address short-term needs, geographic targeting must be updated regularly with indicators of exposure to covariate shocks (floods or droughts). This requires a functional early warning system or community network, but also allows for more geographically refined targeting than with nationally representative survey data. Further, not all households within a shock-exposed area will be affected by a shock, and even if exposed to a shock, some households will have sufficient resources or access to coping mechanisms that help them to avoid poverty and food insecurity. Thus targeting efficiency can often be improved by combining geographic targeting mechanisms with other methods that address the circumstances of individual households.

As indicated in chapter 2 of this book and in the literature, using a combination of targeting methods within a single program can produce better targeting results than relying on a single method (Grosh et al. 2008; Coady, Grosh, and Hoddinott 2004). Combinations of geographic targeting and PMT or geographic targeting and means testing or geographic targeting and community-based targeting are generating promising results in countries like Mexico, Brazil, Kenya, Tanzania, and Niger. Unfortunately, few studies to date provide information on the actual cost of targeting methods, which is needed to analyze the costs and benefits of different methods the combinations of methods.

The current performance of these targeting systems is mixed. The 2011 *Enquête de Suivi de la Pauvreté au Sénégal* (ESPS2) included questions on coverage of a range of social programs. The programs cited include nutritional reinforcement, youth employment programs (*Office Banlieue*), agricultural development, elderly health care (Sésame Plan), food aid, educational support (scholarships), and housing assistance. Some programs were very effective at concentrating on the poorest households, like the nutritional reinforcement and agricultural support programs, while others had significant leakage to the nonpoor, including educational assistance (like scholarships) and food aid. The elderly health care program (Sésame Plan), for example, benefits the better-off 40 percent of households concentrated in urban areas.

Proxy Means Test

The PMT mechanism can guide the selection of beneficiaries based on observable poverty characteristics, which can be extracted from household survey data. The ESPS2 provides a wide range of indicators that help to explain poverty status in Senegal. Certain determinants of poverty, however, can be manipulated if households know that their answer could render them eligible for social assistance, for instance, and others are difficult to observe or verify in the field. Some characteristics, such as size and composition of the household, are more easily verifiable.

This case study looks at two PMT simulations for targeting of the Senegalese safety net programs. The PMTs are evaluated based on their predictive power in identifying poor households. Thus the implicit benchmark is perfect targeting based on current levels of household welfare as observed in the household survey. In other words, predicted household welfare from the PMT model is used to select households for targeting and to estimate inclusion and exclusion errors for the PMT as a targeting tool in Senegal.

PMT Simulation 1

Echevin (2012) provides a *simple PMT simulation*. As described above, the observable household characteristics are chosen to derive the PMT formula through ordinary least squares regression analysis. These characteristics are the ones that can identify the poor and exclude the nonpoor most accurately. Table 9.8 illustrates the coefficients of these characteristics as well as the power of each variable to explain adult-adjusted per capita expenditure (indicated by the R^2).[2] The contribution of each variable in explaining per capita expenditures is ranked from the largest to the smallest contributor. In both urban and rural Senegalese households, having a household of 14 members or more is the biggest determinant of expenditure levels and thereby poverty.

Once the observable characteristics are chosen, a PMT instrument can be created and used by a variety of safety net programs. The coefficients of these characteristics represent weightings associated with levels of household well-being (table 9.8). By adding up the coefficients of these characteristics, we can derive a composite score of household well-being. For instance, in rural areas, a household with 14 members who get their water from a well and only have kerosene lamps would score −0.697. An identical household with access to electricity would score −0.548. In this manner, without directly measuring household consumption or even poverty level, it is possible to classify households as beneficiaries or nonbeneficiaries of a social assistance program according to their composite score.

Given that the PMT method is based on observable household characteristics, it can be adjusted in times of shock. Indeed, the impact of shocks modifies the effect of each observable characteristic of the household. PMT targeting could thus reflect events that affect household well-being.

Table 9.8 Principal Determinants of Poverty Based on Observable Household Characteristics for Rural Areas of Senegal

Characteristic	Coefficient	P-value	Cumulative R^2	Contribution to R^2
14 members or more	−0.319	0.000	0.075	0.075
Rudimentary roof	−0.213	0.000	0.131	0.057
Water from a well	−0.229	0.000	0.172	0.041
Lighting with kerosene lamps	−0.149	0.000	0.181	0.009
Children (0–5 years old) in the household	−0.147	0.000	0.187	0.006
Rudimentary lighting	−0.145	0.000	0.192	0.005
Rudimentary kitchen or cooking	−0.299	0.000	0.196	0.004
Children (6–14) in the household	−0.149	0.000	0.199	0.003
Latrines	−0.073	0.000	0.201	0.002
Piped water	−0.057	0.000	0.201	0.001
Disability	−0.051	0.002	0.202	0.000

Source: Echevin 2012.

PMT Simulation 2

A recent, more *complete PMT formula* features an improved set of variables associated with the adult-adjusted per capita expenditures of Senegalese households. This formula (illustrated in table 9A.1 in the annex to this chapter) was designed with the purpose of further reducing the existing targeting errors. These targeting errors are computed using the poorest 20 percent of households, as well as the 20 percent lowest-PMT-scoring households. The new formula was generated separately for Dakar, other urban areas, and rural areas, so as to account for the unique determinants of well-being in all three regions. As shown in the table, this formula uses a wide range of indicators to identify poor households, reflecting the multidimensional aspect of poverty: socioeconomic characteristics of the household head and members, composition of the household, characteristics of the dwelling, geographic location, and productive and nonproductive assets. The variables used depend on the formula area (Dakar, other urban, or rural): for instance, additional employment characteristics are used for Dakar and other urban areas, but agricultural production and assets are not used for Dakar.

Table 9A.1 indicates that, holding everything else equal, larger households tend to have lower scores for well-being, which is commonly found in PMT formulas. Regarding education, the divide is between household heads with or without higher education, with negative weights associated with all other categories. Indicators of housing quality (access to electricity, formal toilets, access to tap water, cement floor) are also associated with higher scores. Livestock is used to discriminate between households—in rural areas and in urban areas other than Dakar—and is associated with positive weights.

Some belongings are particularly useful for identifying wealthier households: the coefficients associated with owning a car, a truck, and a tractor, for instance, weight heavily in the formula. The region in which the household lives is also an important element of the PMT formula and is associated with some of the highest coefficients. In contrast, only a few services located within 1 kilometer of the house were included in the formula (and only in urban areas other than Dakar), indicating a low potential for nearby services to discriminate poor and nonpoor households in Senegal based on the ESPS2 data set.

Performance of Targeting Mechanisms (Two Simulations)

The simple PMT simulation compared with both actual household welfare and current program eligibility criteria reveals that there is potential to improve targeting outcomes by applying different targeting scenarios to existing safety net programs in Senegal. The simulation done by Echevin (2012) uses nine safety net programs with different targeting scenarios. The base scenario uses the current categorical targeting based on the general characteristics of benefi-ciaries used in Senegal. The second scenario estimates targeting outcomes using the PMT, and the third simulation uses geographic targeting to concentrate resources in the poorest areas in the regions where programs operate, differenti-ated between urban and rural.

The worst targeting outcomes in terms of inclusion errors occur as a result of categorical targeting. Geographic targeting improves outcomes over the base case in all of the simulations. Using a PMT method, however, further improves targeting outcomes in almost all cases. Thus the share of benefits allocated to the poor when using the PMT method is much higher than when using geo-graphic targeting alone. Regarding undercoverage as well, categorical targeting has the worst outcomes and PMT targeting almost always outperforms geo-graphic targeting.

The targeting performance of the complex PMT formula was assessed by looking at the errors of exclusion and inclusion (table 9A.1). Because of the high incidence of poverty in Senegal, the more complete PMT formula was designed with the purpose of limiting the exclusion of poor households from safety net programs as well as the inclusion of nonpoor households in the same programs. The eligibility threshold used in the formula is the lowest quintile of the PMT scores, which was compared to the poorest quintile of the current household welfare distribution to compute targeting errors in the three areas (Dakar, other urban, and rural). The results indicate that errors of exclusion range from 19.7 percent in urban areas (excluding Dakar) to 33.7 percent in rural areas, and errors of inclusion are 35.6 and 44.5 percent, respectively (table 9.9). These lev-els of errors are common for this level of coverage (20 percent of the population) and are relatively low for Dakar and other urban areas where poor households constitute a more homogeneous group in terms of PMT characteristics. Nevertheless, the higher errors of inclusion and exclusion in rural areas—where poverty may be more diverse and harder to identify effectively—signal the need for further information to improve targeting outcomes. Moreover, the increased R^2 compared to the simple PMT formula suggests that, by including additional variables—as in the second formula—we are able to predict consumption more accurately. This makes poor households easier to identify, at the cost, however, of a longer survey with a much larger number of variables.

Table 9.9 Targeting Performance of PMT Formulas in Senegal
% of poor

Type of error	Urban areas (excluding Dakar)	Dakar	Rural areas
Inclusion	35.6	36.3	44.5
Exclusion	19.7	25.9	33.7

Conclusions

Senegal will continue to face both internal and external shocks. The scope, coverage, and effectiveness of the safety net programs (or system) will determine the resulting impact on poor and vulnerable households.

Use of the PMT mechanism can be unified across programs, with specific filters for each program. The PMT mechanism is useful for all poverty-oriented programs that target at the household level. A unified mechanism with specific filters for each program (or a specific target group) is useful across the range of targeted programs in education, health, agriculture, and other key sectors.

The government of Senegal uses a combination of targeting methods for the Programme National de Bourse de Securité Familiale (PNBSF), which aims to provide cash transfers to 250,000 Senegalese households until 2017. This program, which is considered the backbone of the future national social protection system, relies on the development of a registry of potential beneficiaries and the harmonization of targeting methods. As of today, the program combines geographic, community-based, and PMT targeting to select beneficiaries. However, to harmonize the targeting methods of other programs around the PNBSF, the government could consider the following next steps:

- Review the process of implementing the targeting methods based on more recent poverty maps, if available, and of exploring new household surveys and census

- Adapt the targeting formula to specific contexts, like natural disasters, where the impacts of short-term shocks would be incorporated, if needed, by combining geographic targeting on poverty with some shock-related indicators obtained from a shock warning system

- Develop an operational manual to transfer capacities to other institutional actors

- Implement a pilot to test the actual performance of the PMT targeting tool

- Evaluate the efficacy of targeting methods and processes for the first set of households identified for the program

- Discuss findings and results with other international actors and share documents and data to transfer capacities to other institutional actors.

A common targeting tool like the one generated for the PNBSF should be supported by other key elements of a common targeting system. The PMT data requirement and the development of a social registry of potential beneficiaries are based on a common questionnaire that can then be complemented with additional program-specific information, if needed. In addition, an institutional framework that places one operational agency in charge of the targeting process should support the national system. This agency, the Délégation Général de la Protection Social et à la Solidarité, should be responsible for coordinating implementation of the system across the range of agencies. A clear institutional framework would improve the management of the process and provide greater stability in the social protection system in Senegal.

In summary, this chapter has found that errors of inclusion and exclusion are inherent in the PMT method but can be reduced by combining PMT (for targeting chronically poor households) with geographic targeting (that is, for identifying areas affected by the shocks). Furthermore, the establishment of a transparent selection process and verification mechanisms (including community-based mechanisms) would help to reduce the risk that beneficiaries would supply erroneous information in an attempt to claim program eligibility and therefore help to minimize inclusion and exclusion errors.

Annex 9A Detailed Results

Table 9A.1 PMT Formulas for Dakar, Other Urban Areas, and Rural Areas, Senegal

		Weight	
Variable	Urban (other)	Dakar	Rural
Gender of household head			
Female	88.9		28.9
Religion of household head			
Not Muslim			−203.0
Age of household head			
34 years old or less	−9.6		9.7
50 years old or more	4.9		12.4
Education of household head			
No education	−60.9		−263.0
Primary school	−38.9		−248.0
Secondary school 1	−30.0		−225.0
Secondary school 2	−54.6		−311.0
Marital status of household head			
Monogamist	42.2		64.4
Widowed or divorced	−12.5		−5.9
Polygamist	83.7		101.0

(continued next page)

Table 9A.1 (continued)

Variable	Urban (other)	Weight	
		Dakar	Rural
Presence of a disabled household member			
Disabled household member			−51.2
Health insurance			
Household head has a health insurance	30.0		
Agriculture			
The household has agricultural production	−337.0	51.9	
Household head practices agriculture			−39.4
Employment sector of household head			
Agriculture		0.0	−85.8
Fishing or forestry		−372.0	58.2
Industry		−167.0	−30.8
Trade		−170.0	15.6
Services		−179.0	−13.2
Socioeconomic position of household head			
Manager	0.0	0.0	
Qualified worker	−58.6	87.3	
Semiqualified worker	−44.1	0	
Unskilled worker	−82.3	0	
Independent	−106.0	0	
Family help or trainee	−56.4	0	
Other	−122.0	−144.0	
Inactivity		−119.0	−66.8
Independent member			
One member of the household (at least) is an independent worker	46.5		
Wage earner of household head			
Permanent wage earner	106.0	76.6	
Temporary wage earner	−22.3	139.0	
Employment sector of household head			
Public sector	27.6	33.5	−79.3
Private sector (large firm)	136.0	102.0	154.0
Microenterprise	121.0	80.1	5.79
Other household	30.8	−97.3	25.3

(continued next page)

Table 9A.1 (continued)

Variable	Urban (other)	Weight Dakar	Weight Rural
Household size			
Number of people in the household	−125.0	−115.0	
Number of people in the household squared	1.92	2.56	
1 person			694.0
2–3 people			235.0
4–5 people			95.4
7–9 people			−137.0
10 people or more			−207.0
Household composition (number of members)			
5 years old or less	52.1		−28.5
6 to 14 years old	43.5		−18.4
15 to 24 years old	−6.2		−63.3
25 to 64 years old	0.0		−57.1
65 years old or more	−22.7		−56.8
Student			
Household head is enrolled in school		481.0	139.0
Rooms in house			
Two rooms	−27.5	−113.0	116.0
Three rooms	−71.5	−267.0	60.5
Four rooms	−67.4	−287.0	109.0
Five rooms	−67.1	−375.0	86.5
Six rooms	−52.3	−552.0	120.0
Seven rooms or more	−12.4	−625.0	180.0
Number of rooms			
Number of rooms in the house		77.9	
Household members per room			
Number of household members per number of rooms	−38.2	−57.0	
Source of lighting			
Electricity	87.8	72.7	47.2
Lamp (gas, oil)	15.8	0.0	19.9
Other	0.0	0.0	0.0
Bathroom facility			
Formal toilet (with flush)	140.0		71.2
Latrines	80.4		34.4

(continued next page)

Table 9A.1 (continued)

Variable	Urban (other)	Weight Dakar	Weight Rural
Source of drinking water			
Tap	128.0	316.0	39.3
Well	32.6	0.0	−22.8
Drilling	57.3	0.0	162.0
Other	113.0	0.0	0.0
River	119.0	0.0	184.0
Source of energy for cooking			
Electricity or oil	0.0	0.0	0.0
Coal	42.6	−106.0	58.2
Wood	16.8	−199.0	14.7
Natural gas	86.8	−146.0	226.0
Other (garbage, no cooking)	−5.5	−182.0	−123.0
Roof material			
Solid (cement, zinc)			35.4
Floor material			
Solid (cement, tiles)		667.0	54.8
Wall material			
Solid (cement bricks)	31.5		
Garbage service			
Garbage taken away by a garbage service	42.3	54.6	
Internet			
The household has Internet access	16.4		
Type of residence			
Formal residence		52.4	
Kitchen			
Separate room for the kitchen	92.0	88.3	
Type of dwelling			
House with several floors or apartment in a building	0.0	0.0	
Low house	−90.0	−38.8	
Hut or other	−94.4	−107.0	

(continued next page)

Table 9A.1 (continued)

Variable	Urban (other)	Weight Dakar	Weight Rural
Household ownership of this type of animal (several possible)			
Cow(s)			98.9
Goat(s)			14.1
Sheep(s)			31.1
Pig(s)			35.6
Horse(s)			51.3
Poultry			−22.8
Number of animals owned (several possible)			
Cows	4.2		
Goat(s)	1.5		
Sheep(s)	0.0		
Pig(s)	1.4		
Horse(s)	50.4		
Poultry birds	0.5		
Household owns donkey(s)	12.5		
Land			
Household owns agricultural land	312.0		
Cash crops			
Household grows cash crops	128.0		
Fertilizer			
Household uses fertilizer	13.0		
Hired labor			
Household hires labor	−41.8		
Services within 1 kilometer (several possible)			
Primary school	28.4		
Telecenter	14.3		
Internet café	32.2		
Police station	30.6		
Ziguinchor	−346.0		−605.0
Diourbel	0.0		−399.0
Saint-Louis	−101.0		−185.0
Tambacounda	−191.0		−305.0
Kaolack	142.0		−508.0

(continued next page)

Table 9A.1 (continued)

Variable	Urban (other)	Weight Dakar	Rural
Thiès	−121.0		−206.0
Louga	−27.2		−243.0
Fatick	−304.0		−438.0
Kolda	−230.0		−439.0
Matam	−50.9		−131.0
Kaffrine	−160.0		−232.0
Kédougou	−103.0		−646.0
Sédhiou	−101.0		−275.0
Household ownership of this type of asset			
Radio	4.3	77.7	41.7
Television	23.1	136.0	22.3
Cable or private network television			85.2
Bicycle			40.4
Motorcycle	47.0		166.0
Cart	−35.4		10.3
Air conditioner	21.0		54.8
Fan	89.4	80.6	85.7
"*Eponge*" mattress	35.1		51.5
"Spring" mattress	38.7	115.0	
Table	17.3		35.6
Chair		63.1	36.1
Bed	97.7		
Carpet		57.3	20.2
Rug			52.1
Clock or alarm clock	9.3	49.1	12.0
Phone (landline)	77.3	68.0	
Phone (mobile)	93.5		
Phone (landline or mobile)			100.0
Computer	71.8	48.1	55.3
Multimedia player	27.7		
Satellite dish	25.8	62.5	76.5
"*Onduleur*"	25.0		
Flatiron	70.5	196.0	96.6
Modern stove	42.9	44.1	
"*Malgache*" oven	18.2	53.8	84.9
Improved oven	45.1		137.0

(continued next page)

Table 9A.1 (continued)

Variable	Urban (other)	Weight Dakar	Rural
Sewing machine	26.0		
Water heater			174.0
Food processor, mixer			441.0
Fridge or freezer	96.2	47.2	30.0
Natural gas bottle	61.2	21.1	76.1
Electric generator	34.1		
Flashlight	28.8		36.5
Solar panel	202.0		
Car	191.0	112.0	221.0
Truck	239.0	108.0	878.0
Tractor	304.0		
Pirogue	147.0		131.0
Wardrobe	34.4	8.99	2.65
Library	43.4	16.7	17.8
Trunk	13.8		
Armchair			96.2
Plow	20.2		
Pilling machine ("*decortiqueuse*")	63.8		
Net "*a tourner*"	13.7		28.7
Wheelbarrow	24.2		93.8
Seed drill	38.2		
Spray equipment	27.7		66.9
Water barrel	17.3		46.3
Water reservoir			150.0
Hoe ax	−23.5		
Other equipment	53.9	77.1	43.2
Living room	77.1	69.2	42.2
Sleeping room	67.6	125.0	
Constant	12,880	12,730	12,720
Number of observations	2,379	508	2,740
R^2	0.739	0.786	0.653
Errors (%)			
Exclusion	19.7	25.9	33.7
Inclusion	35.6	36.3	44.5

Source: Calculations based on ESPS2 data set.
Note: PMT weights for Dakar, other urban areas, and rural areas. Inclusion and exclusion errors are based on the poorest 20 percent of the population (in each area) and lowest 20 percent of PMT scores (that is, PMT-eligible households). Errors are calculated at the individual levels using ESPS2 weight coefficients.

Notes

1. The agricultural security funds are composed of three funds. (a) The *Fonds de Bonification* was created to improve the access of rural producers to credit by reducing financing charges. It finances the difference between the interest charged by commercial banks and the government-capped interest rate for loans to farmers (7.5 percent). The government pays the spread to the national agricultural bank, the Caisse Nationale du Crédit Agricole du Senegal (CNCAS), which has been operating since 1984 and is the largest source of rural finance. (b) The *Fonds de Garantie* reimburses delinquent loans to the CNCAS up to 75 percent for agriculture and 50 percent for livestock. (c) The *Fonds de Calamité* helps rural producers to cope with natural disasters, allowing them to repay loans and continue their agricultural activities, either by restoring their creditworthiness with the CNCAS or by financing supplies necessary to respond to a shock.
2. Children between 0 and 14 years of age are given a weight of 0.5, and all other household members are given a weight of 1.

References

Coady, David, Margaret Grosh, and John Hoddinott. 2004. *Targeting of Transfers in Developing Countries: Review of Lessons and Experience*. Washington, DC: World Bank.

Diop, M. 2012. "Profile of Social Protection in Senegal: Analysis of the ESPS 2011." World Bank, Washington, DC.

Echevin, Damien. 2012. "Issues and Options in Targeting and Social Transfers in Senegal." Social Safety Net Assessment Background Paper, World Bank, Washington, DC.

Grosh, Margaret, Carlo del Ninno, Emile Tesliuc, and Azedene Ouerghi. 2008. *For Protection and Promotion: The Design and Implementation of Effective Safety Nets*. Washington, DC: World Bank.

IMF (International Monetary Fund). 2005. "Senegal: Selected Issues and Statistical Appendix." Country Report 05/155, IMF, Washington, DC.

———. 2008. *World Economic Outlook 2008: Financial Stress, Downturns, and Recoveries*. Washington, DC: IMF.

Ivanic, Maros, and Will Martin. 2008. *Implications of Higher Global Food Prices for Poverty in Low-Income Countries*. Washington, DC: World Bank.

Measure DHS. 2011. *Senegal Demographic Health Survey/Multiple Indicator Cluster Survey 2010–2011*. Calverton.

Monchuk, Victoria. 2013. *Reducing Poverty and Investing in People: The New Role of Safety Nets in Africa*. Directions in Development. Washington, DC: World Bank.

U.S. Mission to Senegal. 2009. "Senegal: Country Commercial Guide 2009." U.S. Mission to Senegal, Dakar.

World Bank. 2009. "Senegal: Rapid Response Child-Focused Social Cash Transfer and Nutrition Security Project." Report 47740-SN, World Bank, Human Development II, Africa Region, Country Department AFCFl.

———. 2013. "Senegal SP" Safety Net Assessment." Report ACS7005, World Bank, Social Protection and Labor, Africa Region, Washington, DC.

Chapter **10**

Conclusion: Further Investments for Targeting Safety Net Programs

Carlo del Ninno and Bradford Mills

This section distills lessons from the seven case studies and generates guidelines for the targeting of safety net programs in Sub-Saharan Africa. It is possible to improve program targeting of the chronic poor and the vulnerable by adopting appropriate methods and procedures. However, the choice of appropriate targeting methods is contingent on the availability of data and the capacity to implement the methods. Bearing this in mind, we identify critical areas for investments in methods, procedures, and data to facilitate improvements in program targeting.

As emphasized in this publication, safety net programs play a dual role: they enhance the well-being of currently poor households whether or not hit by a shock, and they protect the well-being of households vulnerable to poverty. International literature shows that most successful safety net programs are typically part of long-term interventions that provide consistent assistance to the poorest and that can be scaled up to help vulnerable households respond to shocks. Examples of long-term programs that provide consistent support to chronically poor households include Mexico's Oportunidades, Brazil's Bolsa Familia, and Ethiopia's Productive Safety Net Program. Evidence suggests that long-term programs also can be critically important in protecting households that are vulnerable to poverty in times of crises (see responses to the food, fuel, and financial crisis of 2008 in Brazil, Kyrgyz Republic, and Mexico). Programs can respond to shocks in two ways: by providing additional benefits to current participants where existing coverage is widespread (as in Brazil; Ferreira et al. 2011; World Bank 2013b) and by expanding program coverage to include nonparticipant households exposed to crises (as in Bangladesh on several occasions; Pelham, Clay, and Braunholz 2011; World Bank 2013b).

In Sub-Saharan Africa, safety net programs rarely have been designed as long-term interventions and, as such, have focused on addressing short-term shocks with ad hoc emergency programs that are mostly financed and sometimes implemented by donors (World Bank 2013a).

In the African context, it is also claimed that the first line of defense against shocks for poor families comes from informal social assistance mechanisms whose outreach and strength vary by country and location. A parallel research project has assessed whether such informal arrangements are effective in protecting the vulnerable; the result of a literature review and detailed country studies in Côte d'Ivoire, Rwanda, and Zimbabwe show that informal safety nets do safeguard households but cannot be a substitute for formal programs (Tamiru 2013; World Bank 2012). For one thing, informal forms of assistance often break down following a covariate shock when entire communities are affected adversely, drying up resources available to communities in critical times. For another, informal forms of assistance often fail to meet the needs of socially excluded members of society as well as of some very poor households that are unable to contribute to the common pool of community resources that form the basis of informal support. Therefore, notwithstanding the pervasive prevalence and importance of informal forms of support, formal social assistance programs are needed to fill the gaps in endogenous, community-driven informal mechanisms of support.

Of particular note in Sub-Saharan Africa is the high ratio of need for safety net assistance to available resources. Given resource constraints, programs are often left to target the poorest 20 percent of the population when around 50 percent of the population is officially poor. The need for formal programs and the imbalance between needs and available resources highlight the critical role of targeting programs and resources to the poorest and most vulnerable households. Furthermore, it is important to differentiate between two types of poor households when making resource allocation decisions: (a) households that are chronically poor and need longer-term support to smooth consumption, improve human capital, and make investment decisions that promote their own economic situation and (b) households that need short-term support during periods of shocks or crises. A prerequisite for implementing differential programs targeting these two groups is the ability to identify households needing long-term as opposed to short-term support. Differentiating households with long- and short-term needs remains a crucial challenge in Sub-Saharan Africa, especially when there is considerable movement between the two groups.

Challenges in identifying and targeting the most needy households with different long- and short-term needs fall into three broad areas: targeting methods, implementation processes, and information. As indicated in the literature and the case studies, investments are needed in all three areas. The task can seem overwhelming, but strengthening the safety net through improved program targeting is an investment decision. Like any investment decision, the relevant question is where—given the current state of the system—investments will have the greatest impact at the margin. For each country, methods, process, and information constraints need to be identified and addressed. The magnitude of these constraints also depends on the timeline for implementing a program and the analytical capacity within the country.

The political feasibility and administrative constraints associated with targeting are not a major focus of this book. However, they do play an important role in determining appropriate investments. Administrative constraints may blunt the efficiency of well-designed targeting methods in various ways. Most notably, the capacity to collect and use accurate household data may be hindered and the capacity to deliver assistance to accurately targeted households may be compromised. Similarly, control of social assistance resources can be an important source of political power. Some groups may have a vested interest in undermining efforts to establish quantitative and transparent methods of targeting, as they lose the political power associated with control of social assistance. Politically powerful stakeholders may need to be compensated in other ways when implementing rigorous targeting methods, thus introducing observed and unobserved leakages.

Administrative procedures for removing beneficiaries when situations change also need to be explored when designing program targeting. Crucial questions need to be addressed, such as whether program beneficiaries will need to reapply periodically and be subject to the same targeting procedures as new applicants or whether a validation review of new applicants will be conducted separately. The role of community verification in decisions to remove beneficiaries also needs to be determined. Again, vested political interests are likely to develop that can constrain the use of quantitative and transparent methods. Further lessons on the political feasibility of program targeting and the administrative constraints on program implementation need to be drawn as different targeting methods are employed in Sub-Saharan Africa.

In this concluding section of the book, we summarize the evidence from the country studies and propose some guidance on key investments for countries seeking to improve their safety nets. The following questions are addressed: Will clear and consistent concepts of poverty and vulnerability help to harmonize safety net interventions? Are proxy means test (PMT) models that are based on reliable poverty and vulnerability information a cost-effective investment to reduce exclusion and inclusion errors of the safety net program? Are efforts to increase community involvement in targeting a sound investment? Will the establishment of a unique registry reduce program duplication? Will a formal structured beneficiary identification process reduce errors and program duplication? Should a country invest in program-specific food security questionnaires to identify households that are poor due to their exposure to short-term shocks?

Key Lessons

Table 10.1 summarizes key findings and lessons learned from the case studies in this book. The case studies all document the strong need for safety nets in Sub-Saharan Africa. Chronic poverty is identified as a key concern in most countries. This highlights the need for methods, like PMTs, that specifically identify the chronic poor. However, all countries but Ghana also highlight shocks as an important household risk to be addressed by safety nets. Cameroon, Kenya, Malawi, and Mozambique place particular emphasis on climatic shocks in rural areas, while several countries are particularly concerned about health shocks in the urban context. The emphasis placed in the case studies on vulnerability to shocks highlights the need for complementary methods to address short-term needs as well as chronic long-term poverty.

All countries also have some existing safety net programs in place. Yet these programs are fragmented (Ghana, Kenya, Malawi, Mozambique), suffer from poorly defined, unclear, or overlapping targeting criteria (Cameroon, Ghana, Kenya, Senegal), and have limited coverage (Cameroon, Kenya, Mozambique, Niger, Senegal). Program constraints highlight the need for clear and objective targeting criteria that can be applied transparently to identify and service those households most in need.

In terms of methods, an important lesson that arises is that, although exclusion and inclusion errors are not strictly compatible across case studies, PMTs generally perform well in Sub-Saharan African countries. All case studies conducted ex ante simulations of PMT targeting performance and calculated errors of exclusion and inclusion (although the results are not presented for Mozambique). The incidence of exclusion errors ranges from 14 percent in Niger and 15 percent in urban Cameroon to 40 and 43 percent in Ghana and Kenya, respectively. Similarly, the incidence of inclusion errors ranges from 12 percent in Niger to 52 percent in Malawi. However, the case studies also suggest that PMTs are not a cure-all for improved targeting in Sub-Saharan Africa. Rather, they are one of an array of possible complementary investments.

The magnitude of exclusion and inclusion errors from PMTs varies for several reasons, including the degree of heterogeneity among both the general population and the poor, the level of errors in the measurement of the well-being indicator and covariates, and the relative size of the intended beneficiary population. Several issues associated with variations in PMT performance need further exploration. First, ex ante simulations are in most case studies based on performance within the same data set from which the PMT was generated. Thus the error estimates may be optimistic relative to actual performance in field-level project targeting. The Cameroonian case study addresses this concern by estimating the PMT with a random draw of two-thirds of the national survey

Table 10.1 Summary of Findings and Key Lessons in Select Countries in Sub-Saharan Africa

Country	Risks, poverty, vulnerability	Programs currently in place	Long-term targeting	Short-term targeting	Key lessons
Cameroon	Climatic shocks are prevalent. The chronic poor are concentrated in northern regions.	Regressive universal subsidies; limited targeted programs. Targeted pilots are being implemented.	Geographic, community-based targeting, and PMT. Combining geographic and PMT generates inclusion and exclusion errors under 25%. Quantile regressions limit errors.	Measures impacts of drought with climate data and finds a significant negative impact (9%) on consumption.	Geographic targeting combined with PMT can effectively target the chronic poor. It is important to set up ex post evaluation of cash transfers.
Ghana	Chronic poverty is prevalent.	Multiple programs looking for a common targeting mechanism. The main cash transfer program is piloting a revised PMT.	Revised PMT improves overall targeting performance and performs best in communities with high poverty rates. PMT reduces inclusion errors, but increases exclusion errors when combined with CBT.		CBT can generate good targeting performance, but performance varies widely across communities. PMT performance is more stable and best in high-poverty communities. In all cases, exclusion errors are high due to low coverage of the program.
Kenya	Exposure to shocks is prevalent, particularly among poor households. Rural households are exposed to agroclimatic shocks. Urban households are exposed to employment and security shocks.	Uncoordinated interventions and repeated emergency efforts. The Orphans and Vulnerable Children Program is the largest program. Original targeting with CBT and poverty scorecard is little better than random selection.	Revised PMT alone produces acceptable exclusion (43%) and inclusion (41%) errors.	PMT is improved by adjusting cutoff point in drought areas (geographic targeting) by an estimated 19% reduction in consumption. Performance is improved further by including a food security indicator in drought areas.	The use of geographic targeting of crisis areas and the use of food security indicators can improve targeting in areas exposed to covariate shocks.

(continued next page)

Table 10.1 (continued)

Country	Risks, poverty, vulnerability	Programs currently in place	Long-term targeting	Short-term targeting	Key lessons
Malawi	Exposure to shocks is prevalent, particularly shocks to crop production and food prices. Health-related shocks are also prevalent.	System is fragmented. Social assistance programs cover half the population, but are not responsive to short-term needs.	Proposed PMT method works well, particularly for the extreme poor. PMT performance improves dramatically when combined with geographic targeting to the 6 poorest districts.	Shocks do not have a negative correlation with consumption, but PMT performance improves if conditional on exposure to shocks.	Geographic targeting can dramatically improve PMT performance.
Mozambique	Chronic poverty is widespread, with 50% of households identified as chronically poor. Exposure to climatic shocks is prevalent.	System is fragmented. Only a small share of eligible households receives benefits.		Climatic shocks have a major impact. Floods and cyclones reduce expenditures 32%, droughts and agricultural pests reduce expenditures 17%. Annual exposure to these shocks generates a 4.6% transient poverty rate.	Household budget survey information on shocks and geo-referenced climatic data can be used to target the transient poor.
Niger	More than 20% of population is severely chronically food insecure. Household exposure to shocks is widespread, especially over past 10 years.	Pilot cash transfer safety net was completed in 2012, and new program is being rolled out in several food-insecure regions.	Geographic targeting combined with PMT and community validation generates low exclusion (14%) and inclusion (12%) errors.	Little correlation is found between PMT measure and most common measures of food security (that may be more sensitive to short-term hardship). Strongest correlation for short-term PMT is with measure of household coping strategies.	Food security measures may (noisily) measure different components of food insecurity and show little correlation with chronic poverty. The evaluation of a pilot program finds positive but not statistically significant impact on consumption.
Senegal	Many individuals are poor and vulnerable. Exposure to external (food and fuel) and domestic (agricultural) shocks is widespread.	Current safety nets have limited coverage. Current targeting methods (geographic, categorical, and CBT) show poor results.	PMT coupled with geographic targeting can yield reasonable exclusion errors in coverage of bottom 20% of households.	PMT needs to be improved to be more responsive to short-term shocks.	PMT performance is adequate and can be most responsive to covariate shocks if combined with geographic targeting.

sample, while saving one-third for ex ante targeting simulations. Inclusion and exclusion errors are both relatively low in the simulations. For rural areas, both exclusion and inclusion errors are below 25 percent, while in urban areas with relatively lower rates of poverty, exclusion errors are around 15 percent and inclusion errors are around 35 percent. Thus strong PMT performance does not appear to stem from use of the same data for both PMT estimation and targeting performance simulation.

Other factors may influence PMT performance when applied outside of the survey from which the weights were generated. Relationships between variables and the indicator of well-being may change over time. For example, as technologies like cell phones diffuse throughout the population, they may become less indicative of high levels of well-being. Shifting PMT weight estimates are of particular concern if the national survey from which PMT weights are derived is not recent. Similarly, the PMT may be applied to specific regions or subsamples of the population. Ideally, the survey used to generate PMT weights would also be region or population specific; however, survey sample sizes often preclude such estimates. Two case studies use PMT results from national surveys for out-of-sample targeting. The first, Niger, does not examine the out-of-sample performance of the PMT due to limitations in the data. The second, Ghana, finds that the errors of exclusion are much larger and the errors of inclusion are lower when the PMT is applied for pilot program targeting in a specific area of the country. Further lessons need to be drawn on PMT performance in actual programs, particularly in comparison to predicted performance in ex ante evaluations.

A second concern with PMT performance is that the well-being indicator may not adequately account for differences in household size and composition. Most of the country case studies use per capita expenditures as the welfare indicator, where all household members receive equal weight. Exceptions are Cameroon and Senegal. The Senegal case study employs a weight of 1 for adults and 0.5 for children 0–14 years of age. Cameroon uses a slightly more complex adult-equivalent expenditure measure, where household members are given age-group and gender-specific weights based on recommended daily dietary allowances. In both case studies larger household size is still strongly related to lower adult-equivalent expenditures. Larger households may be poorer, but they are also likely to have economies of scale for expenditures. For example, the Ghana case study finds that PMT and community-based targeting (CBT) methods systematically target groups with different household sizes. The PMT appears biased toward large households with working-age adults, and CBT appears biased toward small households (that is, elderly households and female widows). The case study explores adjusting expenditures by an adult-equivalence scale that includes weighting adults as 1 and children 0–14 years of age as 0.5 and then raising the sum by a power of 0.8 to account for economies of scale in household size. This modified indicator decreases PMT exclusion errors for small households. More ex post evaluations of targeting performance are needed that address the issues of PMT performance in actual field programs and to determine appropriate adjustments of the indicator for economies of scale in household size.

In all of the case studies but Mozambique, programs employ community-based targeting, geographic targeting, or means tests to complement PMTs. The strategy of combining PMTs with some combination of geographic targeting, CBT, and means tests is linked to the idea of using a multidimensional approach to targeting that can potentially improve the identification and targeting of households with long-term and with short-term needs. Nevertheless, care must be taken to maintain a conceptually rigorous framework when generating and evaluating the indicators employed as part of a multidimensional approach.

In the case studies, multiple-method approaches consistently improve targeting performance. The Ghana case study provides an in-depth analysis of the role that community participation can play in improving program targeting. In a comparison of CBT and PMT procedures, the Ghana study finds that, when used alone, the CBT performs slightly worse overall in terms of errors of exclusion and inclusion than PMT. As might be expected, CBT performance also varies more across communities than PMT performance, as the results are dependent on the composition of community members and the community's perception of poverty.[1] In the Ghana case, the types of households erroneously excluded or included differ systematically under CBT and PMT procedures. In general, the CBT procedure appears to identify special cases, while the PMT favors households more aligned with the average poor household in the country. This result is expected since the PMT model is designed based on a model of characteristics of the average poor, and such special and relatively small groups can be overlooked when generating PMT weights. Thus differences in selection are not surprising or necessarily indicative of errors in the process. General CBT procedures also may be more sensitive to short-term changes in household well-being, particularly in response to idiosyncratic and covariate shocks, while a major concern with CBT methods is that family and social network ties will drive up inclusion errors. Potential benefits of CBT procedures in generating community buy-in and agreement on the fairness of beneficiary selection also should not be overlooked. Community participation in the selection of beneficiaries can be particularly important when many households lie close to the program eligibility threshold and, thus, selection outcomes generated only through PMTs can appear to be arbitrary.

However, the addition of more objective PMT procedures has the potential to provide a control on inclusion errors in CBT identification stemming from social networks. The Ghana case study suggests that the use of both CBT and PMT procedures for targeting does, indeed, reduce inclusion errors, although exclusion errors rise as small niche types of poor may be overlooked. More research is needed to understand how CBT and PMT procedures can be designed and implemented as complements. In this vein, the Cameroon case study outlines plans to evaluate CBT and PMT procedures as part of the ex post evaluation of a pilot cash transfer program in a village-randomized design experiment. The results of this targeting experiment should provide further guidance on the efficacy of complementary investments in CBT and data-driven targeting procedures.

In some countries, like Cameroon and Kenya, chronic poverty has a very distinct geographic concentration, making geography an essential component of any targeting effort. Poverty maps are a good source of information for identifying concentrations of the chronic poor, and vulnerability maps can also be employed, like those produced by the Vulnerability Assessment and Mapping of the World Food Program. In many cases, poverty maps can be generated using the same household surveys that are used to generate PMTs.

The results of targeting short-term needs associated with vulnerability to shocks are far more variable across case studies. Shocks do appear to influence observed household expenditures. Four countries have attempted to measure the impact of shocks empirically, and three (Cameroon, Kenya, and Mozambique) have found significant impacts. Data are an important constraint, as four countries (Cameroon, Ghana, Niger, and Senegal) have no household data on exposure to shocks. However, the Cameroon and Mozambique case studies show that, for rainfall-related shocks, data constraints can be overcome partially by making use of geo-referenced rainfall data that are freely available on the Internet to all countries.

While PMTs can be deployed effectively for targeting longer-term assistance to the chronic poor, their efficacy remains an open issue with respect to the identification of beneficiaries for short-term targeting. In the book, methods for augmenting PMT measures with indicators of short-term needs are generically referred to as PMTplus. A key requirement for developing PMTplus methods for short-term targeting is the ability to capture recent changes in household economic well-being in response to negative economic events or "shocks." The case studies explore a variety of methods for effective PMTplus targeting. The Mozambique case study provides a fully specified treatment effects model to estimate the impact of potentially endogenous shocks on household expenditures; with a significant 32 percent reduction in expenditures found for exposure to floods and 17 percent reduction in expenditures found for exposure to droughts and agricultural pests. The impact of these shocks alone generates significant levels of transient poverty in Mozambique, accounting for roughly a 5 percent increase in the rate of total poverty. Weights associated with these shocks can be incorporated into the PMT and used to identify households that are expected to be poor after exposure to a particular shock.

This information can facilitate rapid assistance programs targeting households with short-term needs. However, the method has relatively high data and analytical requirements for estimating the shock weights. Current information constraints on household exposure to shocks suggest that most countries are not ready to make these quantitative investments in order to identify the impacts of shocks.

Alternative, and much simpler, econometric specifications for estimating the impact of shocks that do not rely on household data are also presented in the case studies. In Cameroon and in an alternative model specification for Mozambique, publicly available rainfall data are incorporated directly into the PMT in ordinary least squares (OLS) equations, and significant negative impacts of drought on household well-being are found. Parameter estimates from models incorporating information on regional conditions into specifications can be incorporated into PMTs as part of geographic targeting mechanisms that identify areas experiencing adverse climatic conditions and then adjust PMT scores of households within those regions. Similarly, in Malawi, ex ante targeting simulations are conducted conditional on exposure to shocks, and in most cases PMT performance is found to improve. Nevertheless, rainfall data can only indicate regional exposure to climatic shocks like floods and droughts. Individual household exposure is likely to vary even within areas with widespread regional impacts (del Ninno et al. 2001). Thus climatic data may result in underestimation of the impact of flooding and droughts. The results for Kenya, Mozambique, and Cameroon provide some evidence that this may be the case. In studies on Kenya and Mozambique incorporating information on individual household exposure, droughts are estimated to result in 19 and 17 percent reductions in household expenditures, respectively. In Cameroon, where only regional climatic data are available, droughts are estimated to reduce expenditures 9 percent.

Kenya presents an interesting combination of PMT, geographic targeting, and means test methods for short-term targeting. First, the impact of drought is estimated (a 19 percent reduction in the expenditure measure). Then, in areas where a high proportion of households are affected by the shock, the PMT cutoff point for program eligibility is adjusted upward to reflect this impact. As shown on table 10.2, vulnerable groups A_{12} and A_{22} then become eligible as the PMT cutoff is shifted upward. However, those in group A_{11} are not actually food insecure, even though they are vulnerable, because they are not strongly affected by the shock. Their eligibility stems from an error in geographic targeting due to the fact that the households in the area that are actually affected by the shock are not observed.

In the Kenya case, this error is corrected by incorporating a new geographic targeting and a means test based on food consumption scores to identify food-insecure households below the augmented PMT eligibility

Table 10.2 Targeting Food-Secure and Food-Insecure Households Taking into Account Exposure to Shocks

		Total	After the shock	
			Not affected	Affected
Before the shock				
	Food secure	A	A21	A22
			A11	A12
Food poverty line ↑	Food insecure	B	B11	B12

Table 10.3 Targeting Food-Insecure Households with Means Test after Exposure to Shocks

			After the shock		
				Areas affected by the shock	
		Total	Areas not affected by the shock	Food secure	Food insecure
Before the shock					
	Food secure	A	A20	A21	A22
			A10	A11	A12
Food poverty line ↑	Food insecure	B	B10	B11	B12

threshold. In table 10.3, this is the group of households that are vulnerable in areas affected by the shock (below the augmented threshold) and that are food insecure (indicated as group A_{22}).

The Kenya strategy of combining a PMT with geographic targeting and a means test helps to increase coverage of current programs in the short term, while minimizing inclusion errors in the program.

Since information on exposure to some types of shocks (particularly idiosyncratic) is not available in many countries, the possibility of using different sources of information is worth exploring. For instance, community-based targeting can be used to identify households considered most severely affected by the shock within areas hit by a large covariate shock. But a word of caution is also warranted, as the number of inclusion errors may increase if households behave strategically to gain access to the program when subjective self-assessment measures are employed to identify exposure. This concern applies to most food security measures when used as short-term identification methods (food consumption scores, dietary diversity measures), as they are often rather blunt measures for targeting and prone to manipulation by households.

The Niger case study provides a comprehensive analysis of different potential measures of household food security and how they are correlated with each other and with PMT and expenditure measures. The results suggest that various food security indexes identify very different components of household food security. Further, as PMTs best measure long-term chronic poverty, correlations between food security measures and PMT measures may be weak or nonexistent even without attendant concerns about measurement errors. The finding in Niger is consistent with other studies examining the relationship between food security measures and expenditures. Countering the positive findings in Kenya are the assessments by Migotto et al. (2006) and Wiesmann et al. (2009) that subjective food security indicators are too blunt to be used for targeting economically poor households. Further research is needed on the performance of food security measures relative to actual levels of household well-being, particularly after exposure to short-term shocks.

Improvements in the design of safety net programs can only come from lessons on what works and what does not work with current interventions. In that vein, the Niger case study examines the ex post impact of a rural cash transfer program using a regression discontinuity design; the results are not statistically significant but do suggest that the program has had positive impacts. Impacts are easier to measure accurately if plans for evaluation are in place at the time of program implementation. The Cameroon study lays out the plans for a more controlled experiment to elicit program impacts across a range of expenditure, asset, and schooling indicators. The study should further our understanding of the multifaceted components of program impact. This type of ex post information on targeting performance and program impacts can help to guide further investments in safety nets.

Table 10.4 summarizes the key lessons drawn from across the country case studies. All countries have social safety nets. However, these safety nets tend to be fragmented, are designed largely as an immediate response to shocks, and have limited coverage of poor household populations. Further, targeting criteria are often unclear and inconsistent across programs. Chronic poverty is a key concern of social protection strategies across countries, and PMTs are a widely accepted and adequately performing tool for targeting the chronic poor. However, evaluation of PMT performance is limited by reliance on ex ante evaluation, often with the same data set used to estimate the PMT. Many countries also implement PMTs in combination with other targeting methods like geographic targeting or CBT. More work is needed to understand the performance of PMTs in actual programs and in combination with other methods. Short-term shocks, ranging from large covariate shocks like floods or droughts, to idiosyncratic household shocks like illness or death of earning members generate household vulnerability to poverty in most countries. Improved data

Table 10.4 Summary of Key Lessons Drawn across Country Case Studies

Focus	Key lessons
Social safety nets	All countries have safety nets.
	They are mostly for short-term responses.
	Coverage is limited.
	Targeting criteria are unclear and inconsistent.
Chronic poverty	Chronic poverty is a key concern in all countries.
	PMTs generally perform well in measuring chronic poverty.
	Estimates rely on ex ante evaluations.
	More lessons are needed from in-field performance.
	Most countries employ PMTs with other targeting methods.
	Method complementarities need to be explored.
Short-term needs	Shocks generate short-term risks of poverty in all countries.
	Shocks have a negative impact on household expenditures.
	Better data are needed on shocks and impact.
	Better short-term targeting methods are needed, as is their integration with long-term methods.

are needed on the incidence and magnitude of these shocks, as well as their impact on household expenditures or other indicators of household well-being.

The next two parts of this concluding chapter distill lessons from the case studies into (a) guidelines for improving targeting methods and procedures and (b) guidelines for making future investments in data and information for targeting.

Improving Targeting Methods and Procedures

The choice of targeting methods depends on the objective of the program and the particular circumstances and experiences of each country. This book draws mainly on three methods that can be used in combination to identify households that are either chronically poor or food insecure and households that are vulnerable to these conditions: geographic targeting, community-based targeting, and proxy means testing or means testing. Four considerations govern the choice of method. *First*, the method must meet the main objective of the targeting—that is, to provide regular protection for both those who are unable consistently to secure adequate food (chronically poor or food insecure) and those who can become poor or food insecure in the face of a shock (vulnerable). At the same time, the method must be flexible enough to be used across a safety net of harmonized interventions. In many cases, a combination of methods may be needed to achieve the best targeting results. *Second*, the method of estimating household welfare must be cost-effective. Current household welfare is almost always unknown and costly to verify. Often the most cost-effective procedure for targeting is to generate an accurate prediction of household well-being based on a proxy of household characteristics. Assistance programs also can collaborate with communities in a structured process to generate lists of households that are chronically poor or to employ community validation approaches to help to reduce inclusion or exclusion errors. *Third*, the method must allow for timely identification of potential beneficiaries. Once a shock hits, existing estimates of shock impacts or rapid data collection using means tests in affected areas can help to identify households that are in need but not eligible for assistance based on proxies designed to identify the chronic poor. However, procedures must already be in place to identify major shocks and assess their potential impact. *Fourth*, the method must be compatible with the country's analytical capacity.

With regard to implementation, the seven case studies demonstrate three common steps that are employed in the process of program targeting. The first step is to identify areas with a high concentration of chronic poor or areas in which households are affected by, or prone to, shocks. Identifying these areas allows government and nongovernment groups to focus on concentrations of the chronic poor and respond quickly to the changing needs of vulnerable households in fewer areas.

The second step is to define the role of community input. In most Sub-Saharan Africa communities, residents are, at a minimum, involved in verifying the list of beneficiaries. Increased community involvement can effectively address inherent problems of gathering unbiased information on household well-being and, thus, markedly assist in identifying the poorest and most vulnerable households. However, community members involved in CBT procedures also bring their own interests and agenda. For this reason, procedures need to be put in place to make the selection of beneficiaries objective, transparent, and consistent across areas.

The third step is to use an objective method to rank the level of welfare of potential beneficiaries. A proxy means test and a means test are often used to estimate the welfare of households. While the PMT tries to "estimate" the welfare of households, a means test uses a direct measure of household welfare (for example, declared household income or actual food consumption score). In this book, the PMT is employed in most cases, as the highly informal economy in Sub-Saharan Africa makes declared income or consumption very difficult to verify. PMTs have been developed in Latin American and Eastern European countries and have become a standard method for conducting rigorous objective targeting, because they use a small amount of data on potential beneficiaries to impute well-being from fairly widely available household budget surveys. Analytical requirements are moderate, and, as the case studies indicate, within the capacity of most countries. Targeting accuracy is, for the most part, good. Nevertheless, we do not suggest that PMTs should be the sole method employed for social assistance targeting. Rather, based on experiences with performance, PMTs should become an integral part of targeting processes that involve geographic targeting and community input through validation or active CBT. PMT methods provide a cross-community common structure that is sometimes lacking in CBT methods alone.

Often PMTs are based on OLS regression methods, but when poverty rates are relatively low (for example, in urban Cameroon), quantile regression techniques offer a relatively straight-forward alternative that can substantially improve (decrease) errors of exclusion by giving less importance to well-off households during estimation.

PMTplus is the major methodological extension explored in this book. PMTplus aims to improve the accuracy of PMT performance in predicting the relative ranking of the welfare of households when some households are exposed to short-term shocks. The "best" method for doing so remains open to debate. Household data on shocks, geo-referenced climate data, and community data can all be used to identify exposure. Measures of shock impacts come primarily from carefully constructed econometric studies, and, as the inventory of such estimates increases, it may be possible to simulate impacts quickly with benchmark estimates. However, further work is needed to generate these benchmarks.

In sum, PMT methods for targeting chronic poverty represent good investments in many situations, yet more experience is needed on how best to integrate PMTs with CBT methods and on how to incorporate exposure to short-term shocks through PMTplus methods.

Further Investments in Targeting Procedures

One of the conclusions of the book is that establishing common processes across country assistance programs can generate substantial efficiency gains. The case studies confirm that the fragmentation of assistance program efforts is a dominant feature of social assistance systems in Sub-Saharan Africa.[2] Focusing on the coordination and institutionalization of procedures and the establishment of common criteria and measures for targeting can reduce fragmentation and improve the effectiveness of targeting.

Countrywide coordination efforts should explore the use of common targeting mechanisms and the use of a unified registry of potential beneficiaries. Experiences from social assistance programs worldwide show that the development of a clear, transparent, and measurable concept of poverty for use in targeting criteria and creation of a unified registry increase the efficiency and impact of safety net programs. Brazil, Chile, Colombia, Georgia, Mexico, and Turkey provide examples of success with this strategy. Brazil and Mexico set up these types of systems in the early 2000s and have been running programs with a well-established system since then. A universal registry can still be set up without the need to use common targeting methods across programs, but care needs to be taken to ensure that information collected in the registry meets the targeting needs of individual programs. For example, programs addressing chronic poverty will likely have different targeting criteria than programs responding to short-term crises.

Among the country case studies, Kenya and Ghana have identified the need for a unified registry of potential social assistance participants. As mentioned, a registry facilitates the coordination of benefits across households and shares the costs of data collection across programs. Sub-Saharan African countries should strongly consider developing long-term plans to generate targeting tools that draw on information from a large database of potential applicants contained in a functional registry. Households in the registry can be ranked from the poorest to the least poor when crises hit, and programs can be scaled up rapidly to protect households at the bottom end of the ranking that are most likely to fall into poverty. A registry clearly represents a major investment in uniform procedures and coordination of programs. Thus a major question in determining the efficacy of investments in a registry database is whether the individual programs in the social assistance system have the capacity and commitment to operate in a coordinated fashion and make use of the registry. Presently, most of the existing interventions in Sub-Saharan African countries are fragmented and often try to identify the same population using different methods. Thus investments in the coordination of safety net programs must be made jointly with investments in a unified registry.

As noted repeatedly, further efforts must also be made to document what works and what does not work in the field with regard to both program targeting and program implementation. A registry combined with PMT-based targeting can help to support this type of program history by formally documenting the rationale and procedures associated with the choice of program beneficiaries. Transparent and rationalized decisions also will help to generate continued government and donor support.

Further Investments in Information

Information constraints focus on the information needed to establish reliable estimates of household well-being and identify the chronic and temporary poor in a cost-effective manner. Data for poverty and vulnerability analyses are essential for program targeting, particularly data on indicators of household well-being. Again, investments in information must be viewed through the lens of trade-offs between accuracy and cost-effectiveness. As mentioned, communities can serve as a valuable source of information through CBT procedures. But other investments in quantitative data can be made to improve targeting. Investments can be divided into those that support methods to identify the chronic poor and those that support methods to identify households vulnerable to poverty and food insecurity.

One of the most positive findings to arise from the case studies is that a wealth of national household budget surveys can be used to calibrate proxy means tests. All case study countries have access to a national household budget survey for this purpose. However, the timing, quality, and variables available in the surveys vary widely. Investments in national household budget surveys solely for the purposes of targeting may not be justified. However, national surveys may be modified to include variables that are likely to be important in PMTs. Housing characteristics and asset variables consistently show a high correlation with expenditure indicators, and efforts should be made to include these variables if the country's household budget survey will potentially be used to generate PMTs.

As highlighted, information constraints are most binding when attempting to identify households with short-term needs for social assistance. Households often experience a short-term spell of poverty following exposure to a negative shock to their economic well-being. Ideally, the impact that shocks have on economic well-being would be measured by observations of household well-being pre- and post-shock in household panel data sets. However, such data sets are rarely available in Sub-Saharan African countries and are not available in any of the case study countries. Difficulties in establishing and maintaining panel data sets suggest that conducting a panel survey solely for short-term targeting purposes is probably not warranted or realistic. Nevertheless, using existing panel data sets to establish unbiased estimates of the magnitude of shocks on household well-being can produce reliable estimates that can be employed as benchmark PMT weightings outside of the survey sample. As noted, further research is needed in this area.

Data on household exposure to shocks are weak or nonexistent in many of the country household surveys. Improved targeting of households with short-term needs will require better information on how households are affected by shocks. Better specification of "shock" modules in household budget surveys is one way to improve this information. As the Mozambique and Cameroon data sets demonstrate, useful information on climatic shocks can also be obtained through publicly available geo-referenced rainfall data sets like the National Aeronautics and Space Administration's Climate Resource for Agro-Climatology.[3] Further, these climatic data sets are available over many years, allowing the frequency of exposure to climatic shocks to be assessed.

For example, in a case study of vulnerability in rural Kenya, Christiaensen and Subbarao (2007) employ time-series data on rainfall recorded from 900 stations mapped onto districts and communities to assess community vulnerability to shocks and derive policy recommendations on the appropriate programs to redress vulnerability. Early warning systems can also be used to identify regions with exposure to adverse climatic conditions.

Alternatively, information on short-term household needs also can be collected through direct measures of household food security like food consumption scores or dietary diversity indexes. The Kenya case study indicates that short-term food security indicators can be employed along with PMT measures to improve the targeting of populations exposed to shocks. However, alternative food security indicators appear to measure different components of short-term household needs. Further investments in and analysis of information are needed to identify which indicators work best for exposure to specific types of shocks.

Concluding Comments

This section summarizes suggestions arising from the case studies for potential investments to improve targeting practices. Current standards and critical areas for investments in methods, information, and processes are highlighted in table 10.5. With regard to methods, there is a need for investments to integrate multiple methods of targeting. Understanding the geographic concentration of poverty can enhance the efficiency of program delivery by focusing assistance efforts on areas with the greatest need (due to either consistent chronic poverty or a severe covariate shock). Inclusion errors can be reduced further by investments in proxy means testing and community-based targeting methods that focus on households rather than larger regions.

Improvements in PMT methods focus mainly on increasing the sensitivity of program targeting to short-term changes in households' economic well-being. Investments are possible on three fronts:

- Integration with CBT methods that tend to be better able to measure short-term changes in well-being
- Generation of an effective and rapid means test to identify vulnerable households that have become food insecure in areas exposed to large covariate shocks
- Generation of PMTplus estimates of shock impacts that can be incorporated into PMT rankings of household well-being.

Country-specific choices of where to invest in improved methods will depend largely on available information as well as implementation capacity.

Table 10.5 Summary of Current Standards and Potential Improvements in Targeting Practices

Investment area and current standard	Potential improvement
Targeting methods	
Geographic targeting	Geographically target areas with chronic poverty or high exposure to shocks
Community-based targeting as an alternative to PMT	Integrate CBT with PMT
Proxy means test	Use PMTplus options; adjust PMT weights for exposure to shocks; use rapid means tests for crisis situations
Information	
National household budget survey	Generate household survey information on household exposure to shocks; incorporate geo-referenced data on climatic conditions; incorporate early warning system information
Estimates of poverty	Estimate chronic poverty and vulnerability
Process	
Program-specific criteria and indicators for program targeting	Coordinate targeting criteria and indicators across programs; maintain a common registry database

Further investments are needed to complement widely available household budget surveys, particularly regarding information on the frequency and severity of household exposure to shocks that affect short-term safety net needs. Such information can come from household surveys, broader databases on household conditions, or early warning systems. Further, studies on the characteristics of the chronic poor and the vulnerable can assist in the identification of indicators for targeting as well as critical variables to include in PMT equations. Information from other studies can also be used to generate PMT weights on the impact of exposure to short-term shocks and to identify vulnerable households. For example, general consensus appears to be developing on the magnitude of the impact that droughts have on household consumption; therefore, impacts may not need to be measured for every drought in every country.

Finally, as noted throughout this publication, significant and relatively rapid gains in safety net program efficiency are possible through better coordination among assistance programs. Initial efforts can focus on investments in coordinating program targeting criteria and indicators in order to avoid duplication of efforts and gaps in social assistance program coverage. As coordination across programs increases, the social assistance system can also move toward an investment in a common program registry.

Priorities for investments in targeting systems will be country specific. Many countries still need to make investments in current standards like clear program targeting criteria, national household budget surveys, and geographic, CBT, and

PMT targeting methods. Investments in these standard targeting practices will usually be prioritized above potential improvements on current standards. For those countries looking to move beyond current standards, investments should be driven by need. If poverty is highly concentrated geographically, then investments in geographically refined targeting (possibly combined with methods to identify individual households within areas) will be a priority. If chronic poverty is widespread, then methods to improve PMT performance will be a priority. Similarly, if vulnerability is high due to exposure to shocks, then investments to improve targeting of vulnerable households will be a priority.

Priorities for research on poverty follow directly from issues emerging in the case studies. First, most studies rely on ex ante evaluation of targeting performance. In the case of PMTs this entails using the same sample from which the PMT is derived. A better understanding of ex post targeting performance and the factors that influence performance is needed. Second, complementarities associated with the use of multiple methods for targeting need to be further explored and quantified, particularly with regard to integrating CBT with more quantitative methods. Third, functions and accurate methods for identifying households with short-term needs must be generated and evaluated. As with PMTs, evaluations are best done ex post based on observed targeting performance in crisis situations rather than based on the ex ante simulations presented in the country case studies.

Notes

1. Similar results are found in Rwanda and Indonesia. In Rwanda, CBT performed well, but the addition of PMT improved targeting outcomes. Kakwani and Subbarao (2011) argue that CBT can do a very good job of identifying poor households within a community; horizontal inequity across communities in targeting outcomes can occur since communities have different perceptions of who is extremely poor and who is moderately poor. An experiment in Indonesia that compared CBT, PMT, and a combination of the two reaches a similar conclusion (see Alatas et al. 2012).
2. See the recent review of safety net programs in Africa (Monchuk 2013).
3. See http://power.larc.nasa.gov/cgi-bin/cgiwrap/solar/agro.cgi?email=agroclim@larc .nasa.gov.

References

Alatas, Vivi, Abhijit Banerjee, Rema Hanna, Benjamin A. Olken, and Julia Tobias. 2012. "Targeting the Poor: Evidence from a Field Experiment in Indonesia." *American Economic Review* 102 (4): 1206–40.

Christiaensen, Luc, and Kalanidhi Subbarao. 2007. "Towards an Understanding of Vulnerability in Rural Kenya." *Oxford Journal of African Economies* 14 (4): 520–58.

del Ninno, Carlo, Paul A. Dorosh, Lisa C. Smith, and Dilip K. Roy. 2001. "The 1998 Floods in Bangladesh: Disaster Impacts, Household Coping Strategies, and Response." Research Report 122, International Food Policy Research Institute, Washington, DC.

Ferreira, Francisco H. G., Anna Fruttero, Phillippe Leite, and Leonardo Lucchetti. 2011. *Rising Food Prices and Household Welfare: Evidence from Brazil in 2008.* Discussion Paper 5713. Bonn: IZA.

Kakwani, N., and Kalanidhi Subbarao. 2011. "Improving Community-Based Targeting System: A Case Study of Rwanda." World Bank, Washington, DC.

Migotto, Mauro, Benjamin Davis, Gero Carletto, and Kathleen Beegle. 2006. "Measuring Food Security Using Respondents' Perception of Food Consumption Adequacy." UNU-WIDER Research Paper 2006/88, United National University–World Institute for Development Economics Research, Helsinki.

Monchuk, Victoria. 2013. *Reducing Poverty and Investing in People: The New Role of Safety Nets in Africa.* Directions in Development. Washington, DC: World Bank.

Pelham, Larissa, Edward Clay, and Tim Braunholz. 2011. *Natural Disasters: What Is the Role for Social Safety Nets?* Social Protection Discussion Paper 1102. Washington, DC: World Bank.

Tamiru, Kaleb. 2013. "What Is the Role of Informal Safety Nets in Africa for Social Protection Policy?" World Bank, Washington, DC.

Wiesmann, Doris, Lucy Bassett, Todd Benson, and John Hoddinott. 2009. *Validation of the World Food Programme's Food Consumption Score and Alternative Indicators of Household Food Security.* Discussion Paper 870. Washington, DC: International Food Policy Research Institute.

World Bank. 2012. "Informal Safety Nets in Eastern and Southern Africa: A Synthesis Summary of Literature Review and Field Studies from Côte d'Ivoire, Rwanda, and Zimbabwe." Africa Region Report 77747-AFR, World Bank, Washington, DC.

———. 2013a. *Social Safety Nets in Africa: A Review of the Experiences in 22 Countries.* Washington, DC: World Bank.

———. 2013b. *World Development Report 2014: Risk and Opportunity; Managing Risk for Development.* Washington, DC: World Bank.

Index

Boxes, figures, notes, and tables are indicated by *b*, *f*, *n*, and *t* following the page number.